W9-CFI-810

"As the evangelical voting block fractures and as Billy Graham's capacious shadow fades, a rather significant question looms: Whither American evangelicalism? Perhaps for too long we've relied on political power. Collins, drawing on an insightful exploration of the twentieth century and a deft analysis of the current horizon, points us to the power of common grace and ultimately to the power of the Spirit."

Stephen J. Nichols, author of *Jesus Made in America*

"Kenneth Collins has here issued an invitation to a scholarly forum on evangelical priorities, politics and power in culture and the public square. As at a truly good debate one is forced to think, to agree, to disagree and to admire the skill of the debaters, so it is here. As the fault lines of evangelicalism widen under the tectonic forces of power, postmodernity and personalities, Collins's reflections on teleology, the image of God and the power of the Spirit offer useful bridges to reopen communication between the estranged subcultures of contemporary evangelicalism."

Peter A. Lillback, president, Westminster Theological Seminary

"A major Wesleyan scholar, Kenneth Collins has provided a significant assessment of the promise and problems of modern evangelicalism. From intelligent design to power politics, he has set forth a valuable critique of fundamentalism, neo-evangelicalism, the religious right and the evangelical left. Protestants of different traditions will find Collins a perceptive analyst of the changing dynamics within evangelicalism."

Thomas C. Oden, author of *Classic Christianity: A Systematic Theology*

"*Power, Politics and the Fragmentation of Evangelicalism* is a much-needed critical analysis of evangelical engagements with public policy by a Wesleyan scholar. I strongly recommend it to readers interested in learning about the pitfalls of both the religious right and left. While the book is bound to be controversial, especially among those who advocate evangelical social action, it contains much wisdom and a prophetic warning about how the search for power corrupts religion."

Roger E. Olson, George W. Truett Theological Seminary, Baylor University

"Collins writes with both the wide-ranging knowledge of a historian and the personal engagement of a Wesleyan statesman who has been actively involved in the evangelical movement throughout his career. It would be an understatement to say his provocative narrative of the movement as interpreted through the lens of its various bids for power is as refreshingly honest as it is illuminating. But more importantly, he provides sage guidance and direction for the movement as it seeks to navigate these perilous waters while remaining faithful to the gospel in the twenty-first century."

Jerry Walls, Houston Baptist University

"Kenneth Collins gives us a sweeping overview of the large forces that have led evangelicals, in recent decades, to become major actors in the bitter 'culture wars' that continue to bedevil American society. He makes a justly searing indictment of the principled assault by secularists on religious freedom, while giving sobering admonitions for evangelicals' often defective ways of resisting that assault."

Meic Pearse, Houghton College

Do not allow yourself to be pushed off your story, how you are known in God's love and purpose, by any diminishing 'script' that is out there: whether it is offered by family, 'friends' or by acquaintances. To be sure, you will be surrounded by all sorts of other narratives and definitions of self. Do not buy into them or give them credibility. Know yourself in Christ as the beloved of God in all things. This is part of the truth that will set you free.

—KENNETH J. COLLINS

POWER, POLITICS

AND THE

FRAGMENTATION

OF EVANGELICALISM

FROM THE SCOPES TRIAL TO THE OBAMA ADMINISTRATION

KENNETH J. COLLINS

IVP Academic

An imprint of InterVarsity Press
Downers Grove, Illinois

InterVarsity Press
P.O. Box 1400, Downers Grove, IL 60515-1426
World Wide Web: www.ivpress.com
E-mail: email@ivpress.com

InterVarsity Press® is the book-publishing division of InterVarsity Christian Fellowship/USA®, a movement of students and faculty active on campus at hundreds of universities, colleges and schools of nursing in the United States of America, and a member movement of the International Fellowship of Evangelical Students. For information about local and regional activities, write Public Relations Dept., InterVarsity Christian Fellowship/USA, 6400 Schroeder Rd., P.O. Box 7895, Madison, WI 53707-7895, or visit the IVCF website at <www.intervarsity.org>.

Scripture quotations, unless otherwise noted, are from the New Revised Standard Version of the Bible, copyright 1989 by the Division of Christian Education of the National Council of the Churches of Christ in the USA. Used by permission. All rights reserved.

Cover design: Cindy Kiple
Images: star illustration: © ulimi/iStockphoto
*   ragged black paper: © Petek ARICI/iStockphoto*
Interior design: Beth Hagenberg

ISBN 978-0-8308-3979-8

Printed in the United States of America ∞

Library of Congress Cataloging-in-Publication Data has been requested.

P	19	18	17	16	15	14	13	12	11	10	9	8	7	6	5	4	3	2	1
Y	28	27	26	25	24	23	22	21	20	19	18	17	16	15	14	13	12		

To the memory of

Richard John Neuhaus

an American who knew how

to keep first things first

Contents

Acknowledgments

I would like to thank the following people who read all or parts of the manuscript and offered several helpful suggestions: Jerry Walls, Lawson Stone, Michael Peterson, Joel Scandrett and Christine Johnson.

Introduction

AMERICAN EVANGELICALISM IS THAT FAMILY within the Protestant household, fortified by deep revivalist traditions, that has underscored the importance of the Bible, the atoning work of Jesus Christ, conversion and evangelism.[1] The term evangelicalism itself is contested,[2] but various theological traditions that bear the name invariably express a common interest in the attributes just cited. Part of the rich legacy of this vital movement can be seen in the First and Second Great Awakenings, abolitionism, the Holiness Movement and the progressive movement of the late nineteenth and early twentieth centuries. Its champions range from Jonathan Edwards to Charles Finney, from George Whitefield to Phoebe Palmer, from Billy Sunday to Billy Graham.[3] After the disestablishment of the church during the eighteenth century, in which religion was legally (in the First Amendment to the Constitution) separated from the state, evangelical religion nevertheless flowered in the following century, and it had by that point grown to be culturally powerful. However, by the twentieth century the movement had clearly fallen on hard times. That is, it not only broke up into liberal and conservative wings but was also disinherited by key leaders of American culture who began to look elsewhere for their vision.

---

[1]David W. Bebbington, "Evangelicalism in Its Settings: The British and American Movements Since 1940," in *Evangelicalism*, ed. Mark Noll, David W. Bebbington and George A. Rawlyk (New York: Oxford University Press, 1994), p. 373.

[2]William J. Abraham, *The Coming Great Revival* (San Francisco: Harper & Row, 1984), p. 7.

[3]Though George Whitefield was British he had such a significant impact on American evangelicalism that he must be listed in any major account.

The shifting fortunes of evangelicalism, especially from the nineteenth to the twentieth centuries, led Timothy Smith to employ the ever-changing image of a kaleidoscope to chart this complex movement.[4]

Such a fall from power, and over a relatively brief period of time, makes the study of American evangelicalism a good window not only on the fortunes of Protestantism in the United States but also on the identity of the American nation itself, especially in terms of what it has become as a modern liberal democracy. To explore this engaging story, which has some odd subplots along the way, we will consider different types of power. In other words we will investigate the various dimensions through which American evangelicalism has been expressed in its rich and vibrant life, especially on the national scene. Power is defined in this context, at least initially, in a very basic and general way. It comes in two principal forms: one positive and the other negative. Power in the first sense quite simply entails the ability to do, to effectuate, to achieve desired ends and goals. It is a reflection of interests. Power in the second, so-called negative, sense involves the ability to restrict and constrain; it consists chiefly in inhibiting or outright preventing certain courses of action. This second sense is similar to the nature of power that Martin Luther (1483-1546) had in mind when he described the political use of the moral law in his *Commentary on Galatians*.[5]

Though we have defined power quite broadly, in order to be able to *recognize* the many ways in which the evangelical community in America has expressed its life and purpose as a vibrant community among even larger ones, our approach will nevertheless focus by and large on key powers, especially those that are indicative of the relation between evangelicals and the American nation. In one sense this work is a history of modern American evangelicalism from the 1920s to the present. It tells that story, however, by being attentive to the numerous shifts in fortune that marked the relation of the evangelical community to the broader American nation, especially in terms of cultural, political, intellectual, moral and spiritual power. Indeed, an examination of these same elements will not only help us to comprehend

[4]Timothy Smith, "The Evangelical Kaleidoscope and the Call to Christian Unity," *Christian Scholars Review* 15 (1986): 125.
[5]Jaroslav Pelikan, ed., *Lectures on Galatians*, Luther's Works (1535; reprint, Saint Louis: Concordia, 1963), 26:308-9.

evangelicalism better but also the American nation itself.

Though there are different ways of understanding the relation between culture and politics, our approach will view the former as the larger category as it relates to the entire *society* with respect to knowledge, ideas, customs, traditions, skills, beliefs, language, mores, folkways, artifacts and institutions. The latter category, politics, will be considered more narrowly as referring to government (and influencing it), the powers of distribution, restriction and coercion, as well as to the operations of the state. Indeed, one of the principal arguments of this book is that modern America has developed the unfortunate habit of "politicizing" ever larger areas of human culture that at their best should not in effect be overrun with such influences, with such governmental *power*.

Beyond such considerations the American evangelical story cannot be told apart from attention to the intellectual currents that were such an important part of its heritage extending back to Princeton theologians such as Charles Hodge (1797-1878) and B. B. Warfield (1851-1921), the common sense philosophy of the nineteenth century and the intellectual prowess of Jonathan Edwards (1703-1758) during the eighteenth century. This distinct and considerable intellectual heritage that was a part of the broader cultural power of evangelicals was challenged in the nineteenth century and put aside by cultural elites in the twentieth. Its loss, as well as the ongoing shadow of that loss, have marked evangelical identity ever since. And Wesleyan evangelicals, by and large, have offered modest help in the quest to regain some of this intellectual capital since they were not often asking the question What can I know? (as were their Reformed evangelical cousins) but How can I love? a query emblematic of their own heritage of evangelicalism going back to John Wesley himself.

Given that evangelicals in the United States have championed conversion, or being born again, as being at the heart of genuine Christian experience, it is therefore not surprising to learn that this community has often expressed considerable moral and spiritual concern in the national arena. Emphasizing both personal and social responsibility, the evangelical community has articulated an ethic, among other things, of ministering to the poor, protecting the unborn as well as safeguarding the values pertaining to the family, values that should lead to human flourishing. The irony here, of course, is that in the area of moral power, evangelicals offer researchers abundant evidence of having become increasingly accommodated to American culture instead of transforming it. In fact, the divorce rates among American evangelicals are not very different from the nation at large. And scandals at the national level have rocked the community, though we do not believe that the lens of "scandal" is the most appropriate one to come to terms with the great majority of evangelical Americans, who in so many instances live better lives than some of their leaders.

So then the book will employ an historical narrative (for the most part) while being attentive to the interplay between the evangelical community and a broader national context in terms of a number of powers, and thereby offer a much needed cultural analysis. In chapter one, for example, we will begin by noting the rich cultural legacy of evangelicals hailing from the nineteenth century that was challenged by the rise of higher criticism and evolution, among other things. The cast of characters here, so to speak, will include the Scopes Trial, the rise of the Social Gospel, the Great Reversal and the fundamentalist dilemma that is best expressed in terms of ongoing cultural ambivalence. Moreover, unlike other histories of American evangelicalism we will indicate quite clearly why the turn toward fundamentalism was never undertaken by Wesleyan evangelicals, in any significant way, due to the distinct sense of their own identity and mission.

Chapter two will explore the institutionalization of fundamentalism reflecting its status as an ongoing *subculture*. It will also consider the rise of the neo-evangelicals, who sought to distinguish themselves in several important respects from their fundamentalist brothers and sisters. However, like the fundamentalists, the neo-evangelicals, soon to be known simply as evangelicals, developed an infrastructure to insure that their values and witness would be passed along from generation to generation, given their own standing as a subculture as well. Particular attention will, therefore, be paid to the development of the National Association of Evangelicals, the creation and editorial leadership of *Christianity Today*, the founding of Fuller Theological Seminary and the ministry of Billy Graham. Beyond this, we will consider some of the engaging social developments at the time, especially the civil rights movement, as well as how it was viewed by key evangelical leaders who at times seemed to be more concerned with matters pertaining to their own identity and interests. Beyond this, the coalescing of Wesleyan evangelicals during the 1960s in the face of an overly accommodated mainline denomination (what modern, liberal democracy often does to a communion of faith) will also be examined.

Chapter three will portray the significant political and cultural shift brought into being by Lyndon Baines Johnson in his attempt, among other things, to usher in what he called "The Great Society," that is, one that would eliminate poverty. And the case will be made, interestingly enough, that Richard Nixon, before the whole Watergate fiasco, actually had more in common with Johnson's poverty fighting approaches than is often acknowledged. The fall of Nixon and the corruption of his administration prepared the way for the election of an outsider, Jimmy Carter, the former governor of Georgia, who as a born again Christian was remarkably open about his evangelical faith, though many evangelicals would quickly turn away from his administration. The aftermath of that disillusionment provides some of the context in which to understand the rise of the new religious right in the form of the Moral Majority, and later on the Christian Coalition, and why many Wesleyans opted out. Living in the wake of the historic Supreme Court decision *Roe v. Wade*, many evangelicals not only made their way into the Republican Party and supported a divorced candidate for the presidency in the form of Ronald Reagan, but they also began to look more kindly toward Roman Catholics, who shared some of their key moral concerns.

A great number of evangelicals supported the rise of the intelligent design movement even though, properly speaking, that movement is not even a species of theism since the designer can be understood in various ways, not all of which include the notion of God. At any rate, many evangelicals embraced the movement, and some cheered from the sidelines, simply because in intelligent design they had found a champion who could possibly recover some of the intellectual capital lost during the Scopes Trial, with the hope that this currency could be readily translated into an increased cultural voice. However, because the cultural shadows of Scopes often hung over a consideration of intelligent design, the movement was rarely properly understood. Chapter four then will take great pains to describe intelligent design properly and explore its intellectual challenge and contributions, as well as to note its failures.

Though conservative evangelicals, only a fraction of whom would identify with the religious right, seem to get so much of the attention at the national level, the evangelical left has resurged of late, riding the waves of the popularity of the emergent church and the ministries of Jim Wallis, Tony Campolo and Brian McLaren, and the election of a liberal Democratic president Barack Obama. Chapter five then will take a closer look at this wing of the evangelical community in light of its own writings and against the backdrop of the larger political and cultural changes that have been taking place in the United States from FDR to LBJ and on to Obama. Good windows on the interface between evangelical leftist conceptions of social justice and the modern, liberal democratic state can be illustrated in the recent housing crisis and in the promulgation of the "Manhattan Declaration," a document that none of the names just mentioned saw fit to sign.

The evangelical community, both the right and the left, has in some sense followed broader cultural trends by reducing their *public* voices by and large to a political idiom. Modern liberal democratic states, of course, encourage such developments in a number of ways. The transformation of a full-orbed gospel voice to a political idiom in which *particular* conceptions of social justice, whether from the right or the left, were celebrated, was then brought back into the church (in this evangelicals followed the mainline denominations, though not to the same extent) where it continued to be interlaced with the vocabulary of the gospel itself. In other words, particular conceptions of justice took on an ever larger role such that those evangelicals who thought differently (and there are, after all, many viable ways of understanding social justice) could only feel alienated in such churches. In chapter six then we will detail this problem forthrightly and highlight the ways in which the evangelical community can come to a greater appreciation of the universality of the gospel, its broad catholicity, especially in terms of its transcendent nature. This ongoing political and theological problem likewise demonstrates the necessity of an evangelical political philosophy, one that is informed by Scripture in a preeminent way, as well as by the wisdom of moral and natural law, underscoring those things that pertain to *all* human beings.

The work will conclude with an assessment of the powers (cultural, intellectual, political, etc.) articulated in the largely historical narrative and will suggest the way forward for the evangelical community.

1

Cultural Shifts, the Rise of Fundamentalism
and the Great Reversal

T HOUGH THE CHURCH IN THE UNITED STATES had been officially dis-
established in the First Amendment to the Constitution in 1791, Protestants, many of them evangelicals, almost immediately set out to create a de
facto establishment.[1] The earlier evangelical revivalism of the 1730s and
1740s, informed by a Puritan heritage that sought to dedicate all of the New
World in service to God, pointed the way for nineteenth-century preachers,
who employed similar methods in a Second Great Awakening. Wave after
wave of revivalism flowing from Cane Ridge, Kentucky, in 1801 to the businessmen's revival of 1857, to the holiness camp meetings beginning at
Vineland New Jersey in 1867, and into the pointed preaching of Dwight
Moody (1837-1899) during the latter part of the century, all helped to foster
a genuine Christian culture. The various means of this establishment,
however, were not legal or coercive, but voluntary and persuasive. Revivalism, with its emphasis on the in-breaking of the power of God, now was at
the heart of the methods that had so captivated the nation.

A CULTURAL LEGACY

Revivalists of the period, such as Charles Grandison Finney (1792-1875),

---

[1]Mark D. Regnerus, "Selective Deprivatization Among American Religious Traditions: The Reversal
of the Great Reversal," *Social Forces* 76, no. 4 (1998): 1347-72. Regnerus points out that state estab-
lishments lasted as long as 1833 (cf. p. 1349).

who had left a legal career for preaching, took great pains to proclaim a full-orbed gospel: one that offered hope not simply to individuals but also to society. Indeed, Finney remarked on one occasion to the effect that everywhere the gospel is preached there must also be reform. Likeminded reformist evangelicals helped to establish several voluntary societies to meet both the personal and social needs of the nation, such as the American Bible Society (1816), the American Education Society (1816), the American Sunday School Union (1824), the American Tract Society (1825), the American Temperance Society (1826), the American Peace Society (1828) and the American Antislavery Society (1833) among other groups. These societies, which were not only created to ease the plight of the poor but also to enhance the cultural fingerprint of American Protestants, were marked by generous interdenominational cooperation. The whole cluster of these societies interlaced throughout the nation constituted nothing less than a veritable benevolent empire.

So great was the religious and cultural power of evangelical Protestants in the nineteenth century that by 1870 as George Marsden puts it "almost all American Protestants thought of America as a Christian nation."[2] For example, by 1892 Supreme Court Justice Brewer delivered the opinion of the court (*Church of the Holy Trinity v. the United States*) in declaring that the United States was a Christian nation. Not surprisingly, many Protestants saw their own faith at the heart of the American enterprise, though Roman Catholics, Jews and skeptics naturally objected.[3] Josiah Strong (1847-1916) demonstrated in 1885 with the publication of his best-selling book *Our Country* how quickly the evangelical faith of American Protestants could become amalgamated with the alloys of both ethnicity and race. Mistaking Anglo-Saxon culture for the genius of the gospel itself, Strong declared that "the world's destiny lay with the Anglo-Saxon race."[4] Andre Siegfried continued this tribal theme early into the next century in his book *America Comes of Age* (1927), in which he

---

[2]George M. Marsden, *Fundamentalism and American Culture* (New York: Oxford University Press, 1980), p. 11. Due to the scope and focus of the book, nineteenth-century developments are treated more briefly and to the extent that they illuminate the following century.
[3]Ibid.
[4]George Marsden, *Religion and American Culture* (New York: Harcourt, Brace & World, 1990), p. 116.

raised the question "Will America remain Protestant and Anglo Saxon?"[5] In other words, original stock Protestants, some of whose ancestry went back to the founding of the nation and even earlier, enjoyed and touted their cultural advantages, some of which were reflected in the religious preferences of America.

THE PROGRESSIVE MOVEMENT AND THE GREAT WAR

Many evangelicals brought their religious idealism and moral judgments to the progressive movement that spanned the presidencies of Theodore Roosevelt, William Howard Taft and Woodrow Wilson. In a real sense progressivism, as a political movement, was a response to some of the more troubling aspects of industrialization and urbanization. It therefore sought to bring about a new balance between "Protestant moral values, capitalistic competition, and democratic processes."[6] Among their many reforms progressives helped to pass child labor laws, they developed the notion that charity and welfare should be undertaken by professionals, that is, by social workers, and they supported many of the goals of organized labor.

Voluntary societies to promote social order likewise flourished in the nineteenth century. The Women's Christian Temperance Union, for example, was founded in 1874 and Frances Willard, a Methodist evangelical, provided pivotal leadership from 1879 to 1898. To be sure, many reformers believed that alcohol was destroying the social fabric of the nation, the family in particular. However, what began as a temperance movement (drinking in moderation) soon became a total abstinence crusade, and progressives viewed the alcohol issue in an ultraist way: that is, it was seen as *the* moral issue that if properly addressed would result in numerous social benefits, everything from stable family relationships to increased productivity at work. Class and ethnic issues, however, were also caught up in a prohibition coalition that sought to protect the interests of old stock Americans who felt threatened by the unchurched (largely lower class) and by Catholic, Jewish and Lutheran (drinking) immigrants.[7] The

---

[5]Martin E. Marty, *The Noise of Conflict 1919-1941*, Modern American Religion (Chicago: University of Chicago Press, 1991), 2:63.
[6]Nancy Koester, *The History of Christianity in the United States* (Minneapolis: Fortress Press, 2007).
[7]Martin E. Marty, *Pilgrims in Their Own Land* (Harrisonburg, Va.: Penguin, 1984), p. 377.

Eighteenth Amendment to the Constitution, which banned the manu-
facture and sale of intoxicating beverages, was ratified by the states in October 1919, and it went into effect on January 16, 1920. It represented the
social and cultural power of Protestants who yet remained in earnest to establish a Christian America, one very much in their own image.

One of the greatest reforms undertaken by progressives was undoubtedly women's suffrage. That women did not have the right to vote
seemed to belie the democratic principles that grounded the nation. And
many Christians reasoned that such a failure detracted from the truth that
women, as with men, were created in nothing less than the image and
likeness of God. Harkening back to a 1848 founding convention in a Wesleyan church at Seneca Falls, New York, women's suffrage was yet another
key success of the progressive movement with the passage of the Nineteenth Amendment by Congress in 1919, an amendment that was ratified
by the states the following year.

Despite its many achievements, one of the glaring faults of the progressive era was that its social and cultural vision was largely restricted to
white Americans. Indeed, prejudices against African Americans were not
only extensive but they were also built into the very social mores of the
period. For example, Jim Crow laws that were on the books since the 1880s
gave legal and social force to the physical separation of the races.
Moreover, demonstrating that the Supreme Court itself was not above the
social prejudices of the day, it ruled in *Plessy v. Ferguson* in 1896 that "separate but equal" policies with respect to African Americans were in fact
justified. In addition, some of the worst executive acts against blacks took
place during the presidency of Woodrow Wilson (1856-1924), who brought
several "southern white stereotypes" to the White House.[8] It would take
decades before this blind spot of the reformers was even addressed.

As a reforming Democrat who had earlier cleaned up corruption in
New Jersey as governor, Wilson readily weaved together the narrative of
an American liberal democracy with that of the gospel. According to Mark
Noll this energetic president believed that the American experience "witnessed the fullest manifestation of public Christian values in human

---

[8]Martin E. Marty, *The Irony of It All, 1893-1919*, Modern American Religion (Chicago: University of
Chicago Press, 1986), 1:99.

history."[9] Remembering the Civil War and the disruption it had brought to American society, and with both his father and grandfather having had careers as ministers, Wilson reluctantly entered the Great War as late as 1917 in order to defeat German militarism and to "make the world safe for democracy."[10] William Jennings Bryan (1860-1925), his popular secretary of state, discerned the drift toward war early on and resigned in 1915 on the basis of pacifist principles.

Evangelicals from a number of different social and theological perspectives eventually embraced the war and viewed it, at least to some extent, through the well-worked lens of reform. For example, Columbia University administrators dismissed tenured faculty "for opposing American intervention in the war."[11] And Shailer Mathews (1863-1941), the dean of the divinity school at the University of Chicago, declared that for an American "to refuse to share in the present war . . . is not Christian."[12] Conservative evangelicals, like their liberal theological cousins, conflated patriotism and Christianity as well. Billy Sunday (1862-1935), for example, the slapdash preacher who knew how to captivate an audience, bellowed from the pulpit on occasion that "Christianity and patriotism are synonymous . . . and hell and traitors are synonymous."[13] This was a heady period, to be sure, filled with the all the rhetoric of patriotism, and the American flag was even brought into the churches—and in most cases it remained there.

After the war was over in 1918, the gruesome reality of the carnage (15 million dead) as well as a vision of the vast destruction of resources set in and dispelled the naiveté and optimism that had characterized many of war's supporters, religious leaders among them. The social consequences of the war were also considerable and were evident not only in a loosing of moral strictures that characterized the rise of the jazz age but also in strengthening the forces of secularization, especially among cultural elites, who were by now weary of all idealism, whatever form it took.

---

[9]Mark Noll, *A History of Christianity in the United States and Canada* (Grand Rapids: Eerdmans, 1992), p. 302.

[10]Edward J. Larson, *Summer for the Gods: The Scopes Trial and America's Continuing Debate Over Science and Religion* (New York: Basic Books, 1997), pp. 34-35.

[11]Ibid., p. 61.

[12]Noll, *History of Christianity*, pp. 308-9.

[13]George M. Marsden, *Understanding Fundamentalism and Evangelicalism* (Grand Rapids: Eerdmans, 1991), p. 51.

CULTURAL CHALLENGES TO THE AMERICAN
PROTESTANT EMPIRE

The cultural establishment that Protestants had created in the nineteenth century, largely through the enormous success of revivalism in offering many Americans a common vision and purpose, was challenged by a number of shifting social and cultural realities. Precisely because it is made up of so many diverse elements (intellectual, economic, moral, religious and social), cultural power for any particular group in the life of a nation is at best fleeting. Clearly, culturally privileged groups like to focus on a snapshot, so to speak, of the heights of their power, not realizing of course that the photo will age, no longer depicting the present very accurately. In the same way, American Protestants, though remarkably successful in the nineteenth century, were nevertheless a part of a larger cultural complex that contained any number of factors well beyond their control. What cultural power and influence they had amassed could be viewed as either fortuitous or in a more comforting way as the benevolent providence of God. At any rate, it would not last.

IMMIGRATION

One of the best and most reliable indicators of the religious life of a nation (both present and future) is none other than immigration statistics. In a real sense America has imported its religious makeup. The period between 1870 and 1920, for instance, marks one of the most significant influxes of immigrants in the history of the nation. According to some of the best statistics available, over twenty million people, largely European, passed through the gates of Castle Garden and, after 1892, Ellis Island.[14] Immigrants came from Germany, Ireland, Italy, Russia, Poland and elsewhere. At the turn of the century the numbers swelled from Eastern Europe, which included many Ashkenazi Jews. America was now both more Roman Catholic (Germany, Ireland and Italy) and Jewish (Russia and Poland).

Nativist sentiment quickly emerged among the "old guard" Protestants who felt challenged by the shifting religious composition of the nation. Josiah Strong, for example, maintained that Catholicism threatens many

---

[14]Walter Nugent, *Crossings: The Great Transatlantic Migrations, 1870-1914* (Indianapolis: Indiana University Press, 1992), p. 150.

of America's basic liberties, such as free speech and a free press. "Manifestly there is an irreconcilable difference," he declared, "between papal principles and the fundamental principles of our free institutions."[15] And when the Democratic Party in 1928 nominated the Roman Catholic Alfred E. Smith to be president of the United States, many Protestants warned that he would sell out America to the pope. So great was the concern that even the authors of the *Christian Century* argued that "Catholic teachings and practices clashed with America's democratic principles."[16] And evangelical Protestants, for their part, wondered if the fruit of revivalism and the cultural power it had afforded them could be so easily undone by American bureaucratic policy in the form of mass immigration.

Fearing the wrath of its constituencies, Congress began to pass legislation after the war to restrict immigration. A bill that would exclude migrants who failed a literacy test became law in 1917 over the objections—and veto!—of President Wilson.[17] A few years later Congress passed the Johnson Act (1921) and the Johnson Reid Act (1924), both of which restricted immigration along the lines of "national-origins quotas."[18] The open door of immigration was beginning to close. The World War itself, of course, had interrupted the flow, and with the restrictive legislation of the 1920s followed by the Great Depression of the 1930s transmigration to the United States virtually ceased—at least for a time. And it would not be until much later, that is, during the 1960s, that the country would revamp its immigration policies under the banner of fairness and balance.

INTELLECTUAL CHALLENGES TO THE AMERICAN PROTESTANT EMPIRE

One element of the larger Protestant cultural fingerprint had been the life of the mind that resonated in many respects with American cultural trends throughout a good portion of the nineteenth century. So then in order to appreciate the nature and extent of the intellectual challenges that

---

[15]Edwin Scott Gaustad, *A Religious History of America*, rev. ed. (New York: Harper & Row, 1990), p. 194.

[16]Allan J. Lichtman, *White Protestant Nation: The Rise of the American Conservative Movement* (New York: Grove, 2008), p. 48.

[17]Nugent, *Crossings*, p. 161.

[18]Ibid.

the higher criticism of the Bible and the teaching of evolution posed to so many American Protestants during the early twentieth century (with significant loss of intellectual power in the offing), it is necessary to understand just how they read sacred Scripture. However, in order to comprehend what presuppositions and assumptions evangelical Protestants brought to the Bible, especially toward the end of the nineteenth century, it is necessary to explore their changing views on both American culture and the millennial reign of Christ.

Many of the revivalists around the middle of the nineteenth century, such as Charles Finney, were decidedly postmillennialists. In other words, they believed that the activity of the church was helping to usher in the golden and blessed thousand-year reign of Christ predicted in Revelation 20. However, after the Civil War it became more difficult, but not impossible, to hold such an interpretation of American culture and biblical prophecy. By the 1870s Dwight Moody, a former shoe salesman turned preacher, had now become America's chief evangelist. Though he initially embraced pointed, revivalistic preaching coupled with significant social action along the lines of Finney, after the great Chicago fire in 1871 Moody modified his overall approach to ministry. That is, from now on he largely focused on saving souls. It was almost as if the calamity of the Chicago fire in Moody's eyes was emblematic of the state of the nation. His new outlook was encapsulated in the often repeated observation: "I look upon this world as a wrecked vessel. God has given me a lifeboat and said to me, 'Moody, save all you can.'"[19]

Throughout the remainder of the nineteenth century, Moody preached a premillennial gospel that was pessimistic in terms of the outworking of American culture. Put another way, this popular evangelist was not operating out of a grand Constantinian model in which the Christian faith would make generous and lasting contributions to an American civilization. Instead, he considered that civilization to be in decline, and it would continue in that unenviable state until the second coming of Christ. Moody's new reading of the relation of Christ and culture caught on and many of the leading American evangelists of the period, such as Billy Sunday, Reuben Torrey, W. J. Erdman, J. Wilbur Chapman and George

---

[19]Marsden, *Fundamentalism and American Culture*, p. 38.

Needham, followed in his premillennial footsteps. Like Moody these religious leaders now looked down upon the earlier postmillennialist claim uttered by many of the progressives that the Christian faith would transform American culture in very positive and lasting ways. Instead, they took important steps to separate themselves from what they now judged to be a declining culture. Reflecting on the American scene James Gray remarked, "We cannot absolutely separate ourselves from its society, its literature, its politics, its commerce, but we can separate ourselves from its methods, its spirits, and its aims."[20]

Moody's premillennial cause was helped by the introduction of the teaching of John Nelson Darby (1800-1882), a British evangelist and member of the Plymouth Brethren. Darby taught two key ideas: first there would be a secret rapture of the church, and second there would be a parenthesis in the prophetic clock between the sixty-ninth and seventieth weeks of the book of Daniel. These are two of the basic teachings that constitute the system of theology known as dispensationalism.[21] Arguing that Scripture and the prophetic calendar must be rightly divided, with distinct treatments of the nation of Israel and the church, dispensationalists maintained that God has yet to fulfill several promises to Israel. However, whereas all dispensationalists are premillennialists, arguing that Christ himself will usher in the millennial reign, not all premillennialists are dispensationalists. Nevertheless, both interpretations of the Bible and prophecy depart in key ways from the optimistic and culture-affirming ways of the postmillennialists. By 1917 several professors at the University of Chicago took notice and criticized the premillennialists by arguing that "its leaders were preaching that the current conflict [World War I] was not "the war to end all wars," that the kingdom of God would not come through moral progress, and that the social application of the gospel was a waste of time."[22]

One of the things that united the premillennialists and dispensationalists was that they tended to approach the Bible in a literal way (in line

[20]Ibid., p. 131.

[21]Ernest R. Sandeen, *The Roots of Fundamentalism: British and American Millenarianism, 1800-1930* (Grand Rapids: Baker, 1978), p. 38.

[22]Joel A. Carpenter, *Revive Us Again: The Reawakening of American Fundamentalism* (New York: Oxford University Press, 1997), p. 39.

with their reading of prophecy) that made it difficult for them to embrace the new learning of the nineteenth century in terms of higher criticism of the Bible. Simply put, prophetic judgment had a significant effect on how one viewed the Bible, especially in terms of its authority. And a dispensational reading of Scripture, with all that this entailed, was spread far and wide through the publication of the Scofield Reference Bible in 1909, a work that was later revised in 1917.

Ernest Sandeen put forth the thesis that a coalition of millenarians and conservative Princeton theologians helped to give shape to American fundamentalism. If true, this thesis would suggest that the base of support of fundamentalists (in contrast to H. Richard Niebuhr's claim) was virtually indistinguishable from that of modernists.[23] What makes this coalition so interesting is that many of the conservative theologians at Princeton Seminary, such as Charles Hodge and B. B. Warfield, were neither premillennialists nor dispensationalists, but were actually convinced postmillennialists in their reading of the prophetic calendar.

What drew these millenarians and Princeton scholars together was their common dislike of modernism, a movement that in the judgment of both groups could undermine the inspiration and the authority of Scripture. Indeed, modernism in this context refers to those within the church who were willing to retool, so to speak, significant Christian doctrines in light of both higher criticism and evolutionary theory. For his part Charles Hodge approached the Bible through a Baconian paradigm that placed a premium on induction and empiricism: "The Bible is to the theologian, what nature is to the man of science. It is his store-house of facts."[24] The task of the theologian then, according to Hodge, is "to ascertain, collect and combine all the facts which God has revealed concerning himself and our relation to Him."[25] A. A. Hodge, the son of Charles, along with his colleague B. B. Warfield laid out Princeton's view with respect to Scripture in their salient essay titled "Inspiration," which first appeared in the *Presbyterian Review* in 1881. According to Sandeen,

---

[23]Sandeen, *Roots of Fundamentalism*, p. xvi.
[24]Sydney E. Ahlstrom, ed., *Theology in America: The Major Protestant Voices from Puritanism to Neo-Orthodoxy* (Indianapolis: Bobbs-Merrill, 1967), p. 257.
[25]Ibid., pp. 257-58.

three emphases emerged in this view: first, "the inspiration of the Scriptures [extended] to the words," indicating a plenary verbal view; second, "the Scriptures taught their own inerrancy"; and third, attention was given to "the inspiration of the original autographs," in order no doubt to ward off the charge of error.[26]

Princeton had a tradition of articulating the basic principles of common sense realism that went back to the eighteenth century. To illustrate, John Witherspoon (1723-1794), a Scotsman who became the president of the College of New Jersey (later, Princeton), had imbibed deeply of this philosophy as he grappled with the work of Francis Hutcheson and the skepticism of David Hume (1711-1776).[27] Indeed, Witherspoon's philosophical perspective was in some important ways similar to that found in the writings of the realists Thomas Reid (1710-1796) and his student Dugald Stewart (1753-1828), who both contended that common sense was, after all, a reliable guide to the perception of what is real. Reid defended such realism by affirming that certain principles exist "which the constitution of our nature leads us to believe, and which we are under a necessity to take for granted in the common concerns of life, without being able to give a reason for them."[28] This view, along with its implied methodology, was passed along to Archibald Alexander (1772-1851), who was the first professor of the seminary and one who had been taught by a student of Witherspoon.

Though commonsense realism in America had basically run its course by the mid-nineteenth century, its influence could nevertheless still be discerned in the later writings of Princeton theologians. Professors such as Charles Hodge found the notion that human perceptions reveal the world basically as it is congenial to the larger enterprise of civilization building, of articulating a Christian philosophy in which every thought was taken captive to Christ.[29] This particular cultural synthesis, in which religion

---

[26]Sandeen, *Roots of Fundamentalism,* pp. 123, 125, 127.

[27]See Jack Scott, ed., *An Annotated Edition of Lectures on Moral Philosophy by John Witherspoon* (Newark, Del.: University of Delaware Press, 1982), pp. 35-43 (Hutcheson) and pp. 74-88 (Hume); for a discussion of the ideational relation of Hume and Witherspoon, cf., Henry F. May, *The Enlightenment in America* (Oxford: Oxford University Press, 1976), p. 63ff.

[28]Terence Cuneo and Rene Van Woundenberg, eds., *The Cambridge Companion to Thomas Reid* (Cambridge: Cambridge University Press, 2004), p. 85.

[29]Mark Ellingsen, "Common Sense Realism: The Cutting Edge of Evangelical Identity," *Dialog* 24, no. 3 (1985): 199.

and science each had a vital and largely noncontradictory role to play, however, would not bear the test of time. That is, the largely static conception of science found in the writings of some of the Princeton theologians would not endure. Moreover, subsequent theologians challenged the appropriateness of viewing the Bible, a very diverse body of literature, through the privileged lens of scientific empiricism. The Bible in their judgment was not simply a storehouse of facts.

Higher Criticism of the Bible

A millenarian reading of the Bible in conjunction with the doctrine of inerrancy espoused at Princeton created a cultural and intellectual climate in some of the Protestant denominations that could only spell trouble for someone like Charles A. Briggs (1841-1913), who saw little difficulty in applying higher critical methods to the Bible as he undertook his ministry as a seminary professor. Having studied the works of Johann Eichhorn (1753-1827), F. C. Baur (1792-1860) and Julius Wellhausen (1844-1918), Briggs believed that historical criticism in raising key questions in terms of sources, date, authorship and form—in other words, to consider the Bible in some sense as any piece of literature—did not detract from "the infallibility of Holy Scripture as a rule of faith and practice."[30] Appointed to the Edward Robinson Chair of Biblical Theology at Union Seminary in New York, Briggs delivered his inaugural address in January 1891, in which he "disavowed biblical inerrancy," to the chagrin of several in attendance.[31] He was quickly charged with heresy, was tried by the New York Presbytery, which acquitted him, but was found guilty by the Presbyterian Church General Assembly, which then suspended him from ministry. Briggs recovered somewhat by retaining his position at Union and by his reception into the priesthood of the Episcopal Church in 1899.

Members of the northern Presbyterian denomination who were troubled by the lack of orthodoxy of Union Seminary's graduates persuaded the Presbyterian General Assembly of 1910 to articulate in an unambiguous statement the fundamentals of the Christian faith. The As-

---

[30]Gaustad, *Religious History of America*, p. 256.
[31]Thomas A. Askew and Richard V. Pierard, *The American Church Experience: A Concise History* (Grand Rapids: Baker, 2004), p. 134.

sembly focused on five basic truths: (1) the inerrancy of Scripture, (2) the virgin birth of Christ, (3) the substitutionary atonement of Christ, (4) the bodily resurrection of Jesus, and (5) the authenticity of miracles.[32] A year earlier two Christian laymen, Milton Stewart (1838-1923) and Lyman Stewart (1840-1923), funded the publication of twelve volumes that contained articles supporting the fundamentals of the Christian faith. A. C. Dixon (1854-1925), a popular evangelist and Bible expositor, and R. A. Torrey (1856-1928), who had been called by Moody to head the Bible Institute of the Chicago Evangelization Society, assumed editorial leadership of the project. Eventually these writings were sent free of charge to "ministers of the gospel, missionaries, Sunday School superintendents, and others engaged in aggressive Christian work through out the English speaking world."[33]

In 1917 William Bell Riley (1861-1947), a minister who tried to snuff out the spread of modernism in the Northern Baptist Convention, published *The Menace of Modernism*, in which he railed against those who were transforming the Christian faith in light of the theory of evolution.[34] The following summer Riley, along with a few leaders from the Bible and prophetic conference movement, developed the idea of the World's Christian Fundamentals Association, and the first meeting was held in May 1919.[35] It was not until the following year, however, that the term *fundamentalist* was coined by Curtis Lee Laws, editor of the Baptist paper *The Watchman Examiner*. So defined, a fundamentalist was one who was ever ready "to do battle royal for the Fundamentals."[36] The terminology of Laws, then, was "a protest against the rationalistic interpretation of Christianity which seeks to discredit supernaturalism."[37] Theological modernists soon became fearful of fundamentalist initiatives in the northern churches, and Harry Emerson Fosdick (1878-1969), pastor of the famous Riverside Church in New York, viewed the whole controversy as one between enlightened

---

[32]Marsden, *Fundamentalism and American Culture*, p. 117.
[33]R. A. Torrey and A. C. Dixon, eds., *The Fundamentals: A Testimony to the Truth* (1917; reprint, Grand Rapids: Baker, 1980), 1:5.
[34]Carpenter, *Revive Us Again*, p. 37.
[35]Marsden, *Fundamentalism and American Culture*, p. 158.
[36]Ibid., p. 159.
[37]Marty, *Noise of Conflict*, p. 160.

reason on one side and gross superstition, even ignorance, on the other. In 1922 he queried from the pulpit, "Shall the fundamentalists win?" This probe was quickly answered by Rev. Clarence E. Macartney, senior pastor of Philadelphia's Arch Street Presbyterian Church, who retorted from his own pulpit, "Shall unbelief win?"[38]

In terms of properly assessing fundamentalism beyond the heated objections of its critics, George Marsden's work represents an advance over the carefully argued thesis of Sandeen in that it understands this energetic movement as a complex cultural phenomenon, that is, as a distinct version of evangelicalism "uniquely shaped by the circumstances of America in the early twentieth century."[39] So understood, fundamentalism is "militantly antimodernist Protestant evangelicalism."[40] Or to put it even more succinctly and in a way that Jerry Falwell himself, much later on, would have it: "a fundamentalist is an evangelical who is angry about something."[41]

Marsden's contribution, then, is so valuable because it has contextualized the militancy and anger of fundamentalists against the backdrop of broader American cultural trends rendering such elements intelligible. Again, fundamentalists of the early twentieth century were evangelical Christians "close to the traditions of the dominant American revivalist establishment of the nineteenth century."[42] That is, they were the heirs of this rich cultural legacy that was very much a part of the evangelical narrative and identity. However, by the turn of the century much of this cultural and intellectual capital had been spent. The power of evangelicals who were taking a fundamentalist turn had been dissipated by cultural forms and movements that they could no longer embrace. Evangelicals were now becoming a part of the disinherited; a designation that had always—or so it seemed—pertained to the "other." Now it was evangelicals themselves who were being left behind, and they were angry.

Throughout the 1920s the fundamentalist controversy was largely limited to two denominations: the Northern Baptist Convention and the

---

[38]Douglas A. Sweeney, *The American Evangelical Story: A History of the Movement* (Grand Rapids: Baker Academic, 2005), p. 167.
[39]Marsden, *Fundamentalism and American Culture*, p. 3.
[40]Ibid., p. 4.
[41]Marsden, *Understanding Fundamentalism*, p. 1.
[42]Marsden, *Fundamentalism and American Culture*, p. 4.

Presbyterian Church in the U.S.A., though there were some rumblings among the Disciples of Christ.[43] As a Presbyterian New Testament scholar at Princeton Seminary, John Gresham Machen (1881-1937) challenged not a few of the conclusions that some scholars were drawing in terms of their use of higher criticism. The modernists, as Machen referred to them, struck at the vitals of the Christian faith because like the ancient Gnostics they utilized all the vocabulary of Christianity (grace, redemption, atonement, etc.) but invested this terminology with entirely new meanings.

In his classic critique *Christianity and Liberalism,* which was published in 1923, Machen maintained that "what the liberal theologian has retained after abandoning to the enemy one Christian doctrine after another is not Christianity at all, but a religion which is so entirely different from Christianity as to belong in a distinct category."[44] Mincing no words, Machen contended that liberalism, in making the highest goal of life "the healthy and harmonious and joyous development of existing human faculties," actually descended into paganism.[45] In other words, modernistic liberalism, like ancient paganism, whether in its Greek or Roman forms, was unduly optimistic in terms of the capacity of unassisted human nature, whereas "Christianity is the religion of the broken heart."[46] Again, liberalism is in the imperative mood, while the Christian faith is in the triumphant indicative mood.[47] In short, liberalism "appeals to man's will," Machen declared, "while Christianity announces, first, a gracious act of God."[48]

Though Machen had taught that many true Christian people, not simply liberal opponents of the faith, did not accept the plenary inspiration of the Bible,[49] his views (and those of other fundamentalists) were nevertheless rejected by the Presbyterian Church (PCUSA), which reorganized Princeton Seminary more to its own theological liking in 1929. Effectively forced out of his own educational institution by this de-

---

[43]Mark Ellingsen, *The Evangelical Movement: Growth, Impact, Controversy, Dialog* (Minneapolis: Augsburg, 1988), p. 87.

[44]J. Gresham Machen, *Christianity & Liberalism* (Grand Rapids: Eerdmans, 1990), pp. 6-7. It is Machen himself who makes a strong connection between theological "liberalism" and "modernism."

[45]Ibid., p. 65.

[46]Ibid.

[47]Ibid., p. 47.

[48]Ibid.

[49]Ibid., p. 75.

nominational move, Machen took the lead in establishing Westminster Seminary in Philadelphia that same year, a seminary that remained faithful to the historic Westminster Confession. Machen was suspended from ministry in the Presbyterian Church in 1935, and, along with a few other conservatives, helped to form the Orthodox Presbyterian Church in 1936, which is still in existence today.

Shailer Mathews, representing the outlook of modernism, responded to Machen's argument in his own *The Faith of Modernism*, in 1924. In this work he took on the apologetic task of using the methods of Enlightenment science to discern the central values of the faith in order to meet the needs of the modern world: "An un-theological, practical, scientific age is shaping a religious and moral Christianity which has its own intellectual expression and method, its own uplift and revelation; a religion which is intellectually tenable as it is spiritually inspiring."[50] The goal, of course, was to make the teachings of the Christian faith and the Bible relevant to contemporaries, and thereby maintain the ongoing intellectual power of the faith. As Martin Marty points out, modernists "were genuinely agitated by the idea that, if Fundamentalists won, Christianity would become so implausible that the faith could no longer help shape the culture or attract and 'save' the thoughtful individual."[51] Critics, however, charged that the central doctrines of Christianity were actually transformed in this modernistic apologetic process to the point that they were no longer recognizable. Enlightenment sensibilities and judgments, especially in terms of an empirical method, had essentially displaced the narrative of the Bible.

A second major element of modernism critiqued by Machen and others was its teaching that God is immanent. In other words, the Most High is very close to human beings and is therefore revealed through the slow, gradual processes of human culture. Rejecting the notion of Søren Kierkegaard (1813-1855) that there is an infinite qualitative distinction between God and humanity, the modernists of the early twentieth century ran the risk of confusing the all-too-human with the divine, of mistaking human achievement for the kingdom of God. Reinhold Niebuhr (1892-

---

[50]Shailer Mathews, *The Faith of Modernism* (New York: Macmillan, 1925), p. 13. See also Marty, *Noise of the Conflict*, p. 171.

[51]Marty, *Noise of the Conflict*, p. 168.

1971) criticized this tendency among liberal Protestants of the early twentieth century by pointing out that their faith "involved no discontinuities, no crises, no tragedies or sacrifices, no loss of all things, no cross and resurrection."[52] Such a faith actually extolled not God but humanity.

With such a faith in place, several modernists had little difficulty in redefining some of the basic, traditional teachings of the church for a better cultural fit. Once again, Shailer Mathews, for example, in his pamphlet *Will Christ Come Again?* rejected a literal second coming of Christ and taught instead that the "true Second Coming was the triumph of the ideals of Jesus in human affairs."[53] And Francis John McConnell (1871-1953), Methodist bishop and president of the Federal Council of Churches, quickly mixed American culture with divine action: "I do not misrepresent the churches in the Federal Council when I say that by the sheer magnitude of our enterprise we may take a new place, and make possible a more adequate revelation of God."[54] Elias Sanford recalled the earlier speech of a bishop at the opening of the FCC in which American nationalism was so readily related to the Christian faith: "Let it be ours to sustain that flag and to see to it that wherever that flag goes our holy religion goes, in every part of the world."[55]

Unlike their fundamentalist, premillennial counterparts, the modernists of the early twentieth century, precisely because they continued some of the postmillennial traditions of evangelicalism, were much more susceptible to equating the advance of American civilization with the kingdom of God. It seemed as if a sacred canopy, to borrow the terminology of Peter Berger, was placed atop the narrative of American liberal democracy, with its emphasis on autonomy, freedom and individual rights, such that the elements of the gospel itself took their shape from another source.[56] Such a consideration helps to explain, at least in part, why many liberal modernists began to underscore the importance of social welfare not only as an expression of Christian love, which it clearly was, but

---

[52]Reinhold Niebuhr, cited in ibid., pp. 319-20.
[53]Carpenter, *Revive Us Again*, p. 39.
[54]Francis John McConnell, cited in Marty, *Noise of the Conflict*, p. 36.
[55]Marty, *Noise of the Conflict*, pp. 36-37.
[56]See Peter L. Berger, *The Sacred Canopy: Elements of a Sociological Theory of Religion* (New York: Anchor Books, 1990).

also as the chief means of influencing the culture.[57]

What was at stake, then, in the struggle between fundamentalists and modernists, among other things, was nothing less than the power to influence broader American culture—or so they had thought. And if modernists could claim that fundamentalism was anti-intellectual in its basic rejection of a higher critical approach to the Bible, and therefore not deserving of a larger cultural role, fundamentalists could in turn argue that modernism represented a very acculturated faith, one that could hardly bear the name Christian.

EVOLUTION

Prior to the Civil War evangelical religion and science operated without many of the antagonisms that would later emerge. During this period science was for the most part "practical and utilitarian" in outlook.[58] In other words, it had not yet taken on the "ideal of professionalization and research" that would mark the twentieth century.[59] Moreover, the evangelical religion of the day, fortified in its worldview, once again, by common sense realism was at first largely untroubled by the publication of Charles Darwin's *The Origin of Species* in 1859. The way for embracing evolutionary thought had been prepared for some evangelicals by George Frederick Wright (1838-1921), professor of science and religion at Oberlin College, and Asa Gray (1810-1888), a Harvard botanist, who both put forth a position that "harmonized Darwinism and Christian theism."[60] And John Fiske (1842-1901), philosopher as well as a man of faith, championed Darwin's cause in several essays and contended that "Evolution is God's way of doing things."[61] Evangelical Christians were further reassured that what came to be known as theistic evolution was indeed a viable option for them through the careful work of Henry Drummond (1851-1897), who wrote *Natural Law in the Spiritual World* in 1883.[62]

---

[57]Ibid., p. 216.

[58]Walter H. Conser Jr., *God and the Natural World* (Columbia: University of South Carolina Press, 1993), p. 10.

[59]Ibid., p. 11.

[60]Askew and Pierard, *American Church Experience*, p. 131.

[61]Marsden, *Understanding Fundamentalism*, pp. 36-37.

[62]Winthrop S. Hudson, *Religion in America: An Historical Account of the Development of American Religious Life* (New York: Charles Scribner's, 1973), p. 268.

Interestingly enough, even a fundamentalist such as Reuben Torrey and the Princeton theologian B. B. Warfield accepted theistic evolution. Torrey, for example, exclaimed at one point that a Christian could "believe thoroughly in the absolute infallibility of the Bible and still be an evolutionist of a certain type."[63] And Warfield, for his part, affirmed in a lecture given at Princeton Theological Seminary in 1888 that "I do not think that there is any general statement in the Bible or any part of the account of creation, either as given in Genesis 1 and 2 or elsewhere alluded to, that need be opposed to evolution."[64] Nevertheless all was not well in the evangelical camp simply because no one less than Charles Hodge leveled several serious objections against the new theory. But before a few of these criticisms can be considered, it must be borne in mind that the Darwinism of the latter part of the nineteenth century was much different from that of today. According to Larsen, biologists of this period still defended "a variety of evolutionary mechanisms including Lamarckian ones" (the view that an organism can pass on characteristics that it acquired through experience to its offspring), and the contribution of genetics to evolutionary theory would only come later during the 1930s and 1940s in what would be known as neo-Darwinism.[65]

With these caveats in place, Hodge's criticism of evolution, found both in his essay "What Is Darwinism?" written in 1874, and later in his *Systematic Theology* (1871-1873), struck at the heart of the theory in terms of its basic assumptions and presuppositions. In the second volume of his major theology, for example, in a section on anthropology, Hodge observed:

> The theory in question cannot be true, because it is founded on the assumption of an impossibility. It assumes that matter does the work of mind. This is an impossibility and an absurdity in the judgment of all men except materialists. . . . God, says Darwin, created the unintelligent living cell; . . . after that first step, all else follows by natural law, without purpose and without design.[66]

---

[63]Reuben Torrey, cited in Larson, *Summer for the Gods,* p. 32.

[64]Benjamin B. Warfield, "Evolution or Development," in *Evolution, Science, and Scripture: Selected Writings,* ed. Mark Noll and David Livingstone (Grand Rapids: Baker, 2000), p. 130.

[65]Ibid., p. 26.

[66]Charles Hodge, *Systematic Theology* (Peabody, Mass.: Hendrickson, 1999), 2:15.

Since evolution as taught by Darwin simply focused on material causation, excluding the possibility of the influence of mind or intelligence at the outset (that is, such elements were excluded methodologically), Hodge could only conclude that "the system is thoroughly atheistic, and therefore cannot possibly stand."[67]

In the same year that Hodge published his essay "What Is Darwinism?" John William Draper (1811-1882) exacerbated an already difficult situation in his polemical work *History of the Conflict Between Religion and Science*. Draper's contribution was followed by an equally acerbic work, *A History of the Warfare of Science with Theology in Christendom*, by Andrew Dickson White in 1896. The warfare model articulated in this literature was embraced by several key secularists in the early twentieth century who cared little for religious faith. Clarence Darrow (1857-1938), for instance, lawyer for the defense at the famous Scopes Trial, was taught this perspective by his father, who eagerly consumed the writings of Draper.[68]

Around 1910 American scientists began to distinguish their views very clearly from religious ones, "especially from the academically discredited conservative Biblicist views."[69] And though biologists who espoused Darwin's theory insisted that their work simply touched on empirical, scientific matters, the patterns of belief in terms of this particular population suggested a much different picture. To illustrate, James H. Leuba (1867-1946) of Bryn Mawr University conducted an early survey among professors and discovered unbelief was higher among biologists than other scientists, and the greater the prestige of the scientist the higher level of unbelief.[70] Consequently, "the smallest percentage of believers [was] found among the greatest biologists; they count only 16.9 percent of believers in God."[71] A comparison of this statistic with the percentage of Americans at the time who held theistic views suggests that these biologists, despite their claims to the contrary, were not content to remain within the parameters of the scientific method but instead began to make several philosophical judgments, especially in terms of the question of the existence of

---

[67]Ibid.
[68]Larson, *Summer for the Gods*, p. 22.
[69]Marsden, *Understanding Fundamentalism*, p. 144.
[70]Larson, *Summer of the Gods*, p. 41.
[71]Ibid.

God, that were not warranted by their empirical approach.

The implications of Darwin's theory of evolution, with an emphasis on natural selection, were explored in a number of ways. For example, a half-cousin of Darwin, Sir Francis Galton (1822-1911), was a pioneer in the field of eugenics (the study of breeding in order to improve the human species), having coined the term in 1883. In studying various populations through an adept use of statistics, Galton coined the phrase *nature versus nurture* and became very interested in seeing that the uppercrust be encouraged to marry early through handsome financial incentives. Closer to home Margaret Sanger (1879-1966) adapted the young field of eugenics (literally "born well") to the need for birth control, and in 1921 she established the American Birth Control League (that later became Planned Parenthood). Much more controversial than Galton, her British counterpart, Sanger championed a "negative eugenics" that called for various forms of social intervention in order to eliminate undesirable breeding. Other social activists who held similar views argued for selective breeding and even sterilization to improve the human community. One of Sanger's preferred ways of achieving the goals of negative eugenics was through the restriction of immigrants to the United States, a cause for which she is well known. The American church, however, both Protestant and Roman Catholic, "resented the anti-immigrant thrust of eugenic reformers."[72] Nevertheless, by 1932, according to Lichtman, twenty-seven states had enacted sterilization laws "targeting the least powerful."[73] And Larson points out that by 1935 thirty-five states enacted laws "to compel the sexual segregation and sterilization of certain persons viewed as eugenically unfit."[74]

Yet another implication (mistaken or not) that some drew from Darwin's concept of natural selection was that the survival of the fittest, so to speak, could be understood socially, that is, in terms of the composition of society itself. Herbert Spencer (1820-1903) led the way in this area and developed a line of thought and a set of practices that would later be referred to as social Darwinism. He argued, among other things, that evolution must be understood not simply biologically but also socially, especially in

---

[72]Lichtman, *White Protestant Nation*, p. 37.
[73]Ibid.
[74]Larson, *Summer of the Gods*, p. 27.

terms of wealth and poverty. Influenced by the earlier writings of Thomas Malthus (1766-1834)—who had taught that populations often outrun their food supply with the result that the weak simply perish—Spencer viewed evolution as a "unifying philosophical principle" that could be applied to "social structures, economic developments, race relations, and the growth of nations."[75] Beyond this, William Graham Sumner (1840-1910) offered a few variations on the theme of social Darwinism and considered the on-going influence of religion in society (that some suggested could ame-liorate the hard realities of natural selection) as "sentimental."[76] But if Sumner's judgments were accurate, then perhaps Charles Darwin himself was not a social Darwinist, because in his work *The Descent of Man* he fac-tored in the social instincts of "sympathy" and "moral sentiments" as having consequence in the overall scheme of things.[77] In other words, there is a place for human beneficence and compassion in any social order. The reality is not as stark or as brutal as some of the social Darwinists would have it.

THE SCOPES TRIAL

Almost sixty years after the publication of Darwin's classic, many more evangelicals were beginning to have doubts about the implications of evo-lutionary theory, especially along the lines of Hodge's earlier reflections. William Bell Riley, for instance, head of the World's Christian Fundamen-talist Association, lobbied state legislatures to pass laws against the teaching of evolution, because in his judgment this theory not only under-mined belief in God as the Creator but it also detracted from the dignity of humanity. Riley was successful in the state legislature of Tennessee, which passed the Butler Act in 1925, prohibiting the teaching of evolution. In an attempt to garner publicity for the small town of Dayton, Tennessee (pop-ulation around 1,700), George Rappleyea, manager of the Cumberland Coal and Iron Company, conceived a plan to test the new law by having his young friend, the twenty-four-year-old John T. Scopes, teach evolution in

---

[75]Richard Kyle, *Evangelicalism: An Americanized Christianity* (New Brunswick, N.J.: Transaction, 2006), p. 58.

[76]Marsden, *Religion and American Culture*, p. 123.

[77]Charles Darwin, *The Descent of Man* (New York: A. L. Fowle, 1874).

the classroom. Scopes complied and was indicted on May 25, 1925. A grand jury was assembled and a trial date was set.

Rappleyea's instincts were indeed correct, for in the meantime, before the trial took place, Dayton had attracted national attention. The team of prosecuting attorneys now included William Jennings Bryan, the Great Commoner and three-time presidential candidate. Clarence Darrow, an agnostic who regarded Christianity as a "slave religion" was at the helm of the defense.[78] In his efforts, Darrow was assisted by the American Civil Liberties Union, which took a special interest in the case and framed it in terms of the protection of First Amendment rights. The trial lasted eight days in the sweltering heat of Dayton. In the end Scopes was convicted of violating the Tennessee statute, on July 21, and was fined one hundred dollars. Bryan had won the legal battle but he lost the larger cultural war.

The trial itself was something of a fiasco and was covered by over two hundred reporters from Dayton to London.[79] Complex intellectual issues emerged cartoonlike in some of the national papers, with the fundamentalists being characterized as buffoons. H. L. Mencken (1880-1956), for example, a reporter for the *Baltimore Sun*, derided, misquoted and vilified Bryan so that he appeared as an aging fool. This was neither an accurate nor an even-handed account of the events in Dayton, but rather an argument that proceeded largely by contempt. Revealing a few of his many caustic prejudices a year before the trial, Mencken remarked, "Christendom may be defined briefly as that part of the world in which, if any man stands up in public and solemnly swears that he is a Christian, all his auditors will laugh."[80]

Some small-town newspapers, such as a few in Kansas, for example, were far more accurate in their reporting than the national dailies, and the trial was not depicted as a "public humiliation" of Bryan.[81] Instead this key leader of the Democratic Party (who was so popular that he had won the nomination of his party over incumbent Grover Cleveland in 1896) emerged as a controversial, though honorable man. Bryan was undoubtedly

---

[78]Larson, *Summer of the Gods*, p. 71.

[79]Ibid., p. 142.

[80]H. L. Mencken, cited in *The Evangelicals: What They Believe, Who They Are, Where They Are Changing*, ed. David F. Wells and John D. Woodbridge (Nashville: Abingdon, 1975), p. 123.

[81]Julie A. Scott, "More Than Just Monkey Business," *Kansas History* 30, no. 2 (2007): 78.

one of the most popular progressives of the late-nineteenth and early-twentieth centuries. Combining a commitment to evangelical Christianity with "a willingness to cooperate with those who differed,"[82] Bryan was a national leader who believed that his deeply held faith was not incompatible with the best that a Jeffersonian democracy had to offer.[83] As a key progressive Bryan gave his support to four constitutional amendments that helped to bring some important reforms to the nation: "direct election of Senators, progressive taxation, Prohibition and women's suffrage."[84] Having spent the better part of his career championing the cause of the underdog, Bryan criticized the excesses of capitalism, denounced the unfair practices of trusts and argued for greater government regulation of the banks.[85]

So why then was Bryan opposed to the teaching of evolution in public schools? First, it was not because he was an anti-intellectual, as suggested in Richard Hofstadter's account.[86] Instead, Bryan believed that evolution in its emphasis on natural selection, viewed as a brute and raw struggle for existence (survival of the fittest), would suggest a political approach, offered even by some of the social Darwinists of his day, that left the poor and the downtrodden behind. Moreover, on an international scale, where the forces of *realpolitik* were in play, Bryan viewed World War I as "the European's embracing of the theory of evolution, and applying it to societal struggle for dominance."[87] Second, Bryan thought that the conclusions some would draw from the teaching of evolution would readily undermine belief in God. That is, evolutionary doctrine would not remain simply within the limits of empirical science but would suggest philosophical views, a basic metaphysics, even if only implicitly. "I object to the Darwinian theory," Bryan exclaimed, "because I fear we shall lose the consciousness of God's presence in our daily life, if we must accept the theory that through all the ages no spiritual force has touched the life

---

[82]Marsden, *Fundamentalism and American Culture*, p. 133.

[83]Matthew J. Tontonoz, "The Scopes Trial Revisited: Social Darwinism Versus Social Gospel," *Science as Culture* 17, no. 2 (2008): 134.

[84]Ibid.

[85]Ibid., p. 133.

[86]Richard Hofstadter, *Anti-Intellectualism in American Life* (New York: Vintage Books, 1962), p. 130.

[87]Thomas W. Segady, "Traditional Religion, Fundamentalism, and Institutional Transition in the 20th Century," *Social Science Journal* 43, no. 2 (2006): 204.

of man and shaped the destiny of nations."[88]

About a year before taking on the Scopes case, Clarence Darrow, Bryan's counterpart in the trial, had defended the cause of Nathan Freudenthal Leopold Jr. and Richard Albert Loeb in what was hailed as the trial of the century. The two young, intellectually gifted defendants, one of whom had dabbled in the philosophy of Nietzsche, decided that they would kidnap and kill an innocent teenager (Bobby Franks) simply for the fun of it; that is, to prove that they were genuine "supermen" (*Übermenschen*) not subject to the moral scruples or pangs of conscience of ordinary people. In order to spare their lives Darrow surprised the media and had the two defendants plead guilty. This action resulted in the handing down of two sentences of life imprisonment. In the final hearing, which lasted a whole day, Darrow argued before the judge, and in a way that Bryan found to be deeply troubling, that these youths were the products of their ancestors, and could they really, after all, be held accountable for carrying out the German philosophy that they had learned at the university?

At Dayton, Darrow was adept at spinning the trial in a direction that not only obscured several of the issues at stake but one that also painted Bryan in a very unfavorable light. Upon leaving for Tennessee, Darrow opined, "Nothing will satisfy us but broad victory, a knockout which will have an everlasting precedent to prove that America is founded on liberty and not on narrow, mean, intolerable and brainless prejudice of soulless religio-maniacs."[89] In order to achieve the proper effect Darrow placed Bryan on the stand and grilled him in terms of the early chapters of Genesis, demonstrating that the head of the prosecution was no match for Darrow's rhetorical powers in cross-examination. Bryan was after all a sincere and earnest layman and not a biblical scholar well acquainted with the intricacies of higher criticism. And then in a masterful stroke, "fearing an oratorical tour-de-force from Bryan," Darrow offered no closing summation and thereby denied Bryan the same.[90] In his closing speech, in which his own gifts and arguments would surely come to the forefront, Bryan had hoped to view the trial against the backdrop of the Leopold and

---

[88]William Jennings Bryan, cited in Larson, *Summer for the Gods*, p. 39.
[89]Clarence Darrow, cited in Larson, *Summer for the Gods*, p. 146.
[90]Tontonoz, "Scopes Trial Revisited," p. 122.

Loeb murder, Nietzsche's philosophy, social Darwinism and the eugenics movement. But he never got the chance. Exhausted from the ordeal Bryan died a few days later—and some said as a broken man.

The myth making, however, did not stop with Darrow's rhetorical skills. After the trial many cultural leaders expressed outright disdain toward fundamentalism. In 1931 Frederick Lewis Allen, for example, in his *Only Yesterday: An Informal History of the Nineteen Twenties*, portrayed the Scopes Trial as a defeat for old-time religion, as if this deeply held faith contained nothing of value: "The position of the Fundamentalists seemed almost hopeless. The tide of *all* rational thought in a rational age seemed to be running against them."[91] A couple of years after the trial, in 1927, Sinclair Lewis published his novel *Elmer Gantry* in which the principal character, a preacher, was depicted as a shady, troubled deceiver, ever eager for personal gain at the expense of others.[92] By the time the book was made into a movie in 1960 (in which Burt Lancaster and Jean Simmons starred) the stereotype that ministers were basically dishonorable folk was already well worked in American popular culture.

The chief vehicle, however, for communicating the issues that were on stage at the Scopes Trail was none other than the 1955 play by Jerome Lawrence and Robert Edwin Lee titled *Inherit the Wind*. With a goal of combating the McCarthyism of the period, Lawrence and Lee distorted key elements of the historic trial in order to fit their contemporary purpose, and people of faith, once again, were portrayed as ignorant dupes. When the constitutional scholar Gerald Gunther attended the Broadway performance of the play, he remarked, "For the first time I walked out of a play in disgust. . . . I ended up actually sympathizing with Bryan."[93] As recently as 1994 the National Center for History in Schools recommended that teachers use excerpts from *Inherit the Wind* to teach the views of Bryan and Darrow.[94] And when Tony Randall revived the play on Broadway in 1996,

---

[91]Frederick Lewis Allen, *Only Yesterday: An Informal History of the Nineteen-Twenties* (New York: Harper, 1931), p. 200. See also Brad Harper, "The Scopes Trial, Fundamentalism, and the Creation of an Anti-Culture Culture: Can Evangelical Christians Transcend Their History in the Culture Wars," *Cultural Encounters* 3, no. 1 (2006): 13.

[92]Sinclair Lewis, *Elmer Gantry* (New York: Harcourt, Brace, 1927), pp. 82ff.

[93]Gerald Gunther, cited in Larson, *Summer of the Gods*, p. 242.

[94]Larson, *Summer of the Gods*, p. 244.

the critics hailed it as "pertinent and timely."[95] The irony in all of this, of course, is that the critics of fundamentalism who use the Scopes Trial as their vehicle are supposed to be the critical thinkers, the "bright ones," as it were, and yet they have apparently not even taken the trouble to get the facts straight, much less consider what were the actual (and in many instances reasonable) concerns of a fundamentalist like William Jennings Bryan.

THE WESLEYAN AND PENTECOSTAL DIFFERENCE

Fundamentalism as a distinct movement was a response found principally among Baptists and Presbyterians to rapid cultural and intellectual change in early twentieth-century America. *Militant* opposition to modernism was not, after all, a Methodist theme. Though conservative Wesleyans, broadly understood, clearly did embrace the doctrinal concerns of their Reformed brothers and sisters, and were therefore orthodox, they were never as deeply pained by each cultural turn, each intellectual shift.[96] One of the reasons there was not anything quite like the Briggs trial within the Wesleyan ranks (which would include Methodists, Holiness groups and Pentecostals) was that they were not so much epistemologically (emphasis on knowledge) as they were soteriologically (highlighting redemption) oriented. In other words, Wesleyans at the beginning of the twentieth century were not trying to articulate a cultural philosophy that would constitute the capstone of a Christian civilization in America. That is, they were preoccupied not so much with questions of knowledge or intellect, but with those of salvation. As noted earlier, such an emphasis clearly reflected their rich evangelical pietist heritage that went back to the father of Methodism, John Wesley himself.

Given their concern to underscore the importance of salvation in general and sanctification in particular, of a life marked by the graces of holy love, Wesleyans faced the possible decline and even death of their movement through the specter of ongoing enculturation, of being co-opted by broader American culture, especially in terms of the allure of

---

[95]Ibid., p. 264.

[96]In terms of Darwinism and higher criticism, for instance, Vinson Synan points out that "the holiness and Pentecostal movement generally cite these currents of thought as the 'false doctrines' against which the movement protested" (Vinson Synan, *The Holiness-Pentecostal Movement in the United States* [Grand Rapids: Eerdmans, 1987], p. 57).

wealth and upward mobility. This salient theme has been explored in the past by Donald Dayton in his "embourgeoisement" hypothesis.[97] Riley Case explored this dilemma in terms of distinguishing establishment Methodism with its "tall steeples, rented pews, [and] robed choirs" from populist Methodism with its "log cabins, moral crusades, circuit preachers, revivals [and] camp meetings."[98] But this consideration of nineteenth-century Wesleyans should not be understood simply in terms of class analysis in which economic factors receive the lion's share of attention. For interlaced with the prospect of embourgeoisement, to use Dayton's term, was the preoccupation with holiness, the doctrine of entire sanctification in particular, which many Holiness leaders believed was being shunted aside in the quest for social respectability by "regency" factions within denominations. In other words, as in Wesley's own day, the fear was that riches would empty out the life of the Spirit, wealth would replace redemption itself, such that what remained was simply the form of religion, mahogany Methodism as Case put it, that lacked the vital power of the Spirit of holiness.

One of the key champions of holiness in the nineteenth century was Phoebe Palmer (1807-1874). Her Tuesday meetings, held at her home in New York City, demonstrated a renewed interest in the doctrine of entire sanctification and eventually led to the establishment of the National Camp Meeting Association for the Promotion of Holiness. As holiness proponents stressed the importance of a "second work" of grace, beyond conversion, they were looked upon with disdain by some of the settled clergy of the Methodist Episcopal Church. One Methodist bishop, for instance, complained, "There has sprung up among us a party with holiness as a watchword: they have holiness associations, holiness meetings, holiness preachers, holiness evangelists, and holiness property."[99] Holiness folk both "came out" and were "pushed out" of their larger denominations such that by the end of the nineteenth century a virtual empire of denominations that made holiness their abiding interest was now in existence,

---

[97]Donald Dayton, "The Embourgeoisement of a Vision: Lament of a Radical Evangelical," *The Other Side* 23 (1987): 19.

[98]Riley B. Case, *Evangelical and Methodist: A Popular History* (Nashville: Abingdon, 2004), p. 14.

[99]Marty, *Irony of It All*, pp. 241-42.

including the Wesleyan Methodist Church (1843), the Free Methodist Church (1860), the Church of God Anderson (1881), the Church of the Nazarene, as well as some smaller black Holiness communions such as the Zion Union Apostolic Church (1869).

Through the influence of Palmer, Asa Mahan (1799-1889) and others, many Wesleyans began to identify the doctrine of entire sanctification with the baptism of the Holy Spirit. The Pentecostals who were coalescing around the turn of the century found this teaching congenial. Indeed according to both Synan and Dayton, Pentecostalism is best understood as a child of the holiness movement. Thus, to the second work of grace was added "the 'Pentecostal baptism' with the evidence of speaking in tongues as a 'third blessing,' superimposed [upon] the other two."[100] Pentecostals, like their Holiness cousins, were never content merely with the form of religion but wanted nothing less than the active, real and sustaining power of the Holy Spirit in their daily lives.

Since many, though clearly not all, Pentecostals were Arminian in their theology, they too were unwilling to become too closely identified with fundamentalism.[101] Indeed, the fundamentalist controversy that had so disrupted American Protestantism left the Pentecostals "largely untouched."[102] And since Holiness and Pentecostal groups were major sources of black evangelicalism, African Americans rarely took on the militancy of fundamentalism. Moreover, the fundamentalists themselves rejected Pentecostals outright, viewing them as excessive, even fanatical. In fact, at the 1928 convention of the World's Christian Fundamentals Association, the Pentecostals were "soundly condemned."[103] Consequently those interpreters who view Pentecostalism simply as fundamentalist Christianity with "a doctrine of Spirit baptism and gifts added on," will be very disappointed.[104]

Charles Fox Parham (1873-1929) was the first to teach that the biblical evidence for having received the baptism of the Holy Spirit was the gift of

[100]Synan, *Holiness Pentecostal Movement*, p. 115. See also Donald W. Dayton, *The Theological Roots of Pentecostalism* (Grand Rapids: Francis Asbury Press, 1987), p. 143.

[101]Ibid., p. 205.

[102]Ibid., p. 221.

[103]Ibid., p. 206.

[104]Steven J. Land, *Pentecostal Spirituality: A Passion for the Kingdom* (Sheffield, U.K.: Sheffield Academic Press, 2001), p. 29.

tongues.[105] He viewed this gift as part of the "latter rain" promised in the book of Joel. On December 31, 1900, Parham conducted a watch night service in Topeka, Kansas, at which Agnes N. Ozman began to speak in tongues after midnight, the first day of the new century. Spreading his Pentecostal teaching throughout the Midwest and into Texas, Parham established a Bible school in Houston in December 1905, where he caught the attention of William J. Seymour (1870-1922), a black hotel waiter and preacher. Due to the racism of the time, Seymour had to suffer the indignity of listening to Parham's lectures in the hallway since blacks were not permitted to sit in the same classroom as whites. Having profited from these lectures, Seymour headed west to Los Angeles and began to preach his Pentecostal doctrine in a dilapidated building on Azusa Street in 1906.

Seymour's anointed preaching helped to spark a revival at Azusa Street that lasted from 1906 to 1909. Tears flowed, confessions were made, and people spoke in tongues. One of the many uncanny things about this particular unction of the Spirit, beyond the freedom from the power of sin that it brought, was that the hard and fast lines of racial division were overcome in a unity that mirrored Pentecost. "In an age of Social Darwinism, Jim Crowism, and general white supremacy," Synan observes, "the fact that [blacks] and whites worshipped together in virtual equality among the Pentecostals was a significant exception."[106] Even more poignantly he adds, "The color line was washed away in the blood."[107] Here then was a different kind of power, not that of coercion, influence or social respectability, but of a holy love that brought people together in deep humility and loving communion. Such an anointing took evangelicals back to the roots of their identity as they glorified the Spirit, the One who had tabernacled among them in transforming power.

THE SOCIAL GOSPEL

In the early twentieth century and right on past World War I a number of evangelicals continued in their postmillennial ways, rejected fundamentalism and unflaggingly pursued the quest for a Christian America, despite

---

[105]Synan, *Holiness Pentecostal Movement*, p. 99.
[106]Ibid., p. 165.
[107]Ibid., p. 109.

the significant influx of Jews. Moreover, believing that the "golden age of society was right around the corner,"[108] seminary professors such as Walter Rauschenbusch (1861-1918), who had ministered in Hell's Kitchen in New York City, articulated a theology known as the Social Gospel. Identifying in some important ways the American nation, as a liberal democratic society, with the kingdom of God ("the conception of God can be cleansed from the historic accretions of despotism and be democratized"),[109] Rauschenbusch as well as Washington Gladden (1836-1918), pastor and leader of the progressive movement, created a theological climate in which the social creeds of the Protestant churches emerged. The Methodists, for example, published a social creed in 1908, and it in turn became the basis for several others. Rauschenbusch and Gladden saw clearly the disruptive nature of capitalism to the urban poor who were being left behind.

With an eye on the social dimension of the country, the theologians of this new movement developed the concept of social sin that pertained to the very structures of society. In other words, sin was not simply personal but corporate as well. Rauschenbusch, for example, in his *Christianity and the Social Crisis*, published in 1907, contended that social problems must take the lead. "If the Church has no live and bold thought on this dominant question of modern life," he reasoned, "its teaching authority on all other questions will dwindle and be despised."[110] While many viewed the social definition of sin as helpful, critics of the new terminology quickly pointed out that one was effectively a sinner simply by participating in any modern industrial society, with the result that clear lines of responsibility were blurred.[111] Moreover, upon closer examination the kingdom envisioned in the Social Gospel did not seem to be very different from "the bourgeois idealism of post-Civil War Victorian America and its Anglo-Saxon institutions."[112] This was an old Protestant habit, but it was dressed up in spanking new attire. To be sure, two of the more glaring blind spots of the Social Gospel were gender and race. Rauschenbusch, for example, resisted the Democratic Party plank of 1912 pertaining to women's rights.

---

[108]David Moberg, *The Great Reversal* (Philadelphia: Holman, 1972), p. 32.
[109]Walter Rauschenbusch, *A Theology for the Social Gospel* (Nashville: Abingdon, 1981), p. 187.
[110]Walter Rauschenbusch, *Christianity and the Social Crisis* (New York: Macmillan, 1907), p. 339.
[111]Moberg, *Great Reversal*, p. 122.
[112]Askew and Pierard, *American Church Experience*, p. 147.

"He had no use at all for suffrage," Marty notes.[113] Beyond this, important social justice issues that concerned blacks and others were virtually ignored. "Few pages of the Social Gospel are given over to creativity in respect to native Americans, Orientals, or blacks."[114]

Though the claim is sometimes made that the Social Gospel mirrored the reforming philosophy of the benevolent empire that had arisen in antebellum America, some important differences should be noted. First, many of the Social Gospel leaders engaged in an *ongoing critique* of personal salvation. This is something that Finney, for example, did not do. That is, the gifted evangelist did not play off one good news against the other; he viewed the gospel as one. But Rauschenbusch, for his part, repeatedly complained along the following lines: "The individualist gospel has taught us to see the sinfulness of every human heart. . . . But it has not given us an adequate understanding of the sinfulness of the social order."[115]

Second, Social Gospel pastors were often critical of revivalism's emphasis on instantaneous conversion. Indeed, these preachers, so socially minded, preferred to view salvation by and large as a synergistic process, of divine and human cooperation, in which a premium was placed on the efficaciousness of human activity as men and women served their neighbors in all manner of very tangible social action. Antebellum revivalists, on the other hand, such as Orange Scott (1800-1847) and Luther Lee (1800-1889), while mindful of the necessity of human action in easing the plight of the poor, especially in terms of their abolitionist efforts, were perhaps even more aware of the work that God *alone* could do, that is, in both forgiving sins and renewing the human heart in liberating love.

THE GREAT REVERSAL

What was once held together by nineteenth-century evangelical Protestants, that is, vibrant personal religion *and* extensive social action, broke up in the early twentieth century (sometime between 1900 and 1930) in what Timothy Smith in one of his lectures referred to as "the Great Reversal." Clearly for many of the fundamentalists the Social Gospel was no

---

[113]Marty, *Irony of It All*, p. 292.
[114]Ibid., p. 294.
[115]Rauschenbusch, *Theology of the Social Gospel*, p. 5.

gospel at all.[116] For example, in addressing the World Christian Fundamentalist Association in Philadelphia (1919), Riley fulminated against what he called "social service Christianity" that left out the soul.[117] And Aimee Semple McPherson (1890-1944), of Foursquare Gospel fame, who worked among the poor in Los Angeles, considered all other action than soul winning "basically a waste of time."[118]

The key issue in the breakup of American evangelicalism was not that leaders like Rauschenbusch and Gladden were endorsing social concern. Indeed, the Salvation Army did not miss a beat in its social witness from one century to the next. Rather Social Gospel leaders were perceived by their fundamentalist cousins as undertaking social action "in an exclusivistic way."[119] Such a judgment set up an unfortunate dynamic among fundamentalist evangelicals, who eventually abandoned important parts of their own story ("everywhere there is revival there must also be reform") by deprecating social issues. Moreover, the consequence of this shift was filled with a good deal of irony, for by 1930 the fundamentalists themselves had become as nearly exclusivist as their liberal counterparts. This time, however, the unswerving focus was not on social action but on a personal, individual gospel. The cause of the Great Reversal then was not simply "the fundamentalist *reaction* to the liberal Social Gospel after 1900."[120] It also included the prior action of the Social Gospelers themselves, who had neglected the very depths of personal religion. Even as late as 1966 at the World Congress on Evangelism, Billy Graham, who was by no means a fundamentalist, yet exclaimed: "The 'new' evangelism says soul winning is passé. It wants to apply Christian principles to the social order. Its proponents want to make the prodigal son comfortable, happy and prosperous in the far country without leading him back to the Father."[121]

THE FUNDAMENTALIST DILEMMA

The predicament of fundamentalists in the 1930s was clearly unenviable,

---

[116]Moberg, *Great Reversal*, p. 15.
[117]William Bell Riley, cited in Wells, *Evangelicals*, p. 198.
[118]Ibid., p. 217.
[119]Marsden, *Fundamentalism and American Culture*, p. 92.
[120]Ibid., p. 91 (emphasis added).
[121]Billy Graham, cited in Moberg, *Great Reversal*, p. 16.

for they were alienated on two key levels: first, in terms of their rejection by cultural elites, who as a consequence of their upward mobility often preferred that American civilization contain few religious elements;[122] and second with respect to liberal evangelicals who wanted to create as much distance as possible between themselves and their supposedly anti-intellectual, socially challenged fundamentalist neighbors. Stripped of their dominance in American culture, and having lost any leadership role in the mainline denominations, fundamentalists retreated into an enclave of institutions such as Bible colleges, separatist churches and mission boards that kept their premillennial vision alive.

Many fundamentalists, however, chaffed under this policy of separatism and retreat simply because the quest for a Christian America and the social power and influence it offered had been such an important part of the their own story, especially in terms of the revivalism that played out in the eighteenth and nineteenth centuries. That is, on the one hand, fundamentalists were repulsed by the direction of the country; on the other hand, they wanted to steer the ship, so to speak, thinking that their own moral and spiritual values were the best for the nation. Marsden repeatedly underscored this paradoxical tendency in his own work ("to indentify sometimes with the 'establishment' and sometimes with the 'outsiders'") and argued that fundamentalists "experienced profound ambivalence toward the surrounding culture."[123]

As the country entered an economic depression after the great stock market crash of 1929, many of the churches were depressed as well. As Carpenter notes, "[The] fundamentalists yearned for another Great Awakening that would revive the church's integrity and power, restore the culture's religious character, and bring back national prosperity."[124] But it was not to be. And as they awoke one morning in the middle of the 1930s some fundamentalists began to realize that perhaps the goal of a Christian America was over.[125] They had not, after all, witnessed the

---

[122]Nathan O. Hatch points out that "studies show that those most ready to jettison traditional religious constraints are precisely those whose cultural authority is rising" (Nathan O. Hatch, *The Democratization of American Christianity* [New Haven, Conn.: Yale University Press, 1989], p. 218).

[123]Marsden, *Fundamentalism and American Culture*, pp. 6, viii.

[124]Carpenter, *Revive Us Again*, p. 111.

[125]Robert Handy writes, "Since 1935, the debate over the relation of church and state has often been

arrival of the New Israel as they had hoped. Instead, they found themselves exiled to a land that had never been in their vision—Babylon, a very American Babylon.

clouded by lack of clear recognition that the Protestant era of American history has indeed come to an end" (Robert T. Handy, *A Christian America, Protestant Hopes and Historical Realities* [New York: Oxford University Press, 1971], p. 214).

2

Fundamentalism, Neo-Evangelicalism
and the Search for Power

The stock boom of the Roaring Twenties saw a rise in the stock market's value from 105 points at the beginning of the decade to a whopping 380 points at its end. The wild speculation that drove the boom eventually came crashing down on October 29, 1929, in a huge bust otherwise known as Black Tuesday. President Herbert Hoover (1874-1964) signed a large tax cut into law that same year to ease the burden on the average American, but his endorsement of the Smooth-Hawley Tariff the following year raised import duties to an all-time high and sparked a trade war that resulted in business stagnation and further market declines. By the time that Franklin D. Roosevelt (1882-1945) took office in March 1933, the market index ebbed at around 60 points.

The Great Depression and Its Aftermath

Robert Handy has argued that an already depressed Protestantism, having experienced several cultural shocks, was overtaken by the broadening economic depression. Two indicators of this decline can be seen in the falling church attendance[1] on the one hand (and not limited by the way to rural areas) and the diminished status of the clergy on the other.[2] During the

---

[1]Though church attendance may have been in decline, church affiliation was not. See Sydney E. Ahlstrom, *A Religious History of the American People*, vol. 2 (Garden City, N.Y.: Image Books, 1975), p. 448.
[2]Robert T. Handy, *A Christian America, Protestant Hopes and Historical Realities* (New York: Oxford University Press, 1971), p. 433.

economic downturn Protestantism experienced a spiritual lethargy such that it could no longer view itself as the nation's religion. Simply put, "the 'Protestant era' in America," Handy contended, "was brought to a close."[3]

Even with these general trends in American religion there were yet signs of vitality, especially among fundamentalists. Theological liberals at the time, however, sometimes painted a very quaint picture of American religion and apparently exchanged hard demographics for wishful thinking. The editors of the *Christian Century*, for example, opined that fundamentalism was "an event now passed, a brief, dysfunctional mutation away from the main line of religious evolution."[4] And in an article produced for the *Encyclopedia of the Social Sciences* in 1937, H. Richard Niebuhr described American evangelicalism in the *past* tense.[5] A more accurate assessment of the fortunes of the fundamentalists during the economic downturn, as unemployment rates were rising, can be found in the work of Joel Carpenter. Noting that fundamentalists were indeed at their "lowest point of visibility and respect during the 1930s," Carpenter goes on to point out that they were nevertheless "thriving and picking up institutional momentum."[6] Fundamentalists withdrew from the culture—or were rather dismissed from it—but they immediately set about to build an infrastructure in terms of education institutions, often in the form of Bible colleges, that kept their theological vision as well as their plausibility structures alive.[7] Beyond this, even the ideal of a liberal arts college yet remained an important part of the fundamentalist witness. To illustrate, during the 1930s Gordon College was established in Boston; Bob Jones College was relocated to Cleveland, Tennessee, in 1933; and William Jennings Bryan University was founded in 1930 in Dayton, Tennessee.[8]

With an educational infrastructure in place, fundamentalism focused on both ministry at home and missions abroad. Southern Baptists, for ex-

---

[3]Ibid., p. 442.
[4]Joel A. Carpenter, *Revive Us Again: The Reawakening of American Fundamentalism* (New York: Oxford University Press, 1997), p. 13.
[5]D. G. Hart, *That Old Time Religion in Modern America: Evangelical Protestantism in the Twentieth Century* (Chicago: I. R. Dee, 2002), p. 56.
[6]Carpenter, *Revive Us Again*, p. 32.
[7]Ibid., p. 86.
[8]Ibid., p. 21.

ample, gained about a million and a half members between 1926 and 1940.[9] And though the Pentecostals of the Assemblies of God were hardly fundamentalists, yet as a conservative faith that was in earnest to maintain both the form (orthodoxy) and the power of religion (baptism of the Holy Spirit), their numbers swelled fourfold during this same period.[10] Meanwhile mainline Protestant denominations that followed modernist trends in the name of relevance declined in terms of virtually every statistic imaginable: from membership to baptisms, from Sunday school enrollments to total receipts.[11]

Fundamentalists regrouped yet again during the 1930s by beginning to develop the media expertise for which they have become known. At first it appeared as if fundamentalists would be locked out of radio broadcasting. Theological liberals in the Federal Council of Churches, for example, petitioned CBS and NBC to stop the sale of religious programming so that their own supposedly "nonsectarian" offerings could be given exclusive free air time.[12] This scheme, however, quickly fell apart since the sale of religious broadcasting was far too lucrative a market to shut down. A successful radio evangelist who emerged in this newly acquired social and cultural space was Charles Fuller (1887-1968), a former citrus-packing businessman, whose broadcast *The Old Fashioned Revival Hour* became "the most widely heard religious program in the nation."[13] With 152 stations along the Mutual Systems network and an estimated audience approaching twenty million by 1939, Fuller had found a wide following for his fundamentalist beliefs.[14]

While unemployment rates continued to rise (they jumped from 8.7 percent in 1930 to 19 percent in 1938), the fundamentalists quietly built the institutions that would give their movement strength and vitality in the days ahead. Coming out of a vital Puritan Reformed heritage that placed a premium on education, several fundamentalists came together and formed important publishing houses. In time, Grand Rapids, Michigan, became a

---

[9]Ibid., p. 31.
[10]Ibid.
[11]Ibid.
[12]Ibid., p. 131.
[13]Ibid., p. 111.
[14]Ibid., p. 24.

virtual mecca of publishing with the establishment of William B. Eerdmans
Publishing Company and the Zondervan Publishing House during the
1930s. Created through the ministry of Dwight Moody much earlier in
1894, Moody Press, perhaps the most important at this time, continued to
serve the fundamentalist community throughout the economic malaise.

With educational institutions, media and publishing houses in place,
fundamentalists were coalescing during their cultural exile and hoping for
better days. This period of regrouping, which lasted from 1926 to the 1940s
must not, however, be mistaken for the demise of the movement itself as
some historians have suggested.[15] On the contrary, fundamentalism was by
far "the most influential evangelical movement in the United States during
the second quarter of the twentieth century."[16] The movement was licking
its wounds, so to speak, but it was still standing despite the wishes from
many corners of American culture, both within and outside the church,
that it simply go away.[17]

To a certain extent fundamentalists themselves were responsible for
their own exile from the levers of cultural power during the 1930s. Indeed,
the idea of separation was so strong within the movement that fundamentalists refused to cooperate with those who were not doctrinally orthodox
(such as theological liberals) or those they judged to have corrupted the
faith (such as Roman Catholics). And fundamentalists thought even less of
the trends beyond the church, the pop culture of the decade for instance,
especially the latest offerings from Hollywood. And yet due to their strong
sense of being responsible for the nation, a sense that had flowered during
the great evangelical revivals of the nineteenth century, fundamentalists
remained both ambivalent and conflicted.[18] On the one hand they wanted
to separate in order to maintain the purity of the faith. On the other hand
they wanted to lead the nation in order to establish a genuinely Christian
culture. What fundamentalism had actually done well during this period,

---

[15]David F. Wells and John D. Woodbridge, eds., *The Evangelicals: What They Believe, Who They Are,
Where They Are Changing* (Nashville: Abingdon, 1975), p. 127.

[16]Carpenter, *Revive Us Again*, p. 237.

[17]Douglas A. Sweeney, *The American Evangelical Story: A History of the Movement* (Grand Rapids:
Baker Academic, 2005), p. 170.

[18]George M. Marsden, *Fundamentalism and American Culture* (New York: Oxford University Press,
1980), p. viii.

despite its faults and setbacks, was to preserve the supernatural dimension of the faith that would once again be appreciated by so many believers in the decades ahead.[19]

THE NEW DEAL

During his acceptance speech at the 1932 Democratic convention (a convention that in many ways mimicked the techniques of revivalism) Franklin D. Roosevelt promised the country a "New Deal." This era ushered in by Roosevelt can be viewed, on the one hand, as an appropriate response to the economic suffering brought about by the Great Depression. On the other hand it can be seen as entailing an unprecedented intervention by the federal government in the economic life of the nation as well as a massive increase in public welfare to ease the burden of the economically depressed. Promising to help the person at the bottom of the economic pyramid, Roosevelt handily defeated Herbert Hoover, his Republican opponent, in the 1932 election by over seven million votes. Hoover had garnered only 59 electoral votes to Roosevelt's 472.

During the course of his first year in office Roosevelt not only championed several pieces of economic and social legislation but he also established new government agencies, including the Emergency Banking Act, the Tennessee Valley Authority and the Federal Emergency Relief Administration. But perhaps the most important act passed during this early period, and no doubt the most controversial of all, was the National Industrial Recovery Act (NIRA) which was at the heart of the president's New Deal agenda. On May 27, 1935, however, the Supreme Court (*Schechter Poultry Corp v. United States*) in a 9-0 decision deemed this act to be unconstitutional.

Fearing that the goals of his administration might be undermined by a "conservative" court, Roosevelt concocted a plan shortly after he took office for a second term in January 1937 that would add a Supreme Court justice for every current member who still sat on the court at seventy years and six months of age. This attempt to "stack" the court apparently had its effect since the following year the Supreme Court upheld both the

---

[19]Donald G. Bloesch, *The Future of Evangelical Christianity: A Call for Unity Amidst Diversity* (Colorado Springs: Helmers & Howard, 1988), p. 29.

Wagner Act and the Social Security Act, two important pieces of social welfare legislation. A journalist at the time, Ray Tucker, remarked, "The Court's record remains 100 percent New Deal since the day the 'packing' proposal was introduced."[20] Later the World Christian Fundamentalist Association went on record in opposing FDR along similar lines. In May 1940, for example, it "denounced the administration for supporting the 'lawless sit down strike,' [and] attempting to destroy the constitution through court packing."[21]

In winning the 1936 election, Roosevelt and the Democratic Party appeared to be unstoppable. Alf Landon, the Republican Governor of Kansas, had run an ineffective campaign that left Roosevelt with 61 percent of the popular vote and all the electoral college votes but eight. It was the largest electoral landslide in U.S. history. With overwhelming majorities in both houses the Democratic Party was on the verge of rendering the Republicans obsolete—or so it seemed. The GOP, for example, held only 89 House and 16 Senate seats. Failing in the gubernatorial contest in New Jersey in 1937, the Republican Party held "seven governorships with a combined population less than that of New York State."[22] The Republicans rebounded somewhat in the off-year elections of 1938 and nearly doubled their number of house seats by picking up "eighty one [congressional seats] along with eight Senate seats and fourteen governorships." Such gains still left Democrats in control of Congress with "60 percent of House and 70 percent of Senate seats."[23]

With both houses in his grip, and with a relatively docile Supreme Court in place, President Roosevelt not only changed the power ratio between the federal government and the states, but he also oversaw a federal bureaucracy that was supplanting local, ethnic and religious benevolent institutions that were unable to keep pace with the increasing need during the depression years. Rejecting the New Deal's "secular activism, its relativistic ethics, and its collectivist measures," fundamentalists and evangelicals maintained that the policies of the New Deal "discouraged the

---

[20]Allan J. Lichtman, *White Protestant Nation: The Rise of the American Conservative Movement* (New York: Grove Press, 2008), p. 95.
[21]Ibid., pp. 113-14.
[22]Ibid., p. 92.
[23]Ibid., p. 104.

Christian virtues of self-help, thrift, and charity, and instead encouraged sloth, dissolution, and dependence." Even more pointedly, an article in the *Sunday School Times* warned, "Redemption from economic calamity could not be found in a liberal state that 'leaves out God and leaves out sin.'"[24]

Theological liberals during the 1930s by and large embraced Roosevelt's big-government ways. Some of those who carried the torch of the Social Gospel during this decade, such as Harry Hopkins (1890-1946) and Mary McLeod Bethune (1875-1955), were actually advisers to the president himself. They, like so many others from the political left, believed that the problems of urbanization and industrialization were simply too great for local resources to handle. However, in offering relief to the nation's poor, Roosevelt was urged by Hopkins to do so in an accountable way, one that would avoid the dole. Even before the president took office, however, his social and economic critics were already well engaged. In a gesture of support for the new president, Harry Emerson Fosdick, the liberal paladin who was now well ensconced at the Riverside Church in Manhattan, signed a letter composed by several businessmen, administrators and religious leaders, including the president of the American Federation of Labor as well as Rabbi Stephen Wise. After urging the "whole people to declare in unison their confidence and faith in our President," the authors of this letter appealed to the American people to "cooperate with the President *in taking such action* as will guarantee economic stability, restore confidence and thereby relieve unemployment and widespread distress."[25] In light of such comments, it was not just fundamentalists who were now concerned with the blending of religious faith with American culture and politics.

THE SHIFTING THEOLOGICAL CONTEXT

The theological predicament of liberal Protestantism in America was now complicated by a theology of crisis, which like much else in theology was a European import. Hailing in a real sense from the publication of the *Römerbrief* by Karl Barth in 1919 (2nd ed. 1922), this early theological em-

---

[24]Ibid., pp. 78-79.
[25]"Letter Urging Support of the President," March 6, 1933, www.presidency.ucsb.edu/ws/index
    .php?pid=14639 (emphasis added).

phasis grew out of the disillusionment following World War I. Faced with the tasks of a pastorate in Switzerland, Barth came to the uncomfortable conclusion that his theological education, which had included immersion in the liberal theology of Friedrich Schleiermacher (1768-1834) and Adolf von Harnack (1851-1930) had left him ill-prepared. He therefore began to retool, so to speak, in order to articulate a theology that was informed by the insights of Søren Kierkegaard, the Protestant Reformers and others. In Barth's able hands, theological and cultural reflection (evidencing a larger theology of history) would become the mechanism whereby he would critique the culturally accommodating ways of the German Christians during the Nazi period. Indeed, in 1934, the Barmen Declaration, a statement of the Confessing Church contra the German Christians, was written by and clearly reflected Barth's new perspective.

As significant as Barth was to theology in Europe, it was his colleagues Emil Brunner (1889-1966) and Reinhold Niebuhr (1892-1971) who perhaps had a greater impact on the American scene, at least prior to World War II. Brunner, for example, lectured during the academic year of 1937-1938 at Princeton Theological Seminary. Grappling with the prospects of a vital Christian faith in a scientifically and empirically oriented culture, this Swiss theologian demonstrated that the robust and generous truth of the Bible must not be subsumed under an I-It paradigm that was much more appropriate for the examination of *objects*.[26] Influenced by the Jewish theologian Martin Buber (1878-1965) in several respects, Brunner made the I-Thou relation, the truth of personal correspondence, the pivot of his theology. Such a move softened the sharp edges of the conflict between religion and science and in a way, so some claimed, far better than what theological liberals had to offer.

Home-grown theologian Reinhold Niebuhr was born in Missouri and later attended Yale University, where he received his Bachelor of Divinity degree in 1914. Serving at the Bethel Evangelical Church in Detroit from 1915 to 1928, Niebuhr became increasingly aware of the oppressive work conditions in the auto industry and he often railed against Henry Ford. Though he had initially been a socialist and even advocated some of the

---

[26]See Emil Brunner, *The Divine-Human Encounter* (Westport, Conn.: Greenwood Press, 1943), pp. 45-47.

planks of the Communist Party USA, Niebuhr's political thought was changing during the 1930s. Important in this regard was the publication of his classic text *Moral Man and Immoral Society* in 1932, in which he challenged the naiveté of liberalism, both secular and religious, in its failure to be conscious "of the basic difference between the morality of individuals and the morality of collectives, whether races, classes or nations."[27] In other words, evil on the personal dimension is only compounded on the group level where other factors and dynamics come into play. If individuals are selfish, groups are inordinately so.

In his writings and sermons Niebuhr continued to develop the doctrine of original sin (one that had been virtually abandoned by theological liberals due to the erroneous conclusions they had drawn from evolutionary theory), such that by the time German tanks smashed into Poland in September 1939, he had been disabused of his earlier pacifism. Articulating a theological stance that would come to be known as "Christian Realism," Niebuhr maintained that Hitler and the evil of Nazism must be opposed—by force. While a professor of practical theology at Union Seminary in New York at the outbreak of the war, Niebuhr, always quick in debate, made sport of Harry Emerson Fosdick's hastily assembled Ministers' No War Committee, "a clumsily named group . . . worthy of derision."[28] To be sure, Protestants, for the most part, supported the war effort, though they avoided "the unrestrained capitulation to the war spirit which had left them disgraced after 1918."[29] The theology of Niebuhr and others had indeed made a difference. It complicated the assessment of good and evil, especially in noting the ironies entailed in the use of power, and it therefore made the whole matter of war that much more serious.

THE RISE OF THE NEO-EVANGELICALS

Dissatisfied with some of these new trends in theology, because they did not emphasize propositional revelation; with modernism because it was culturally accommodated; and with fundamentalism itself because it was

[27]Reinhold Niebuhr, *Moral Man and Immoral Society* (New York: Charles Scribner, 1932), p. ix.

[28]Reinhold Niebuhr, cited in Martin E. Marty, *The Noise of Conflict 1919-1941*, Modern American Religion (Chicago: University of Chicago Press, 1991), 2:47.

[29]Sidney Ahlstrom, *A Religious History of the American People* (Garden City, New York: Image Books, 1975), 2:444.

militant, socially vacuous and separatist, a group within the fundamentalist household began to distinguish themselves with the label "neo-evangelical." This language, which may not have been used until as late as 1948 (although some historians prefer the period of the forming of the National Association of Evangelicals in 1942), was likely suggested by Harold John Ockenga (1905-1985), pastor of the Park Street Church in Boston, and it sought to emphasize the irenic, progressive nature of the movement and that it did indeed have a social message.[30] Fundamentalist detractors, however, quickly criticized the neo-evangelicals and claimed that the new terminology sounded a lot like neo-orthodoxy, a theological movement that was in some sense a reaction against nineteenth-century liberal theology.[31] Of course, the term *evangelical* itself already had a rich history, and several instances can be found in English literature during the sixteenth century, especially in the writings of Richard Hooker (1554-1600), in particular *The Laws of Ecclesiastical Polity.*

In time the *neo* prefix simply dropped out and this North American group that began forming in the 1940s, with a Reformed fundamentalist heritage, was simply known as "evangelical." This was a subtle move but one with enormous theological implications for a group largely with a Presbyterian, Congregationalist and Baptist fundamentalist heritage. The designation "evangelical" meant that their major concerns (the earlier Briggs heresy trial, for instance) should have typified all evangelicals—but they clearly did not. For their part Wesleyan evangelicals looked upon such claims with some degree of amusement, since John Wesley, the father of Methodism, had already employed the term *evangelical* over thirty times in his own writings to refer not to any great intellectual or cultural struggle but to the salvific effects of the great evangelical revival in England during the eighteenth century.[32]

At any rate, the neo-evangelicals considered themselves reformers in a number of ways. First, the militant, aggressive spirit of fundamentalism had to be thrown off. Fundamentalists, of course, did not view the matter

---

[30]George M. Marsden, *Reforming Fundamentalism: Fuller Seminary and the New Evangelicalism* (Grand Rapids: Eerdmans, 1987), pp. 146, 3.

[31]Ibid., p.169.

[32]John Wesley, "The Spirit of Bondage and of Adoption," in *The Works of John Wesley*, vols. 1-4, *Sermons*, ed. Albert C. Outler (Nashville: Abingdon, 1984), 1:251.

quite this way, and a recent spokesperson, Ernest Pickering, objects to the reasoning entailed in this judgment in his following observation: "To be militant does not mean to be nasty, vituperative, or mean-spirited. Failure to understand this truth causes some to disdain the term 'militant.'" And in order that readers would not mistake his meaning he adds: "No one was more loving than the Apostle Paul, but no one was more bold and specific in his defense of the faith."[33]

Second, the neo-evangelicals especially disliked "the doctrinal and the cultural implications of a thoroughgoing dispensationalism."[34] In particular they rejected the separatist tendencies of fundamentalism that rendered the movement socially and politically disengaged. In 1947, for example, Carl F. H. Henry (1913-2003) published *The Uneasy Conscience of Fundamentalism* and criticized fundamentalism as "the modern priest and Levite, by-passing suffering humanity."[35] Henry and other neo-evangelicals, however, were careful not "to confuse their renewed social interest with the social gospel"[36] which, in their judgment, was far too critical of personal religion. However, some of the harshest criticism of the fundamentalists came from the pen of Edward J. Carnell (1919-1967), a Baptist pastor and later president of Fuller Seminary. Among other things, Carnell claimed that fundamentalists defined its status "by negation," that is, all who disagreed with them were rendered apostate. Again, Carnell considered fundamentalism to be a "perversion of orthodoxy," and he lambasted it for its supposed "cultic mentality."[37] Beyond this, Sherman Roddy, son of a Fuller professor, excoriated fundamentalists as "religious, social, psychological and economic 'have nots.'"[38] Theological liberals could hardly have said more.

In criticizing their fundamentalist cousins, neo-evangelicals may have given an ear to several of the arguments of theological modernists. In other words, as Jon Stone points out, in distinguishing themselves from

---

[33]Ernest D. Pickering, *The Tragedy of Compromise: The Origin and Impact of the New Evangelicalism* (Greenville, S.C.: Bob Jones University Press, 1994), p. 162.
[34]Marsden, *Reforming Fundamentalism*, p. 6.
[35]Carl F. H. Henry, *The Uneasy Conscience of Fundamentalism* (Grand Rapids: Eerdmans, 1947), p. 17.
[36]Jon R. Stone, *On the Boundaries of American Evangelicalism: The Postwar Evangelical Coalition* (New York: St. Martin's Press, 1997), p. 119.
[37]Ibid., pp. 113, 115.
[38]Ibid., p. 111.

fundamentalists, evangelicals may yet have had cause for concern especially as they "soon became aware of their own increasingly leftward drift toward liberalism."[39] This drift could be discerned, in part, in the evangelical quest for greater cultural respectability. The question, of course, was how far left could neo-evangelicals go and yet maintain their evangelical identity?[40] It is almost as if evangelical understanding during the 1940s was being formed with an eye on two key movements, not one: fundamentalism, of course, but also liberalism. That is, theological liberalism as a dialogue partner had never really dropped out.

Third, the ongoing attraction of theological liberalism for neo-evangelicals, not of course in terms of its doctrinal confusion but with respect to its institutional power, is evident in the nearly obsessive evangelical quest for intellectual respectability. Carnell, for example, bewailed the lack of academic prowess among fundamentalists and thought them to be both rigid and dull. Desiring the approval of those well beyond the evangelical community, Carnell opined, "I want to command the attention of Tillich and Bennet: then I shall be in a better place to be of service to the evangelicals. We need prestige desperately."[41] Picking up the intellectual mantel supposedly dropped in his fundamentalist roots, Carl Henry, for his part, undertook an engaging and lively critique of modern thought in his *Remaking the Modern Mind*, written in 1946. Indeed, Henry had charged that the "fundamentalists' lack of engagement with modern intellectual trends had done incalculable damage to the faith."[42]

The grasp for intellectual legitimacy was perhaps nowhere more evident than in the eager pursuit of Ivy league doctoral degrees by the up-and-coming evangelicals. Indeed, during the 1940s more than a dozen evangelicals were earning such degrees at Harvard.[43] Eleven of these scholars were from a fundamentalist background and three were from a Wesleyan-Holiness evangelical one.[44] Beyond this, evangelicals began to form academic

---

[39]Ibid., p. 119.

[40]Ibid. I have focused on evangelical identity and not an "orthodox" one, as Stone has done.

[41]Edward John Carnell, cited in Rolland D. McCune, *Promise Unfulfilled: The Failed Strategy of Modern Evangelicalism* (Greenville, S.C.: Ambassador International, 2004), p. 45.

[42]Carpenter, *Revive Us Again*, p. 200.

[43]Ibid., p. 191.

[44]Ibid.

organizations that would foster and sustain this intellectual interest, including the American Scientific Affiliation (ASA), founded in 1941, and the Evangelical Theological Society (ETS), established in 1949. The Wesleyan counterpart, that is, the Wesleyan Theological Society (WTS) did not emerge until much later in 1965.

Though evangelicals were in earnest to set themselves apart from their fundamentalist heritage with respect to militancy, social action and the life of the mind, one area in which they continued to bear the marks of this complicated heritage was on the topic of the inspiration and authority of the Bible. The common sense realism taken up by the earlier Princeton theologians and passed along to a younger generation of scholars in the form of a theological rationalism that focused on propositional revelation and the correspondence theory of truth could be readily seen in Henry's discussion of the authority of Scripture in his major theological work, *God, Revelation and Authority*. Moreover, one of the basic requirements to become a member of the Evangelical Theological Society, beyond holding the appropriate academic degree, was to affirm that "The Bible alone and the Bible in its entirety, is the word of God written, and therefore inerrant in the autographs."[45] By way of contrast, no such requirement was a part of the Wesleyan Theological Society at least since 1970,[46] and this fact helps to explain, at least in part, why there are so few Wesleyans in ETS.

The Infrastructure of Neo-Evangelicalism

One of the strengths of fundamentalism during its years of isolation and regrouping was its ability to create viable institutions to sustain its witness. In a similar fashion the neo-evangelicals quickly set about to establish structures that would carry its distinct voice from one generation to the next. Four such institutions are noteworthy: (1) the National Association of Evangelicals, (2) *Christianity Today* magazine (3) Fuller Theo-

---

[45]Hart, *That Old Time Religion in Modern America*, pp. 125-26.

[46]The doctrinal statement on Scripture in the first volume of the *Wesleyan Theological Journal*, produced in 1966 was as follows: "That both Old and New Testaments constitute the divinely-inspired Word of God, inerrant in the originals, and the final authority for life and truth" (vol. 1, no. 1 [spring 1966]). This language, however, was modified in the 1970 edition of the journal that now reads: "In the plenary-dynamic and unique inspiration of the Bible as the divine Word of God, the only infallible (i.e., "absolutely trustworthy and unfailing in effectiveness or operation"), sufficient and authoritative rule of faith and practice . . ." (vol. 5, no. 1 [spring 1970]).

logical Seminary, and (4) the ministry of Billy Graham.

The National Association of Evangelicals. In wanting to avoid "the ecclesiastical regimentation" of liberalism on the one hand and "the doctrinal regimentation" of fundamentalism on the other,[47] J. Elwin Wright and a few of his colleagues met at the Coronado Hotel in St. Louis on April 7-8, 1942, and put together a framework out of which the National Association of Evangelicals (NAE) arose. Unlike the fundamentalists with their separatist tendencies, Wright invited people from every evangelical sector to this groundbreaking meeting.[48] Among those in attendance were Pentecostals, Anabaptists, Wesleyan-Holiness folk and "other non-fundamentalist Christians."[49] After this initial gathering, a group of more than six hundred delegates met in Chicago the following year and ratified a constitution. Harold Ockenga was elected president and Leslie R. Marston (1894-1979), a Free Methodist bishop, became the first vice president.[50] So successful was this new institution that by 1947 the NAE represented "thirty denominations, totaling 1,300, 000 members."[51]

The hope of many of these early evangelical leaders, of course, was that the NAE would reawaken a dynamic religious tradition that held together both the personal and social witness that was so much a part of nineteenth-century revivalism—and to do so in a spirit of Christian charity. But several fundamentalists at the time urged their key proponents to ignore this neo-evangelical institution, and pressure, even intimidation, was applied.[52] For example, Ralph Davis, who was to be a part of the inner circle of the NAE, abruptly withdrew.[53] And so long as V. Raymond Edman was president of Wheaton College (1940-1965) this prestigious school refused to identify with the NAE. In a similar fashion Dallas Theological Seminary failed to join the association "even though its president, Lewis Sperry Chafer, had signed the call to the St. Louis meeting."[54]

---

[47]Stone, *On the Boundaries*, p. 132.
[48]George Marsden, *Evangelicalism and Modern America* (Grand Rapids: Eerdmans, 1984), p. 12.
[49]Christian Smith, *American Evangelicalism: Embattled and Thriving* (Chicago: University of Chicago Press, 1998), p. 11.
[50]Carpenter, *Revive Us Again*, p. 149.
[51]Marsden, *Evangelicalism and Modern America*, p. 13.
[52]Carpenter, *Revive Us Again*, p. 152.
[53]Ibid., p. 152.
[54]Ibid.

Of those few Roman Catholics who paid attention to the rise of the NAE, there was at least some cause for concern. Indeed, in indicating why evangelicals needed to come together in the first place to form the NAE, Ockenga highlighted three great threats to America and the cause of Christ, namely, "Roman Catholicism, liberal theology, and secularism."[55] Catholics naturally feared a revival of nativist sentiment, the kind that had played out in the mid-nineteenth century when the Know Nothing Party formed in the wake of massive immigration from Ireland and Germany. Was the creation of the NAE a bold attempt to rekindle the old fires of a quest for a Christian America, and one that left those beyond Protestantism on the sidelines? The subsequent history of the NAE, however, proved such fears to be unfounded. To be sure, one of the great political stories of the 1990s was that of evangelicals and Catholics *together*, a remarkable coalition that will be explored in the following chapter.

Christianity Today. In order to strengthen the cultural and intellectual voice of fundamentalists turned neo-evangelicals, *Christianity Today* was founded in 1956 at the urging of Billy Graham (1918-) and his father-in-law L. Nelson Bell (1894-1973). This bimonthly magazine, which has become the flagship of the evangelical world, was in some sense a response to the mainline *Christian Century*, and Carl F. H. Henry was its first editor. Offering laity and clergy alike thoughtful essays on theology, church life and social issues from an evangelical point of view, *Christianity Today* quickly attracted a faithful following and eventually overtook *Christian Century* in terms of subscriptions. J. Howard Pew (1882-1971), the noted philanthropist, helped to finance the magazine during its early years. However, with the money came also editorial pressure, and Henry was eventually replaced by Harold Lindsell, whose editorials were far more congenial to Pew's conservative politics.

Fuller Theological Seminary. The idea for a seminary that would give expression to the intellectual interests of the neo-evangelicals came from Charles Fuller, the engaging radio evangelist whose broadcasts were now more popular than those of Bob Hope and Charlie McCarthy.[56] One night

---

[55]D. G. Hart, *Deconstructing Evangelicalism: Conservative Protestantism in the Age of Billy Graham* (Grand Rapids: Baker Academic, 2004), p. 113.
[56]Randall Balmer, *Encyclopedia of Evangelicalism* (Waco, Tex.: Baylor University Press, 2004), p. 275.

in November 1939 God awoke Fuller and placed a burden on his heart for a "Christ-centered, Spirit-directed training school, where Christian men and women could be trained in the things of God."[57] With the proper funding in place, once again with the help of Pew, Fuller Theological Seminary opened its doors almost a decade later in 1947 in Pasadena, California. In his excellent study *Reforming Fundamentalism: Fuller Seminary and the New Evangelicalism*, Marsden points out that the school was bound by allegiance to three major religious movements: classical Protestant Christianity, American evangelicalism and fundamentalism.[58] However, contrary to the founding dream of Fuller, women were neither permitted to enroll in the first class nor were they allowed "to sit in on the courses."[59]

Harold Ockenga was appointed the first president of Fuller, though he still retained his pastorate in Boston. In terms of the life of the mind he believed that conservative evangelicals were the "heirs to Reformation culture . . . [that led] to the amazing rise of power of the West."[60] Ever energetic and marked by an abundance of vision, Ockenga assembled a faculty that drew from some of the best conservative scholars of the day: "Everett Harrison (1902-1999) in Bible, Carl Henry in theology, Harold Lindsell (1913-1998), in history and missions, and Wilbur Smith (1894-1976) in apologetics."[61] Fuller's fundamentalist critics, however, were not impressed. In fact, they charged that many members of Fuller's faculty "seemed sympathetic with neo-orthodoxy."[62]

Sensing a leftward drift in theological education, fundamentalists repeatedly claimed that Fuller was going "soft" on the inspiration and authority of the Bible in general and the doctrine of biblical inerrancy in particular. Modifying its stance on inerrancy at a faculty and trustee planning conference in 1962, Fuller opened itself up to ongoing criticism that appeared to grow in volume as the decade progressed.[63] Indeed, C. Davis Weyerhaeuser, David Allan Hubbard and even Dan Fuller, the son of the

[57]Rolland D. McCune, *Promise Unfulfilled: The Failed Strategy of Modern Evangelicalism* (Greenville, S.C.: Ambassador International, 2004), p. 42.

[58]Marsden, *Reforming Fundamentalism*, p. 3.

[59]Ibid., p. 123.

[60]Ibid., p. 63.

[61]Sweeney, *American Evangelical Story*, p. 175.

[62]Balmer, *Encyclopedia of Evangelicalism*, p. 277.

[63]Sweeney, *American Evangelical Story*, pp. 177-78.

school's namesake, were all caught up in this conflict surrounding Scripture, and they were often put on the defensive. When Hubbard was later appointed the president of the seminary in 1963, some of the faculty left for the more conservative pastures of Trinity Evangelical Divinity School.

The new seminary had its critics, not only from the theological right but also from the left. Indeed, tensions between the evangelicals and their mainline counterparts increased as denominational officials made it clear that they did not appreciate the competition in a field that they had considered very much their own. To illustrate, the Presbyterian Church in the U.S.A. had been served by several independent seminaries in the past, but not by one like the evangelical startup at Fuller.[64] Hiding behind a number of theological and academic objections, the Presbytery of Los Angeles in the fall of 1948 sent a warning along the following lines to all Presbyterian students who attended Fuller: "Theological training at Fuller was entirely unacceptable . . . and if students wished to remain under the care of the presbytery, they would have to leave Fuller by January 1949."[65] Fuller eventually overcame much of this opposition through the sheer intellectual weight of its gifted faculty. By the 1960s (especially in establishing the Schools of Psychology and World Mission) the seminary had already demonstrated that the terms *evangelical* and *academic* go hand in hand.

The Ministry of Billy Graham. Born on a dairy farm near Charlotte, North Carolina, in 1918, William Franklin Graham grew up in an evangelical Presbyterian home. Having experienced a powerful religious conversion in 1934 under the ministry of Mordecai Ham, Billy Graham enrolled at Bob Jones College (now a university) two years later. However, chaffing under the strict rules and regimentation of this school, Graham remained there only briefly. In 1937 he headed for the more favorable quarters of the Florida Bible Institute and then on to Wheaton College in 1940, where he graduated three years later. At Wheaton he met and later married Ruth Bell (1920-2007), the daughter of L. Nelson Bell, a missionary to China, and cofounder of *Christianity Today*, as noted earlier.

Following the call of an evangelist, Graham was already beginning to preach more widely as a staff member of Youth for Christ in 1946. Three

---

[64]Marsden, *Reforming Fundamentalism*, p. 96.
[65]Ibid.

years later he conducted an evangelistic campaign in Los Angeles that was to launch his career as one of America's most remarkable and gifted preachers. During his many nights of preaching, in which several prominent personalities were converted, Graham had the good fortune to catch the attention of William Randolph Hearst, the newspaper magnate, who in liking his preaching and especially his politics urged his reporters to "puff Graham."[66] Touching on the themes of marriage, the home, crime, big business, the role of the United States in the world, the importance of moral law and an "unchecked crime wave," there was actually much that could have been of interest to Hearst.[67]

Though Graham was well appreciated for his clear gospel preaching that offered hope to so many suffering people, some began to ask if he was intermingling the Christian faith and the American way of life: "America is truly the last bulwark of Christian civilization," he intoned. "If America falls, Western culture will disintegrate."[68] Again, and in a way that left some Americans out, Graham declared from the pulpit, "if you would be a true patriot, then become a Christian. If you would be a loyal American then become a loyal Christian."[69] The Jewish theologian Will Herberg (1901-1977), author of *Protestant, Catholic and Jew*, dismissed Billy Graham not so much for his alleged Americanized faith but because for all "the power and fervor of his crusades," he still spoke "in the language of individualistic piety which in lesser men [than the admired Graham] frequently degenerates into a smug and nagging moralism."[70]

In late December 1949 Graham began a revival campaign in Boston, which had been organized for the most part by Ockenga's Park Street Church. His gifted preaching was so successful here and elsewhere that his reputation now preceded him wherever he went. During a five-week crusade in Washington, D.C., in 1952, Graham was introduced by no one less than Sam Rayburn, the Speaker of the House, who declared from the

---

[66]Hart, *That Old Time Religion in Modern America*, p. 84.

[67]Carpenter, *Revive Us Again*, p. 223.

[68]Billy Graham, cited in Richard Kyle, *Evangelicalism: An Americanized Christianity* (New Brunswick, N.J.: Transaction, 2006), p. 139.

[69]Ibid.

[70]Will Herberg, cited in Martin E. Marty, *Under God Indivisible 1941-1960*, Modern American Religion (Chicago: University of Chicago Press, 1996), 3:338.

Capitol steps, "This country needs a revival, and I believe Billy Graham is bringing it to us."[71] Indicating something of the religious climate of 1950s America, Graham's service was not only "permitted by an unprecedented act of Congress" but was also carried "on radio and television across the nation."[72] And though the *Christian Century* ignored the revivals conducted by Graham in 1949 and 1950, others were beginning to take notice.[73] By 1958 President Henry Pitney Van Dusen of Union Seminary was already talking about a "third force" in American religion beyond the mainline Protestant denominations and Roman Catholicism.[74]

A turning point came in 1957 when Graham was invited by the Protestant Council of the city of New York to conduct a crusade. Employing an "inclusive approach" in evangelism, Graham cooperated with theological liberals, who at times sat on his platforms. This collaboration was too much for fundamentalists, who claimed that Graham was watering down the faith and compromising with the principal enemies of the gospel. Graham's response, in part, was similar to that given by John Wesley to his own eighteenth-century critics: "The one badge of Christian discipleship is not orthodoxy but love."[75] Fundamentalists, however, were by no means pleased with this answer. The New York campaign "put in place permanently the old fissure that the new evangelicals created back in the 1940s."[76] Moreover, at least one British evangelical was likewise concerned about Graham's "ecumenical" approach. Martin Lloyd Jones, for example, said that he would make a bargain with Graham "if he would stop the general sponsorship of his campaigns—stop having liberals and Roman Catholics on the platform—and drop the invitation system, I would wholeheartedly support him and chair the Congress."[77] Graham naturally declined the offer. The neo-evangelicals then, for the

---

[71]Sam Rayburn, cited in Wells, *Evangelicals*, p. 227.
[72]Ibid.
[73]Carpenter, *Revive Us Again*, p. 233.
[74]Wells, *Evangelicals*, p. 222.
[75]Iain H. Murray, *Evangelicalism Divided: A Record of Crucial Change in the Years 1950-2000* (Edinburgh: Banner of Truth Trust, 2000), p. 33. In his sermon "The Catholic Spirit," Wesley takes as his text 2 Kings 10:15: "Is thine heart right, as my heart is with thy heart? And Jehonadab answered, It is. If it be, give me thine hand" (Wesley, *Sermons*, 2:81).
[76]McCune, *Promise Unfulfilled*, p. 55.
[77]Murray, *Evangelicalism Divided*, p. 33.

most part, were leaving fundamentalism and its separatist attitudes behind. As McCune points out, "Graham brought an end to evangelical unity."[78] Nevertheless, back in 1950 Graham had written to Bob Jones Sr., well-known fundamentalist leader, as follows: "I need your advice and counsel and covet your long years of experience. . . . All of us young evangelists look up to you as a father."[79] One wonders, however, if Graham would have written the same letter in 1957.

Beyond the National Association of Evangelicals, *Christianity Today*, Fuller Theological Seminary and the ministry of Billy Graham, the distinctly evangelical voice in America was augmented by other important institutions as well such as the InterVarsity Christian Fellowship, which originated in Great Britain and was brought to the United States in 1941; Youth for Christ, which conducted mass rallies among teenagers and young adults during the 1940s in England, the United States and Canada; and Campus Crusade for Christ, which was founded by Bill Bright and his wife, Vonette Bright, as a ministry to students at UCLA in 1951. All of these institutions typified the strong evangelical desire for evangelism, to share the good news of the grace of God manifested in Jesus Christ in as broad a manner as possible.

THE POPULARITY OF RELIGION AND THE THREAT OF COMMUNISM

After World War II religion prospered in America. Church affiliation, for example, rose from 49 percent in 1940 to 55 percent in 1950 and on up to 69 percent by 1960.[80] One of the most significant gains was during the period from 1950 to 1956 when affiliation climbed from 55 to 62 percent.[81] During the postwar baby boom, while the country was listening to doo-wop and getting back to work, it was also, remarkably enough, going to church. Finding this trend congenial to his own personal style, President Eisenhower (1890-1969) began all his cabinet meetings with a silent prayer, he supported the National Day of Prayer that Congress created in 1952, and

---

[78]McCune, *Promise Unfulfilled*, p. 55.
[79]Pickering, *Tragedy of Compromise*, p. 51.
[80]Ahlstrom, *Religious History of the American People*, p. 448.
[81]Ibid.

he became the first president to attend a weekly prayer breakfast.[82] "Our government makes no sense, unless it is founded in a deeply felt religious faith," he declared, "and I don't care what it is."[83]

The early 1950s were also known as the time when the Pledge of Allegiance was modified to reflect not only the religious sentiment of the people but also a growing fear of communism. To illustrate, the pledge had originally been composed by Francis Bellamy, a Baptist minister, in 1892 to honor the four-hundredth anniversary of the arrival of Christopher Columbus in the new world.[84] In August 1945 Congress made Bellamy's work "the official pledge of allegiance to the nation's flag."[85] A few years later, in 1953, Congressman Louis C. Rabault from Michigan introduced a House Joint Resolution that proposed the phrase "under God" be added to the pledge.[86] In June the following year both houses of Congress passed the resolution to include the phrase and president Eisenhower signed the legislation into law on Flag Day.[87] The anticommunist flavor of the newly revised pledge was revealed in the early observations of Rabault, who warned: "From the root of atheism stems the evil weed of communism. Unless we are willing to affirm our belief in the existence of God, we open the floodgates to tyranny and oppression."[88] And as Lee Canipe points out, "Including God in the nation's pledge would send a clear message to the world that, unlike communist regimes that denied God's existence, the United States recognized a Supreme Being."[89] Moreover, a Gallup poll in 1958 revealed that 80 percent of the American electorate would not "vote for an atheist for President under *any* circumstances."[90]

The 1950s were a heady time to be an evangelical in America, and key elements of the neo-evangelical infrastructure took up the anticommunist cause and thereby blended American religion and politics in new cul-

---

[82]Lichtman, *White Protestant Nation*, p. 193.

[83]Dwight D. Eisenhower, cited in Kyle, *Evangelicalism*, p. 132.

[84]Lee Canipe, "Under God and Anti-Communist: How the Pledge of Allegiance Got Religion in Cold War America," *Journal of Church and State* 45, no. 2 (2003): 310.

[85]Ibid., p. 310.

[86]Ibid., p. 314.

[87]Ibid., p. 319.

[88]Louis Rabault, cited in ibid., p. 317.

[89]Canipe, "Under God and Anti-Communist," p. 315.

[90]Eric R Crouse, "Popular Cold Warriors: Conservative Protestants, Communism, and Culture in Early Cold War America," *Journal of Religion and Popular Culture* 2, no. 2002 (2002): 2.

turally limited formations. Earlier during his Los Angeles campaign, for instance, Billy Graham had pulled out the stops, so to speak, and excoriated communism as "a religion that is inspired, directed and motivated by the Devil himself who had declared war against Almighty God."[91] Congressman Frank W. Boykin of Alabama quickly discerned the usefulness of a powerful voice such as Graham's.[92] The thought began to emerge in the minds of several politicians that "the greatest and most effective weapon against Communism today is to be [a] born again Christian."[93]

Carl F. H. Henry, for his part, defended the actions of the House Un-American Activities Committee and urged Americans to resist "the monstrous evil of Communism."[94] *Christianity Today* not only began to view missionary activity as the "first line of priestly defense against communism,"[95] but it also invited Herbert Hoover in 1960 to write a three part anticommunism series with the titles: "The Communist Menace: Red Goal and Christian Ideals," "Communist Propaganda and the Christian Pulpit," and "Soviet Rule or Christian Renewal?"[96] And the National Association of Evangelicals, not to be outdone in its criticism of communism, published a brochure which stated, "Communism is Satanic and must be dealt with as such."[97]

The old Christian right, which was headed up by Carl McIntire (1906-2002) and Billy James Hargis (1925-2004), was even more vocal in its opposition to communism than many of the neo-evangelicals. McIntire was a Bible Presbyterian Church fundamentalist preacher who in 1941 established the militant and separatist American Council of Christian Churches (ACCC) in New York City in opposition to the Federal Council of Churches. Seven years later he founded the International Council of Christian Churches (ICCC) as a counterpoise to the liberal World

---

[91]Billy Graham, cited in ibid., p. 6.

[92]Richard Pierard, "From Evangelical Exclusivism to Ecumenical Openness: Billy Graham and Sociopolitical Issues," *Journal of Ecumenical Studies* 20, no. 3 (1983): 430.

[93]Ibid., p. 439.

[94]Carl F. H. Henry, cited in Crouse, *Popular Cold Warriors*, p. 7.

[95]Kenneth D. Wald, "The Religious Dimension of American Anti-Communism," *Journal of Church and State* 36, no. 3 (1994): 489.

[96]Crouse, *Popular Cold Warriors*, p. 8.

[97]Alex Karmarkovic, "American Evangelical Responses to the Russian Revolution and the Rise of Communism in the Twentieth Century," *Fides et Historia* 4, no. 2 (1972): 18.

Council of Churches. Viewing many evangelicals as "weak-kneed and heretical," McIntire claimed that such believers "do more harm to the cause of the Gospel and the purity of the Church than the liberals themselves."[98] This animated radio preacher denounced "the NCC and WCC, the Roman Catholic Church, the Revised Standard Version (RSV) [and] civil rights."[99] Known as an extremist in evangelical circles, McIntire was so bitterly opposed to communism that he began to claim that "the United States had a duty under God to attack the Soviet Union with atomic weapons."[100]

Though most Americans rejected the animated anticommunist rhetoric of McIntire as unbalanced, they nevertheless thought that the communist threat was real. For example, in a survey conducted during the 1950s, it was learned that "91 percent of Americans held that high school teachers who were admitted Communists should be fired and 77 percent approved having their American citizenship taken away."[101] Playing on such fears, Senator Joseph McCarthy (1908-1957) addressed the very real problem of communist infiltration of the U.S. government, but he did so in such a reckless manner that he cast aspersion on the innocent and "cause[d] untold grief to the country he claimed to love."[102]

Already by 1939 the United States had cracked the Soviet diplomatic code, though the contents of the "decrypted cables (code named Venona)" would not be made available to the public until as late as 1995.[103] This information, along with that gathered by Soviet agents Igor Gouzenko, Elizabeth Bentley, and Louis Budenz revealed that Alger Hiss, the diplomat from the State Department who had advised FDR at Yalta and who by the way often referred to Joseph Stalin as "Uncle Joe," was in fact a communist spy as Whittaker Chambers had claimed all along.[104] Beyond this, the Venona Report laid bare, to the consternation of many liberal Democrats, just how extensive communist infiltration actually was

---

[98]Kyle, Evangelicalism, p. 136.

[99]Richard Quebedeaux, The Young Evangelicals (New York: Harper & Row, 1974), p. 24.

[100]Barry N. Hankins, American Evangelicals: A Contemporary History of a Mainstream Religious Movement (Lanham, Md.: Rowman & Littlefield, 2008), p. 140.

[101]Crouse, Popular Cold Warriors, p. 3.

[102]William J. Bennett, America: The Last Best Hope, vol. 2, From a World at War to the Triumph of Freedom (Nashville: Thomas Nelson, 2007), p. 303.

[103]Lichtman, White Protestant Nation, p. 201.

[104]Ibid., p. 149.

during FDR's administration. To illustrate, Laurence Duggan (1905-1948), a member of the State Department who fell to his death from a Manhattan high rise, and Harry Dexter White (1892-1948), U.S. Treasury Department official who was cozy with the economist John Maynard Keynes (1883-1946), were both Soviet agents.[105] Two weeks before his death in Warm Springs, Georgia, President Roosevelt observed in anguish, though it should have hardly been a shock, "[Stalin] has broken every one of the promises he made at Yalta."[106]

WESLEYAN EVANGELICALS COALESCE

Because Wesleyan evangelicals (which would include many Pentecostals) never had a significant fundamentalist faction to distinguish themselves against, the trajectory of the movement was somewhat different from that of their Reformed evangelical cousins. Many Wesleyans, for example, were already situated in evangelical denominations well before they joined the NAE. This had been the result of the "come out" or "pushed out" (depending on the perspective) sifting that took place much earlier. That is, during the latter part of the nineteenth and into the twentieth centuries the Holiness movement distinguished itself not from fundamentalism but from culturally accommodated, liberal mainline denominations. Of course not all Wesleyan evangelicals were a part of distinct Holiness bodies. Indeed, many remained within Methodist mainline denominations such as the Methodist Episcopal Church, the Methodist Protestant Church and the Methodist Episcopal Church, South, that would eventually come together to form the Methodist Church in 1939. Twenty-nine years later, in 1968, the Evangelical United Brethren, a small conservative denomination, joined hands with the larger, mainline Methodist church to form the United Methodist Church, which remains the largest mainline Protestant denomination in America even today.

The coalescing period for Wesleyan evangelicals was not the 1940s, as it was for the neo-evangelicals, but the 1960s. In 1966, for example, Charles W. Keysor (1925-1985) wrote a groundbreaking article, "Methodism's Silent Majority," in the *New Christian Advocate* and contended that the denomi-

---

[105]Bennett, *America*, p. 250.
[106]Ibid.

nation "seriously underestimated the evangelical sentiments of its clergy and its membership."[107] Out of the response to this honest and engaging article the renewal movement Good News took shape and the first issue of the magazine of the same name appeared in the spring of 1967, that is, about a year after the *New Christian Advocate Article.*[108]

As a renewal movement Good News was not "primarily a conservative reaction to the social and political unrest of the 1960s and 1970s."[109] Such a designation would stack the deck, so to speak, by mistakenly claiming that the larger mainline body or the broader culture itself was ever the leader while Good News was merely a reaction against such leadership. On the contrary, Good News represented in a very positive fashion, and in an abundance of tempered leadership, an authentic Wesleyan Methodist witness with an eye ever on the renewal of the church. In short, Good News as a movement was none other than a "populist evangelicalism,"[110] that maintained among other things that the essence of the Christian faith can be found in what is now called "convertive or conversional piety,"[111] that is, in the new birth that celebrates Jesus Christ as a risen Lord and powerful Savior, one who sets the captives free.[112]

No sooner had the United Methodist Church formed in 1968 that it began its decades long precipitous decline, such that more than a few folk in the erstwhile Evangelical United Brethren began to question what they had done. Part of the problem was that the educational materials for Methodist youth had in effect displaced the narrative of the gospel with the reigning leftist politics of the day. This extensive cultural accommodation of the church, especially in its Sunday school materials, was challenged once again by Charles Keysor, who drafted the pungent editorial "Cyanide in the Church School" for the January-March 1970 issue of *Good News* magazine.[113]

---

[107]Charles W. Keysor, cited in Balmer, *Encyclopedia of Evangelicalism*, p. 291.
[108]Riley B. Case, *Evangelical and Methodist: A Popular History* (Nashville: Abingdon, 2004), p. 30.
[109]Ibid., p. 12.
[110]Ibid.
[111]Roger E. Olson, *Reformed and Always Reforming* (Grand Rapids: Baker Academic, 2007), p. 80. Olson's description of this terminology highlights the theme of "real Christianity," so important to both historic Pietism and Wesleyan evangelicalism.
[112]Case, *Evangelical and Methodist*, p. 15.
[113]Ibid., p. 45.

Beyond this, the ongoing doctrinal slippage championed by Methodist mainline leaders (who in many instances had confused undigested higher criticism for sound biblical scholarship) had been so great that evangelical Methodists were compelled by the love of Christ to gather in North Carolina in 1975 and issue "An Affirmation of Scriptural Christianity for United Methodists," a document otherwise known as the Junaluska Affirmation. This document underscored such vital Christian doctrines as "human depravity, the authority of the Bible, the necessity of sanctification, and the centrality of Christ in the salvation process."[114] In addition the work stressed the importance of ameliorating the plight of the poor by engaging in all manner of social action, deeds of kindness and mercy in particular.[115]

Astute Wesleyan theologians such as Thomas C. Oden discerned that the theological problems confronted by Wesleyan evangelicals (as denominational leaders in an uncritical way slapped the name of Jesus onto leftist Americana) were precisely those taken up by other evangelicals and even by conservative Roman Catholics well beyond the evangelical family. Indeed, Oden invited Christians from diverse theological traditions to cooperate in articulating orthodox Christian belief for a new age through careful and renewed study of the early church fathers (paleo-orthodoxy). His seminal work, which included many publishing projects, built important theological bridges that are still in place today.[116]

THE CIVIL RIGHTS MOVEMENT

During the decade of the 1950s a million blacks left the South, and three-fourths of black Americans lived in urban areas by 1965.[117] With "less than one half of one percent of black Protestants [worshiping] in nonsegregated congregations," the quip of Yale Divinity School's dean, Liston Pope, was unfortunately true: "It is appalling that the most segregated hour of Christian America is eleven o'clock on Sunday morning."[118] In this segre-

---

[114]Balmer, *Encyclopedia of Evangelicalism*, p. 376.
[115]Ibid.
[116]One of the most important publishing projects along these lines is the Ancient Christian Commentary on Scripture series (Oden is the general editor) published by InterVarsity Press.
[117]Ahlstrom, *Religious History of the American People*, p. 572.
[118]Marty, *Under God Indivisible*, pp. 381, 387.

gated and hostile culture in which Jim Crow still ruled the day, Rosa Parks, a forty-two year old seamstress, took a stand on December 1, 1955, and refused to give up her seat to a white passenger on a bus in Montgomery, Alabama. Her subsequent arrest, for violating what had been a Southern custom, resulted in a boycott of the bus system, which not only lasted more than a year, nearly crippling the company, but it also helped to spark the civil rights movement in America. Perhaps Parks had been emboldened by the Supreme Court's decision *Brown v. Board of Education* a year earlier, in which the court unanimously agreed that segregation in public schools was unconstitutional. What was good for the schools should be good for the transportation system as well.

Martin Luther King Jr. (1929-1968), a Baptist minister and graduate of Boston University, helped to lead the boycott in Montgomery, and in 1957 he established the Southern Christian Leadership Conference, of which he was made the first president. Labeled as a friend of communists by J. Edgar Hoover, King struggled to gain acceptance by white evangelical and fundamentalist ministers who looked askance at his political inclinations and tactics.[119] Jerry Falwell (1933-2007), for example, founding pastor of the Thomas Road Baptist Church, declared during King's Selma campaign, "I must personally say that I do question the sincerity and non-violent intentions of some civil rights leaders such as Dr. Martin Luther King Jr."[120] Moreover, having already penned the classic jeremiad on social action, *The Uneasy Conscience of Modern Fundamentalism*, as noted earlier, Carl F. H. Henry should have been an early and vocal supporter of King and the broader civil rights movement, but unfortunately he was not.

Three key factors prevented or deflected Henry's involvement. First, Henry was politically and theologically separated from the civil rights movement in that many of its white supporters were not middle-class evangelicals like himself but "northern liberal Christians, Catholics, Jews and non-Christians.[121] In other words Henry, like so many other northern evangelicals at the time, was preoccupied with evangelism and with

---

[119]Martin E. Marty, *Pilgrims in Their Own Land* (Harrisonburg, Va.: Penguin, 1984), p. 442.

[120]James M. Washington, ed., *The Essential Writings and Speeches of Martin Luther King, Jr.* (New York: HarperCollins, 1991), pp. xiv-xv.

[121]Michael O. Emerson and Christian Smith, *Divided by Faith: Evangelical Religion and the Problem of Race in America* (New York: Oxford University Press, 2000), p. 46.

"fighting communism and theological liberalism."[122] Second, even as late as 1965 (after King had written "Letter from a Birmingham Jail") Henry showed "little sympathy for social agitation on behalf of black rights."[123] Indeed, in a way that seemed to undermine the thrust of his earlier thesis that had pointed to structural evil, Henry argued "that racial discrimination could be overcome only by personal Christian behavior and a heart free of bias."[124] Third, in stressing law and order, Henry rejected the civil disobedience advocated by King and considered it disruptive.

In a similar fashion the editors of *Christianity Today*, fearing "disrespect for law implicit in mob demonstrations and resistance," were also not in the forefront on civil rights issues.[125] In the editorial pages of the magazine from 1956 to 1986, the topic of civil rights received "steady declining attention."[126] And when the topic was broached after all, for example in the March 18, 1957, issue, both articles offered little support to the social justice efforts of King.[127] Two years later an editorial on "Race Tension and Social Change" attempted to articulate an "evangelical moderate stance" that avoided all the messy elements of a struggle for social justice.[128] It contended, in the absence of very much theoretical reflection, that evangelicals should avoid "the trap of being a segregationist or an integrationist."[129] As Hammond points out, "Neo-evangelicals found themselves opposing the civil rights movement because many black leaders were associated with and were supported by the liberal wing of Christianity."[130] The logic here is inescapable but no less troubling: the friend of my "enemy" is also my enemy. And just as *Christian Century* ignored Billy Graham at the height of his early campaigns, so too *Christianity Today* ignored King. In fact, the Baptist minister was not even men-

[122]Ibid.

[123]Curtis J. Evans, "White Evangelical Protestant Responses to the Civil Rights Movement," *Harvard Theological Review* 102, no. 2 (2009): 266.

[124]Ibid.

[125]Michael D. Hammond, "Conscience in Conflict: Neo-Evangelicals and Race in the 1950s" (Ph.D. diss., Wheaton College Graduate School, 2002), pp. 116-17.

[126]Corwin E. Smidt, *Contemporary Evangelical Political Involvement* (Lanham, Md.: University Press of America, 1989), p. 41.

[127]Hammond, "Conscience in Conflict," p. 106.

[128]Ibid., p. 113.

[129]Ibid.

[130]Ibid., p. 150.

tioned in the magazine until January 17, 1964, when the editors noted briefly "that he had been chosen *Time's* 'Man of the Year!'"[131]

In 1950 Billy Graham followed local customs in the South, and as a result his crusades were initially segregated. A couple of years later in Jackson, Mississippi, Graham agreed to segregate the audience but he rejected the suggestion of Governor Hugh White "to conduct separate meetings for blacks."[132] At this same meeting the popular evangelist criticized segregation, but when his outspokenness disturbed some of the white Southerners present, Graham related to a local newspaper: "I feel that I have been misinterpreted on racial segregation. We follow the existing social customs in whatever part of the country in which we minister."[133] Accordingly, when the crusade moved farther north to Washington, D.C., that same year, with a much different environment, Graham changed his approach and now integrated the seating.[134]

Though some scholars discern a turning point for Graham on the race issue in 1953, we argue that it actually occurred the following year. To illustrate, when Graham was in Chattanooga, Tennessee, in 1953, he did indeed remove the ropes separating whites from blacks in the auditorium (though few took advantage of the open seating). However, a few months later, while conducting a campaign in Dallas, Texas, Graham once again "accepted segregated seating."[135] It was not until the Supreme Court ruled in 1954 in its landmark decision cited earlier (*Brown v. Board of Education*) that Graham was now emboldened to violate "local custom," whether in the North or the South. In a *Life* magazine article two years later Graham declared, "We have decided to hold no more crusades unless all of any race can sit where they please. . . . Where men are standing at the foot of the Cross, there are no racial barriers."[136]

By 1957 Graham not only took steps to integrate his own evangelistic as-

---

[131] Evans, "White Evangelical Protestant," p. 268.
[132] Harold Myra and Marshall Shelley, "Jesus and Justice: How Billy Graham Tactfully Led Evangelicals on Race at His First New York City Crusade," *Christianity Today* 49 (2005): 58.
[133] Emerson and Smith, *Divided by Faith*, p. 47.
[134] But it should also be noted that when Graham addressed the Southern Baptist Convention a few months later, he called for "integrating Baptist colleges" (see Hammond, "Conscience in Conflict," p. 23).
[135] Emerson and Smith, *Divided by Faith*, p. 47.
[136] Hammond, "Conscience in Conflict," p. 29.

sociation but he also invited Martin Luther King Jr. to give the invocation at a crusade in New York City. King's prayer opened with "a call to forgiveness [and] . . . for a brotherhood that transcends race or color."[137] Graham heartily agreed with King's vision, but like his fellow evangelical Carl Henry he took issue with the black preacher's methods. As a friend of presidents (an unofficial adviser to the Eisenhower White House) and as a champion of good order, Graham simply would not advocate civil disobedience—in the sense of Gandhi or otherwise. When pushed Graham would break local custom and tradition if necessary, and even then it was often done in an ambivalent way, "but he would not break the law."[138] So fearful was Graham of the specter of disorder in American society that when the Civil Rights Act of 1964 was passed under President Lyndon Johnson, he urged Dr. King to call on black leaders "to declare a moratorium on demonstrations until people have an opportunity to digest the new Civil Rights act."[139]

Beyond this, the broader evangelical community itself repeatedly criticized civil rights marches and legislation. Charles Stanley (1932-), the popular Southern preacher, actually positioned guards outside "his" church during the 1970s "to keep African-Americans out."[140] And the fundamentalist Bob Jones University refused to admit black students until 1971, when married African American couples were allowed for the first time, so fearful were the administrators and board members of interracial marriage.[141] Unmarried black students were finally admitted in 1975, but a strict prohibition on interracial dating remained.[142] Consequently, even into the 1970s white evangelicals, as Hankins observes, "[were] among the least likely segments of society to support racial justice."[143]

MARTIN LUTHER KING JR.

A year after President Kennedy (1917-1963) called out the troops to quell

---

[137]Ibid., p. 32.
[138]Myra and Shelley, "Jesus and Justice," p. 59.
[139]Evans, "White Evangelical Protestant," p. 260.
[140]Balmer, *Encyclopedia of Evangelicalism*, p. 651.
[141]Ibid., p. 89.
[142]Ibid.
[143]Hankins, *American Evangelicals*, p. 127.

the riots surrounding James Meredith (1933-), the first black student to enroll at the University of Mississippi, Martin Luther King Jr. was arrested on April 16, 1963, in Birmingham, Alabama. Growing up in a Baptist church in which his father was a pastor, King learned early on that the Christian faith is a universal religion that transcends race, ethnicity, gender, social class or cultural origin. During the time he attended Crozer Theological Seminary in Chester, Pennsylvania, King began to think deeply about social justice issues and became acquainted with the writings of Walter Rauschenbusch, especially his *Christianity and the Social Crisis*. Though King found much to his liking in Social Gospel thought, he differed from Rauschenbusch and others whom he believed came "perilously close to identifying the kingdom of God with a particular social and economic system—a temptation which the church should never give into."[144]

While he was in prison King penned a letter ("Letter from Birmingham Jail") that not only revealed why he and the civil rights movement could no longer wait ("justice too long delayed is justice denied"), but also argued for an understanding of justice that was well rooted in both moral philosophy and the Christian faith.[145] Appealing to the writings of Augustine (354-430) and Thomas Aquinas (1225-1274), King maintained that the laws of many Southern states, such as Alabama and Mississippi, were invalid because they were out of harmony with the natural law and the eternal law that is above it. Put another way, such laws failed to accord to black Americans those benefits and prerogatives that pertain to them precisely as human beings. "An unjust law," King wrote in this letter, "is a code that a majority inflicts on a minority that is not binding on itself. This difference is made legal."[146]

Having a theoretical basis for distinguishing an unjust law from a just one, King developed a sophisticated distinction between the legal and the moral, a distinction that several evangelicals were reluctant to acknowledge. In this line of reasoning some laws may be on the books, so to speak, but because they deny basic human rights to a sector of the popu-

---

[144]James M. Washington, ed., *The Essential Writings and Speeches of Martin Luther King, Jr.* (New York: HarperCollins, 1991), p. 37.
[145]Ibid., p. 292.
[146]Ibid., p. 294.

lation, such laws must be deemed immoral. Or as King himself put it, a law so construed is necessarily unjust for "it does not square with the law of God, so for that reason it is unjust and any law that degrades the human personality is an unjust law."[147] So then, part of King's strategy to further the civil rights of black Americans was to challenge such unjust laws through the use of nonviolent civil disobedience, a tactic he had learned from Gandhi. Such civil disobedience always upset the law-and-order crowd, who argued in terms of respect for the law of the land above all, or at best they championed gradual, less disruptive forms of change. To this and similar objections, King replied, "And I submit that the individual who disobeys the law, whose conscience tells him it is unjust and who is willing to accept the penalty by staying in jail until that law is altered, is expressing at the moment the very highest respect for the law."[148]

Though the strategy employed by King invited criticism from evangelicals and others, there was a genius in his method of wedding a natural law critique of unjust state laws to nonviolent civil disobedience. If King had promoted violence in a struggle to address injustices then the inevitable police crackdown would have hardly evoked sympathy for the movement. "They got what they deserved," would have been the quick, almost unthinking reply. But King did something very different. His goal, of course, was to demonstrate that the legal sometimes is immoral because the state has simply codified the all-too-common prejudices of the majority. In order, however, to get the average American to hear this plea of injustice, King had to break through the normal social filters such as a concern for law and order that would most often cut off any sympathetic response in its tracks. King, however, would eventually get the ear of the American people through a strategy of nonviolence coupled with his generous moral concern.

The stage was set the following month in May, 1963, for a heroic contest between nonviolent civil rights protestors who had God's moral law on their side and Bull Connor, the Commissioner of Public Safety in Birmingham, Alabama, who had his dogs and police. Television cameras caught the graphic violence of Conner's directives. Black activists were

---

[147]Ibid., p. 49.
[148]Ibid.

smashed into storefronts by hoses, pummeled by the billy sticks of cops, and bitten by attack dogs as they patiently suffered for their cause. Americans, indeed the world, looked on this spectacle in horror as the cameras rolled. Ironically enough, the law-and-order argument was being turned on its head, and Conner's lackeys now appeared to be shameful as new heroes were being born. Moreover, a fund of sympathy, wide and deep, was evoked that day for King's cause. Such an identification, sustained by strong emotion, represented nothing less than the illuminating grace of God breaking through, a grace that darkness and hatred could by no means overcome. And so while neo-evangelicals were positioning themselves between fundamentalism and liberalism, as they were preoccupied with fighting communism and developing a unified cultural voice, the actions of King demonstrated a much different kind of power, not that of coercion and force, but one that, remarkably enough, refused to speak the language of Babylon.

3

Evangelicals, the Religious Right and the Moral Life of the Nation

L YNDON BAINES JOHNSON (1908-1973), a Democrat from Texas known for his political wheeling and dealing as the United States Senate majority leader, was thrust into the presidency upon the assassination of John F. Kennedy. Though the charm and wit of Kennedy were clearly not passed along to the new president, Johnson did inherit an ugly war in Southeast Asia that not only rent the country but also helped to unravel his own administration. Due to their ongoing fear of atheistic and often violent communism, American evangelicals by and large supported Johnson's war in Vietnam. J. Howard Pew, who had funded various evangelical causes, put pressure on the community to take "pronationalist and procapitalist positions," though Carl Henry, his editor at *Christianity Today*, once again did not appear to be sufficiently militant in this area.[1] Demonstrating his own support of the American military, Billy Graham, the friend of presidents, visited the troops in Vietnam, and if he had any misgivings about the war itself, he did not make them public.[2]

The nation, however, was badly divided. While veterans groups produced buttons that read "Victory in Vietnam," students, radicals and anar-

---

[1]George M. Marsden, *Understanding Fundamentalism and Evangelicalism* (Grand Rapids: Eerdmans, 1991), p. 74.
[2]Nancy Koester, *The History of Christianity in the United States* (Minneapolis: Fortress Press, 2007), p. 183.

chists took to the streets and raged against the American government. Abbie Hoffman, Rennie Davis and Alan Ginsberg were the newfangled, self-appointed prophets. Because of the mishandling of the war by the administration, the Democratic Convention in Chicago in 1968 became a focal point for the antiwar protests. Misjudging the situation, Mayor Richard J. Daly added fuel to the demonstrations by unleashing the Chicago police, who beat students and even roughed up some reporters, Dan Rather among them, in a frenzy that played out to the disgust of the American people on the evening news. The year 1968 had been a particularly violent one with the assassinations of Martin Luther King Jr. in April and Robert F. Kennedy in June, and riots erupted in Washington, D.C., ten blocks from the White House in the aftermath of King's death. By this time some Americans, evangelicals among them, began to wonder if the American social fabric itself was unraveling.

When an unpopular war divides a people, when protestors repeatedly challenge the legitimacy of the government as well as the social mores of the nation, then such a society may undergo rapid social and cultural change, especially in terms of its moral life. Indeed, according to some observers the 1960s resulted in the "institutionalization of immoralist radicalism."[3] In other words, this decade witnessed the loosing of a traditional moral order, heretofore sustained by family and church, to make room for the new left's vision of drugs, promiscuous sex and the "decline of artistic and intellectual standards."[4] According to Robert Bork, a later Supreme Court nominee, hedonism and narcissism ruled the day as the 1960s generation "combined moral relativism with political absolutism."[5]

Charles Krauthammer, for his part, argued that it was "not enough for the deviant to be normalized. The normal must be found to be deviant," with animus directed especially toward middle-class values that were deemed to be "oppressive and shot through with pathologies."[6] The idea of being countercultural soon issued in a rejection of tradition, with all its ac-

---

[3]Roger Kimball, *The Long March: How the Cultural Revolution of the 1960s Changed America* (San Francisco: Encounter Books, 2000), p. 41.
[4]Ibid.
[5]Robert H. Bork, *Slouching Towards Gomorrah: Modern Liberalism and American Decline* (New York: Regan Books, 1996), p. 51.
[6]Charles Krauthammer, cited in ibid., pp. 3-4.

cumulated wisdom from the past, to celebrate the present generation itself as the premier locus of authority. This dynamic can be seen especially in terms of the shifting sexual ethic of America during this period. With the advent of the birth control pill in 1960, and with the radical challenge of traditional sexual mores in the name of "free love," the illegitimacy rate in America rose from the 1960s and onward in a precipitous way. Senator Daniel Patrick Moynihan conducted a famous study in the mid-1960s on poverty and concluded, among other things, that out-of-wedlock births were 3 percent for whites and nearly 24 percent for blacks. "A little more than thirty years later," as Ron Sider points out, "33 percent of all our children are born to unmarried women. The white illegitimacy rate is now 25 percent and the black rate 70 percent."[7] More recently, according to the *New York Times*, "Unmarried mothers gave birth to 4 out of every 10 babies born in the United States in 2007."[8] And the trend continues.

Such disturbing statistics are clearly the ongoing results of the sexual revolution of the 1960s, a revolution that promised freedom but actually left considerable poverty in its wake, especially in the form of single motherhood. In fact, there is no better predicator of poverty in America today, with all its attendant social problems, than the number of unwed mothers. The irony here is too poignant to be missed. That is, the new left's hedonistic individualism actually undermined its own calls for equality and a concern for the poor by creating a troubled underclass that would only increase from decade to decade. As Gertrude Himmelfarb pointed out, "Having been spared the class revolution that Marx predicated, we have succumbed to the cultural revolution. What was, only a few decades ago, a subculture in American society has been assimilated into the dominant culture."[9]

THE GREAT SOCIETY AND AN ACTIVIST SUPREME COURT

Continuing in the line of Franklin Roosevelt, who believed that the federal government must intervene in the economic life of the nation in order to

---

[7]Ronald J. Sider, *Just Generosity: A New Vision for Overcoming Poverty in America* (Grand Rapids: Baker, 1999), p. 122.

[8]Gardiner Harris, "Out of Wedlock Birthrates Are Soaring, U.S. Reports," *New York Times*, May 13, 2009, www.nytimes.com/2009/05/13/health/13mothers.html.

[9]Gertrude Himmelfarb, *One Nation, Two Cultures* (New York: Alfred A. Knopf, 1999), p. 118.

bring about social justice, President Johnson, in an address before the graduating class at the University of Michigan on May 22, 1964, laid out in broad strokes his vision for what he called "the Great Society," one that would supposedly be more compassionate and just, but that in the end laid the groundwork for a burgeoning American welfare state.

Though several politicians had underestimated Lyndon Johnson, he turned out to be remarkably adept at political persuasion, and many of his social programs were enacted into law. To illustrate, during his administration Johnson guided legislation that led to the creation of the Medicare and Medicaid programs; he established federal education funding that spent about a billion dollars early on to assist low income children; he created the Office of Economic Opportunity (OEO); he enhanced the Food Stamp Program; he organized the Job Corps and Vista (Volunteers in Service to America); and he helped to establish the Corporation for Public Broadcasting as well as the National Foundation on the Arts and Humanities among several other things. This litany of social service projects undertaken by the Johnson administration constituted what its advocates thought to be a veritable benevolent empire, but unlike the project of nineteenth-century evangelicals, the Great Society did not proceed with local and private support and in a voluntary way; instead, it operated largely at the federal level by amassing public tax dollars in order to redistribute them in accordance with its own political and social vision. According to one critic the Great Society "accomplished the most thorough-going redistribution of wealth and status in the name of equality that this country had ever experienced."[10]

One way of redistributing wealth was to enhance the federal welfare program Aid to Families with Dependent Children (AFDC), which had been started in the mid-1930s under the Roosevelt administration. During the 1960s, however, this program had developed some nasty unintended consequences, especially for black households. By tying cash payments to the number of children in a home the program actually increased, even promoted, the number of unwed mothers. By reducing payments if the father remained anywhere near the home, the program basically destroyed

---

[10]Bork, *Slouching Towards Gomorrah*, p. 67.

the black family for generations to come.

The gradual move toward a modern liberal democratic welfare state that hailed from the 1930s in which dependency on the federal government was encouraged must not be viewed utterly in a partisan way as if only members of the Democratic Party were the key players. Richard M. Nixon (1913-1994), for example, continued in the Great Society ways of Johnson and instituted a Family Assistance Plan (FAP) that offered guaranteed minimum incomes to families; he expanded Social Security benefits; he created the Supplemental Security Income Program that provided funds for the aged, blind and disabled; and he cobbled together a budget in which social spending exceeded military outlays.[11] In fact, Nixon incurred more federal debt than LBJ and speculated about forming a new majority party that would embrace the Democrat John Connally as a running mate.[12]

It would be a mistake, however, to view the Great Society that LBJ sought to bring about simply in economic terms. Operating from a larger vision of social justice, President Johnson supported civil rights legislation working its way through Congress during his administration that was sorely needed to address injustices with respect to the African American community and in terms of American women of all races. The effort here went back to the Kennedy administration (JFK's speech on June 11, 1963), though it was Johnson who finally signed the historic legislation on July 2, 1964. The effects of the passage of the civil rights act were seen chiefly in three areas: voter registration, the public schools, and the workplace.

During this time of so many different kinds of change, evangelicals had the distinct sense that as the role of the government increased in the lives of Americans, the traditional efforts of the church in the area of responsible and accountable charity were being increasingly undermined. Put another way, the temporal ministries of the church were being weakened, eviscerated, by an overweening federal government. Beyond this, evangelicals perceived once again that what cultural power they had was slipping away in light of some key decisions made by the Supreme Court. Earlier, at

---

[11]Allan J. Lichtman, *White Protestant Nation: The Rise of the American Conservative Movement* (New York: Grove Press, 2008), pp. 282, 294.

[12]Ibid., p. 296.

the turn of the century about 75 percent of America's major school districts began the day with Bible reading and prayer.[13] And even as late as 1931 the Supreme Court had declared in *United States v. Macintosh* that "We are a Christian people."[14] But by the 1960s all of this had changed. In 1962, for example, in *Engel v. Vitale* the Court ruled against school prayer by declaring "it is no part of the business of government to compose official prayers to be recited as part of a religious program."[15] And the following year the *Court in School District of Abington v. Schempp* ruled that "ritual Bible reading and recitation of the Lord's Prayer in the public schools were likewise unconstitutional."[16] As one author put it, "evangelicals had been caught completely off guard by the Court's decision."[17] According to Ronald C. Doll, professor of education at Hunter College in New York City, the Court "not only secularized the schools but made it possible for children to be taught atheism or agnosticism without any opposing perspective."[18]

The public outcry in light of these two court decisions was considerable and unabated—and not simply among evangelicals. To be sure, even today a majority of the American people favor prayer in schools. For example, a George Gallup survey conducted in 2005 revealed that "76% of Americans favor a constitutional amendment to allow *voluntary* prayer in public schools."[19] However, during the decade of the 1960s, as these judgments were handed down by the Supreme Court, evangelicals began to believe that an already engorged state was seeking to privatize all religious expression, to remove every vestige of religion from public life under the banner of a pluralistic liberal democracy. Indeed, the Supreme Court in its 1947 decision *Everson v. Board of Education* had already lifted the lan-

[13]D. G. Hart, *That Old Time Religion in Modern America: Evangelical Protestantism in the Twentieth Century* (Chicago: I. R. Dee, 2002), p. 97.

[14]Martin E. Marty, *The Noise of Conflict 1919-1941*, Modern American Religion (Chicago: University of Chicago Press, 1991), 2:296.

[15]David F. Wells and John D. Woodbridge, eds., *The Evangelicals: What They Believe, Who They Are, Where They Are Changing* (Nashville: Abingdon, 1975), p. 230.

[16]Edwin Scott Gaustad, *A Religious History of America*, rev. ed. (New York: Harper & Row, 1990), pp. 358-59.

[17]Ronald C. Doll, cited in Hart, *That Old Time Religion in Modern America*, p. 155.

[18]Ibid., p. 155.

[19]David W. Moore, "Public Favors Voluntary Prayer for Public Schools," *Gallup*, August 26, 2005, www.gallup.com/poll/18136/public-favors-voluntary-prayer-public-schools.aspx.

guage of a "wall of separation" from the letter of Thomas Jefferson to the Baptists of Danbury in 1802.[20] The result of this judicial move that was clearly evident in the rulings of the 1960s (and was no doubt informed by the countercultural movements then in play) was not simply to privatize religious expression and thereby in many instances render it irrelevant, but also to declare in an even more problematic way that the public square was not cultural space but that it belonged to the state. Put another way, it is one thing to maintain separation of church and state (a view that even some evangelicals will favor in order to protect the church). It is quite another thing, however, to enforce a separation of church and culture in the name of an increasingly powerful federal state. The one allows for genuine religious liberty; the other can only render believers second-class citizens. Evangelicals naturally chafed under these court rulings, and so in 1973 when the blockbuster decision *Roe v. Wade* was handed down, which made abortion legal by considering it a "private" matter, some evangelicals began to wonder if the government was downright hostile to people of faith.

SOCIAL ACTION AND THE YOUNG EVANGELICALS

At least a decade behind American cultural trends, evangelical social action surged during the 1970s. "A new, younger generation of 'radical evangelicals,'" David Gushee points out, "felt that Henry and the neo-evangelicals had not gone far enough in their critique of capitalism and social injustices in American society."[21] Accordingly, in 1973 the Chicago Declaration of Evangelical Social Concern was issued by Ron Sider and others to give added focus to an emergent evangelical social witness. Many evangelicals recognized that the normal outworking of capitalism often issues in some cruel consequences for the poor and that entire segments of society need help in order to improve their lot in life. The Chicago Declaration states, "We acknowledge that God requires justice. . . . Although the Lord calls us to defend the social and economic rights of the poor and oppressed, we

---

[20]Stephen L. Carter, *God's Name in Vain: The Wrongs and Rights of Religion in Politics* (New York: Basic Books, 2000), p. 74.

[21]David P. Gushee, *Christians and Politics Beyond the Culture Wars: An Agenda for Engagement* (Grand Rapids: Baker, 2000), p. 20.

have mostly remained silent."[22] With this and other goals in mind, racial and gender equality among them, Evangelicals for Social Action was formed in 1978 to broaden the evangelical social and political footprint even though the old line, as represented by Bernard Ramm, had already complained much earlier that "the one who affirms [that Christian ethics touches on political, social and economic aspects of modern life] would have a difficult case to prove from the pages of the New Testament."[23]

Remarkably well intentioned, a movement dubbed the "young evangelicals" were eager to "apply the Gospel to every dimension of life" that would include personal, social, economic and political elements.[24] Richard Quebedeaux chronicled the rise of this movement in a sanguine account published in 1974. The young evangelicals as well as their older supporters had supposedly "freed themselves completely from the old prejudices associated with the Fundamentalist-Modernist controversy and its aftermath and [were] ready to move forward."[25] Critical of the "antiquated social mores and the cultural baggage of revivalism," the young evangelicals, however, were often scattershot in their criticism of church and society, were largely unaware of the threat that a large burgeoning welfare state posed to the life of the churches, demonstrated little awareness of political philosophy, whether the writings of John Locke (1632-1704) or of Jean Jacques Rousseau (1712-1778), and never took the trouble to articulate what problems an American liberal democracy posed to people of faith in general and evangelicals in particular.[26]

Even Quebedeaux, who followed this movement closely, was far less optimistic in a second book produced a few years later, titled *The Worldly Evangelicals*. He notes, for example, that not only had the young evangelicals become worldly, but also, oddly enough, that had been their very design. In other words, having started out with the intention of changing the world, the worldly evangelicals soon deemed it necessary to become

---

[22]"The Chicago Declaration of Evangelical Social Concern," *Center for Public Justice*, November 25, 1973, www.cpjustice.org/stories/storyReader$928.

[23]Bernard Ramm, cited in Jon R. Stone, *On the Boundaries of American Evangelicalism: The Postwar Evangelical Coalition* (New York: St. Martin's Press, 1997), p. 88.

[24]Richard Quebedeaux, *The Young Evangelicals* (New York: Harper & Row, 1974), p. 40.

[25]Ibid., p. 54.

[26]Ibid., p. 99.

"respectable by the world's standards," with the noble goal, of course, of gaining a hearing. This was the same siren song that Carnell had heard years earlier. The result of this move, Quebedeaux notes, was not that the worldly evangelicals were respected by the American cultural elite but that they became "harder and harder to distinguish from other people."[27] Having set out to change the world, the worldly evangelicals had been transformed by American culture. This was an old story, to be sure, and one that has been repeated all too often.

WATERGATE AND THE ELECTION OF AN EVANGELICAL PRESIDENT

While the young evangelicals were coming together, many Americans were surprised to learn of the extent of the paranoia that had surrounded the Nixon administration. In the spring of 1972 few Americans, not even Democrats, doubted that the president would win reelection. And yet operatives from the White House orchestrated a risky break-in of the Democratic headquarters at the Watergate Hotel in Washington, D.C., on May 28 and June 17 of that year. The last incursion led to the arrest of the burglars and ultimately to the unraveling of the Nixon presidency. As the case unfolded, White House conversations that had been secretly recorded on tape were eventually (and after much legal wrangling) turned over to John Sirica, chief judge of the United States District Court in Washington, D.C. Upon listening to the tapes, Billy Graham, who had earlier held Nixon in high esteem, was downright sickened. In fact, he was so upset after listening to these conversations, "peppered as they were with profanities and racial epithets for his [Nixon's] Democratic opponents, that he wept, felt nauseated, and then vomited for hours."[28]

When Nixon's vice president Spiro T. Agnew (1918-1996) pleaded no contest to a bribery charge, he was replaced in 1973 by Gerald R. Ford (1913-2006), minority leader of the House, under the provisions of the 25th Amendment. At first evangelicals were pleased with this appointment, given the quiet though solid religious commitment of Ford. But when

---

[27]Richard Quebedeaux, *The Worldly Evangelicals* (San Francisco: Harper & Row, 1978), p. 14.
[28]Charles Marsh, *Wayward Christian Soldiers: Freeing the Gospel from Political Captivity* (Oxford: Oxford University Press, 2007), p. 60.

Nixon resigned in 1974 and as Ford prepared for the upcoming election, he made the statement that "there is no Soviet domination in Eastern Europe," to the chagrin of most Americans.[29] Moreover, when his wife, Betty, outspoken as she was, undermined the pro-life platform of the party, support quickly evaporated among evangelicals, and Ford lost the election to a Southern Democrat by a narrow margin.[30]

The election of Jimmy Carter (1924-), former governor of Georgia, naval officer and erstwhile peanut farmer, "arrested the drift of evangelicals to the Republican Party," at least for a while, that had been occurring since the time of Barry Goldwater's bid for the White House.[31] In the wake of the Watergate scandal Carter's more relaxed style as well as his promise to the nation that "I will never lie to you" were greatly appreciated.[32] In a departure from the pomp and circumstance ways of former presidents, Carter walked in the streets of Washington, D.C., on inaugural day, forgoing the usual limousine ride; he dispensed with "Hail to the Chief," and he even sold the presidential yacht, the USS *Sequoia*.[33] And unlike the more reticent Gerald Ford, Jimmy Carter was open, even exuberant, about his evangelical faith. The language of born again Christianity flowed from his Southern Baptist lips (though he eventually left the denomination in 2000) and quickly became a part of the national vocabulary. According to George Gallup, during the year of Carter's election, "one person in three (34 percent) claimed to have had a 'born again' experience."[34] Having emerged from its subculture during the 1940s, evangelicalism had finally come to political power in the 1970s.[35] This had been a slow train coming, but evangelicals had clearly put a vital infrastructure in place that prepared them for better days. Indeed, Carter did for evangelicals what Kennedy had done for Roman Catholics. As Mark Noll observes, "Carter

---

[29]William J. Bennett, *America: The Last Best Hope*, vol. 2, *From a World at War to the Triumph of Freedom* (Nashville: Thomas Nelson, 2007), p. 458.

[30]Ibid.

[31]Richard Kyle, *Evangelicalism: An Americanized Christianity* (New Brunswick, N.J.: Transaction Publishers, 2006), p. 195.

[32]"Jimmy Carter," *The American Experience*, PBS, www.pbs.org/wgbh/amex/carter/filmmore/pt .html.

[33]Bennett, *America*, p. 460.

[34]Corwin E. Smidt, *Contemporary Evangelical Political Involvement* (Lanham, Md.: University Press of America, 1989), p. 2.

[35]Kyle, *Evangelicalism*, p. 8.

brought religion and politics into closer public contact than they had been since the era of Woodrow Wilson and William Jennings Bryan."[36] *Newsweek* magazine fittingly declared 1976 "the Year of the Evangelical."

But all was not well. In fact, even before Carter was elected president a squabble broke out between his staff and Jerry Falwell over an interview of the candidate in *Playboy* magazine. On his own national television program that aired from Lynchburg, Virginia, Falwell criticized Carter for this lapse of judgment. To his surprise, Falwell, who was then the pastor of the Thomas Road Baptist Church, received a phone call in his office from Carter's special assistant, Jody Powell, ordering him to "back off."[37] Falwell, however, was not about to be silenced on a matter the he considered to be of great moral importance. For his part, Carter later referred to the whole affair as "his initial baptism into the world of politics."[38]

As a Baptist, and as one who identified with the free church tradition, Jimmy Carter believed that "one's personal morals should be kept separate from public policy."[39] Such a political philosophy set the president on a collision course with some of his fellow evangelicals who preferred the more Puritan view that "Christian morality should be enforced legally."[40] Flash points quickly emerged with respect to secularism, homosexuality, abortion and even the definition of a family. To illustrate, in 1979 Adrian Rogers, the president of the Southern Baptist Convention, chided the president during a meeting in the oval office in the following words: "Mr. President, I hope you will abandon your commitment as a secular humanist."[41] Beyond this, as Hart points out, though Carter "talked a good game, [he] showed greater tolerance on gay rights and feminist issues than many evangelicals could bear."[42] In fact, after he left the presidency Carter came out in favor of "civil unions" for homosexuals.[43] And in terms of abortion,

---

[36]Mark Noll, *The Old Religion in the New World: The History of North American Christianity* (Grand Rapids: Eerdmans, 2002), p. 170.

[37]Gushee, *Christians and Politics*, p. 22.

[38]Ibid.

[39]Kyle, *Evangelicalism*, p. 196.

[40]Ibid.

[41]Adrian Rogers, cited in D. Michael Lindsay, *Faith in the Halls of Power: How Evangelicals Joined the American Elite* (New York: Oxford University Press, 2007), p. 55.

[42]Hart, *Old Time Religion in America*, p. 162.

[43]Jimmy Carter, *Our Endangered Values: America's Moral Crisis* (New York: Simon & Schuster, 2005), p. 69.

though the president waxed eloquently about eliminating *the need* for abortion, in the end he actually increased the resources for federally funded birth control clinics.[44] Tim LaHaye, noted evangelical leader, was so exasperated by these and other policies that he exclaimed: "God we have got to get this man out of the White House."[45]

During the 1970s evangelicals were by and large reluctant to embrace the feminist cause, especially in its second wave as expressed, for example, in the writings of Shulamith Firestone (*The Dialectic of Sex*) and Carol Hanisch, who had popularized the phrase "the personal is political." Many evangelicals read the Bible in ways that made it difficult for them to contextualize the apostle Paul's statements on women, especially those found in First Corinthians. In other words, first-century teachings that arose, in part, in light of the cultural sensibilities of the Middle East were readily universalized and immediately applied to modern settings and a diversity of locales. In 1972 Alice Paul drafted the substance of what became a proposal to alter the Constitution of the United States, known as the Equal Rights Amendment. This amendment quickly passed both houses of Congress by the necessary two-thirds majority, but it also had to be ratified within seven years (though an extension of three years was granted) by three-fourths of the states in order to become the law of the land. The language of the proposed amendment was brief and straightforward:

> *Section 1.* Equality of rights under the law shall not be denied or abridged by the United States or by any state on account of sex.
> *Section 2.* The Congress shall have the power to enforce, by appropriate legislation, the provisions of this article.
> *Section 3.* This amendment shall take effect two years after the date of ratification.[46]

During his presidency Carter strongly supported the passage of this amendment, though his critics charged that such an endorsement was due to the inordinate influence of his wife, Rosalyn, upon him, and that he had failed

---

[44]Bennett, *America*, pp. 460-61.
[45]Tim LaHaye, cited in Barry N. Hankins, *American Evangelicals: A Contemporary History of a Mainstream Religious Movement* (Lanham, Md.: Rowman & Littlefield, 2008), p. 144.
[46]Roberta W. Francis, "Frequently Asked Questions," *The Equal Rights Amendment*, www.equalrightsamendment.org/faq.htm.

to take into account the social and moral consequences of this legislation. The president's sharpest critic on this topic, however, was not an evangelical but a well educated, articulate and vocal conservative Roman Catholic, Phyllis Schlafly (1924-). The ERA, she argued, "dissolved men's obligation to support their wives and children, forced women into the workplace, and relegated their children to day-care centers." In addition, "it legalized homosexual marriage and required government to pay for abortions."[47] Whether Schlafy's allegations were accurate or not, she nevertheless succeeded in changing the tone of the national conversation that was now marked by considerable ambiguity. Consequently the ERA failed to pass by three states (thirty-eight states were needed) by the deadline of June 30, 1982.

A good window on Carter's social ethic, especially as it related to matters of human sexuality, can be found in his call for a national conference on the family that was held in 1980. The original intent of this gathering had been to strengthen the American family. Conservative Catholics and evangelicals therefore eagerly participated until they began to realize that the president had stacked the conference with members who not only "refused to privilege heterosexual families" but who also championed "abortion rights, the ERA and national health insurance."[48] The tipping point for many came in the form of a change in the name of the conference from Conference on the Family (traditionally consisting of two parents rearing their children) to Conference on Families (any assemblage of people living together). Richard John Neuhaus (1936-2009), a Missouri Synod Lutheran pastor at the time, resigned from the conference and walked out in protest. And evangelical leaders quickly realized that there was little difference between Carter's views and the Democratic Party line on most social issues.[49] "This ill-fated Conference," as Damon Linker points out, "played a crucial role in fostering . . . evangelical disaffection."[50]

The greatest achievement of the Carter administration was arguably the Camp David Accords, the agreement between Egypt and Israel that led to a cessation of hostilities between the two nations (though hardly peace) as

---

[47]Phyllis Schlafly, cited in Lichtman, *White Protestant Nation*, p. 320.

[48]Ibid., p. 348.

[49]Ibid., p. 331.

[50]Damon Linker, *The Theocons: Secular America under Siege* (New York: Anchor Books, 2006), p. 44.

well as to the return of the Sinai to Egypt. But even here, in an area of significant progress, there was room for significant evangelical dissatisfaction. The Accords, which were made up of two agreements (*A Framework for Peace in the Middle East* and *A Framework for the Conclusion of a Peace Treaty Between Egypt and Israel*), contained language that suggested the future creation of an autonomous, self-governing authority in the West Bank and Gaza, language that many Arabs interpreted as the creation of a Palestinian state. This two-state solution, though favored by Carter, was rejected by many evangelicals, dispensationalists among them, who believed that the entirety of the land of Palestine quite simply belonged to the Jews.[51] How could the Jewish people hand over land that had been promised to them (think of Jerusalem) by no one less than Almighty God? The logic was compelling for some evangelicals but challenged by others—even by the evangelical left.[52]

Add to these presidential difficulties the national humiliation of the Iranian hostage crisis, which lasted four hundred and forty four days, as well as the infamous Carter "malaise" speech (though he never used this exact word), riddled as it was with self-doubt and accusations that the American people were caught up in a "crisis of confidence," and it can easily be seen why not simply evangelicals but also the broader American public had turned on this once popular president. For their part evangelicals believed that the administration was "completely adrift."[53] "One of the great ironies of the twentieth century," Randall Balmer notes, "is that the very people who emerged to help elect Carter in 1976 turned rabidly against him four years later."[54]

THE RISE OF THE NEW RELIGIOUS RIGHT

Emerging in the late 1970s in the midst of the troubled Carter administration, the religious right embraced such groups as the Moral Majority,

---

[51]For a recent expression of Carter's views on this topic see Jimmy Carter, *Palestine: Peace Not Apartheid* (New York: Simon & Schuster, 2006).

[52]Tony Campolo, *Red Letter Christians: A Citizen's Guide to Faith and Politics* (Ventura, Calif.: Regal, 2008), p. 114.

[53]Lindsay, *Faith in the Halls of Power*, p. 55.

[54]Randall Balmer, *The Making of Evangelicalism: From Revivalism to Politics and Beyond* (Waco, Tex.: Baylor University Press, 2010), p. 56.

who made Jerry Falwell a household name, Focus on the Family, headed up by the Nazarene psychologist James Dobson, and Concerned Women of America, founded by Beverly LaHaye, wife of the well-known pastor and author (who later cowrote the Left Behind series). The religious right, though it would exercise significant political power (especially within the Republican Party), nevertheless represented only a fraction of evangelicals, though it embraced many fundamentalists as well. Indeed, according to the best estimates, "Fully 70 percent of evangelicals in America do *not* identify with the Religious Right."[55]

Remarkably enough, the very founding of the Moral Majority (and therefore the religious right as well) is a topic much disputed by scholars. Historian Randall Balmer, for instance, maintains that the infamous *Roe v. Wade* Supreme Court decision did not precipitate the rise of the Moral Majority, as is popularly believed. Instead he chronicles a narrative that devolves upon Bob Jones University and its struggle to retain its tax-exempt status in the eyes of the IRS. To illustrate, in 1971 a District Court in the case *Green v. Connally* handed down a judgment that supported the IRS in its intent to remove the tax-exempt status from institutions that engaged in racial discrimination "be they churches, clubs or schools."[56] Sensing the cultural and political winds, the administrators at Bob Jones University, an institution that previously had perpetrated the discriminatory and unjust practice of racial segregation, decided to admit only *married* African American students in 1971, so great was the fear of miscegenation.[57] Four years later the university reluctantly admitted single black students while at the same time it rigorously enforced a policy that prohibited interracial dating, the violation of which constituted grounds for dismissal.

Encouraged by the decision of *Green v. Connally*, the IRS officially revoked the tax-exempt status of Bob Jones University on January 19, 1976, though it made this action retroactive to 1970, "when the school had first been formally notified of the IRS policy."[58] According to Balmer's interpre-

---

[55]Lindsay, *Faith in the Halls of Power*, p. 28 (emphasis added).
[56]Balmer, *Making of Evangelicalism*, p. 63.
[57]Ibid.
[58]Ibid.

tation, Paul Weyrich (1942-2008), famous for his statement "I don't want everybody to vote. Elections are not won by the majority of the people," saw an opportunity to advance his political agenda. The conservative activist redefined the contest between the university and the IRS not as one of overt racism (which it clearly was) but as a David-and-Goliath conflict of a powerful government agency against "the sanctity of the evangelical subculture."[59] Balmer notes that during the 1990s Weyrich recalled what had galvanized the religious right in the following words: "What changed their mind was Jimmy Carter's intervention against Christian schools, trying to deny them tax-exempt status on the basis of so-called de facto segregation."[60] But this chronology, this account of the matter, is surely incorrect, for the crucial IRS decision against Christian schools occurred on January 19, 1976, that is, a full year and a day before James Earl Carter Jr. was inaugurated the thirty-ninth president of the United States. Was the animus directed against Carter by the religious right that animated and confused?

According to syndicated columnist Cal Thomas, the rise of the Moral Majority was the brain child of three men: Howard Phillips, president of the Conservative Caucus, and Jewish; Paul Weyrich, president of the committee for the survival of a Free Congress, a Catholic at the time; and Jerry Falwell, a fundamentalist Baptist.[61] It was Weyrich who actually came up with the name Moral Majority, though Falwell embraced it immediately. Ed Dobson, a former assistant of Jerry Falwell, has corroborated some aspects of Balmer's narrative in maintaining that "The Religious New Right did not start because of a concern about abortion."[62] And though this statement may be accurate with respect to the intentions of the founders of the Moral Majority, it clearly does *not* explain the motivations of the vast numbers of people who eventually joined the movement. For that story we must look elsewhere.

Operating from a different vantage point, Sabrina Ramet, professor of political science at the Norwegian University of Science and Technology,

[59]Ibid., p. 64.
[60]Paul Weyrich, cited in ibid.
[61]Cal Thomas and Ed Dobson, *Blinded by Might* (Grand Rapids: Zondervan, 1999), p. 14.
[62]Ed Dobson, cited in Balmer, *Making of Evangelicalism*, p. 65.

observes, "The Christian Right emerged in the course of the 1970s in response to a *number* of developments," including the spread of drugs, the celebration of free love, the proliferation of premarital (and extramarital) sex, fallout from *Roe v. Wade* and the 1977 gay rights referendum in Dade County, which sparked the activism of Anita Bryant who formed the organization Save Our Children.[63] Moreover, in his book on American religion Thomas Askew contends that the Moral Majority was set up during the Carter administration as a counter to the "secular humanism, the relativistic, materialistic ideology of a small liberal elite who controlled the media, education, the government bureaucracies, and the courts."[64] And Kyle, for his part, views the formation of the Moral Majority in terms of a "reaction to government decisions regarding abortion, homosexuality, feminism, and prayer in schools."[65]

At any rate, once the political action structures of the Moral Majority were in place, this movement evoked an animated, even visceral, response from cultural elites who had been schooled on the notion that religious folk in modern liberal democracies are best seen and not heard. Oddly enough, social scientific studies were conducted to determine if activism in the Moral Majority constituted evidence of psychological pathology![66] Beyond this, the editorial pages of the *New York Times* railed against the movement and its leaders. In fact, so fearful were some Hollywood elites, who enjoyed the generous profits from a vulgar cultural gravy train, that Norman Lear, the well-known TV producer, helped to create the left-leaning People for the American Way, an organization located in Washington, D.C., that even today *monitors* right-wing activities. In short, "Secular Americans recoiled in horror in the face of the Reverend Falwell and his Moral Majority," as Susan Harding notes, "not only because the direction of history as we understood it had been contradicted but also be-

---

[63]Sabrina Ramet, "'Fighting for the Christian Nation': The Christian Right and American Politics," *Journal of Human Rights* 4, no. 3 (2005): 432 (emphasis added).

[64]Thomas A. Askew and Richard V. Pierard, *The American Church Experience: A Concise History* (Grand Rapids: Baker, 2004), p. 223.

[65]Kyle, *Evangelicalism*, p. 199.

[66]Clyde Wilcox, "Rethinking the Reasonableness of the Right," *Review of Religious Research* 36, no. 3 (1995): 271. Wilcox concluded, however, that the "data suggest that activism in the Moral Majority was not generally attributable to pathological sources" (ibid., p. 271).

cause *our* religious-cultural order was being turned upside down."[67]

The stated goals of the Moral Majority, an organization that embraced Protestants, Catholics and Jews, were actually more benign than some of its detractors had imagined. To illustrate, it affirmed the separation of church and state; it was pro-life, pro-traditional family; it was opposed to illegal drugs and pornography; it supported the state of Israel and the Jewish people; it championed a strong national defense; it supported equal rights for women, though it rejected the ERA as the wrong means to insure those rights; and it encouraged its state organizations to be indigenous and autonomous.[68] And though the early leadership, for fear of being misunderstood, also affirmed that the Moral Majority was not a political party and did not endorse candidates for election, it nevertheless had a significant impact on its own membership and beyond in terms of the ongoing drift of evangelicals and fundamentalists into the Republican Party.

Another significant group of the emerging religious right was Focus on the Family. It was established in 1977 by the Wesleyan-Holiness evangelical (Church of the Nazarene) psychologist James C. Dobson, who not only taught pediatrics at the University of Southern California School of Medicine but also was well known for his best-selling book *Dare to Discipline*, which sold more than 4.5 million copies.[69] In this work he challenged the permissive rearing methods of Dr. Benjamin Spock, a cultural icon, and offered instead the value of disciplining children, within a context of loving care and concern, as creating an environment in which children would flourish. With such an emphasis of its founder in place, Focus on the Family underscored the integrity of the family and the attendant issues of human sexuality. The organization naturally came into conflict with the sexual preferences of the counterculture that hailed from the 1960s but had now become in many respects mainstream.

Women bore the brunt of America's shifting sexual ethic in which out-of-wedlock births often resulted in women being abandoned to raise their children alone and often in poverty. Accordingly, Concerned Women of

---

[67]Susan Harding, "American Protestant Moralism and the Secular Imagination," *Social Research* 76, no. 4 (2009): 1303 (emphasis added).

[68]Thomas and Dobson, *Blinded by Might*, pp. 38-39.

[69]Hankins, *American Evangelicals*, p. 156.

America (CWA) was created by Beverly LaHaye in 1979 in order to promote scriptural values for women as they faced the many challenges of modern culture. In a way similar to Focus on the Family, CWA wanted to restore the integrity of the family, which was being undermined by a sexual ethic that was irresponsible, libertine and especially damaged women and their children. Concerned Women of America identified six core issues that it would continually address: the family, the sanctity of human life, education, pornography, religious liberty, and national sovereignty. From the beginning the group has been politically active, and its current president, Wendy Wright has been listed among "The 100 Most Powerful Women of Washington."[70]

THE CHRISTIAN COALITION

By the summer of 1980 relations between Jimmy Carter and what should have been his evangelical base had already deteriorated. The president was considered "a dangerous apostate," and he was denounced "for immoral views on the social issues by hordes of groups."[71] Moreover, outright public bickering erupted between Carter and various fundamentalist leaders. Jerry Falwell, for example, continued to lampoon the administration, and Carter shot back, "Jerry Falwell can go straight to hell," and then catching himself he added: "and I mean that in a Christian way."[72]

With the help of evangelicals and the religious right, Ronald Reagan (1911-2004) won the 1980 election by defeating Carter in a landslide. The Republican candidate won forty-four states and garnered 489 electoral votes to Carter's 49. Two thirds of white evangelicals had voted for Reagan.[73] Cal Thomas viewed this landslide as a vindication of conservative Christians since the debacle of the Scopes trial.[74] In one sense, however, this was an odd political marriage, for though Reagan often spoke of God, he hardly ever attended church; though he was a champion

---

[70]www.c-fam.org/About-Us/staff/wendy_wright.html.

[71]Ralph Reed, *Active Faith: How Christians Are Changing the Soul of American Politics* (New York: Free Press, 1996), p. 94.

[72]Jimmy Carter, cited in ibid.

[73]Sara Diamond, "On the Road to Political Power and Theocracy," Political Research Associates, www.publiceye.org/eyes/sd_theo.html.

[74]Thomas and Dobson, *Blinded by Might*, p. 40.

of family values, he was divorced and "rarely saw his grandchildren,"[75] and though he advocated economic responsibility, he set the nation down a course of deficit spending with his huge tax cuts and ever-increasing un-balanced federal budgets.[76] But Reagan paid attention to the religious right and the broader evangelical movement; he took them seriously. For ex-ample, during his first term in office, and after his handlers had specifically advised against it, Reagan became the first president to address the Na-tional Association of Evangelicals, first in 1983 and then the following year as well. In fact, Reagan delivered his famous "Soviet-Union-as-the-Evil-Empire" speech before a warm evangelical audience at the NAE in Or-lando in 1983.

For evangelicals Reagan was a champion who unabashedly communi-cated many of the values they held dear: belief in God, respect for country, honesty, fair play, hard work and family responsibility. They especially liked his able defense of the very least of all, the unborn. Indeed, not only did Reagan embrace pro-life forces during his eight years as president but he also declared February 22 (the anniversary of *Roe v. Wade*) as "National Sanctity of Human Life Day."[77] So concerned was Reagan about the sanctify of human life that he composed a book, while he was president, specifically devoted to the topic of abortion, titled *Abortion and the Con-science of the Nation*. Moreover, Reagan realized that if Americans ever wit-nessed an abortion, which some members of the National Organization of Women had referred to as a simple medical procedure, then their con-sciences would indeed be pricked. To that end, he let it be known that the film *The Silent Scream* had been shown at the White House itself. Several in the prochoice movement fulminated against the president for having the bad taste, as they put it, of showing such a controversial film. Reagan, however, remained firm in his convictions. But given the president's views on this weighty moral issue, evangelicals could hardly comprehend why he appointed Sandra Day O'Connor to the Supreme Court in 1981.

George H. W. Bush, Reagan's vice president and the man who would

---

[75]Dinesh D'Souza, *Ronald Reagan: How an Ordinary Man Became an Extraordinary Leader* (New York: Touchstone, 1997), p. 8.

[76]U.S. Government Spending, www.usgovernmentspending.com/federal_debt_chart.html.

[77]Gaustad, *Religious History of a America*, p. 369.

succeed him in office, was never warmly embraced by evangelicals. They remembered all too well his numerous criticisms of Reagan as they both had vied for the Republican nomination in 1980, especially his comment about "voodoo economics." Indeed, Bush was seen by some as a liberal Republican or at best a moderate who liked to bask in the glow of Reagan's popular conservatism. For all these reasons and more, Pat Robertson, a Baptist leader and head of the Christian Broadcasting Network, entered the Republican presidential contest in 1988 in order to give evangelicals greater voice in the national arena. He came out of the gate finishing a strong second in the Iowa caucus behind Bob Dole but ahead of Bush. Robertson, however, finished poorly in New Hampshire and won in only four states: Washington, Nevada, Alaska and Hawaii. Upon withdrawing from the presidential contest, Robertson garnered the energy as well as the organizational savvy that had emerged during his campaign and channeled it into the founding of the Christian Coalition in 1989, an advocacy group that embraced evangelicals, fundamentalists and charismatics. Since the Moral Majority had closed its doors this same year, many viewed the Coalition as the natural successor to Falwell's group, though the Thomas Road Baptist Church preacher, himself, looked to James Dobson, the Nazarene leader, as his successor on the Christian right.

Robertson was impressed with the political instincts of Ralph Reed, a young and energetic graduate of the University of Georgia, a school where he was involved in the College Republicans club. Converted at an Assemblies of God church in suburban Washington, Reed was remarkably ambitious, politically speaking, and he initially set out not so much to serve the Lord (indeed he later repented of some of his early ruthless political behavior) but to "become the next Lee Atwater—a bare-knuckled, brass-tacks practitioner of hardball politics."[78] With a knack for political mobilization, Reed convinced Robertson that the way to be most politically effective was to begin small; that is, to start at the grass-roots level by establishing state and local chapters of an up-and-coming movement. "The Christian community got it backwards in the 1980s," Reed later wrote, "We tried to charge Washington when

---

[78]Randall Balmer, *Encyclopedia of Evangelicalism* (Waco, Tex.: Baylor University Press, 2004), p. 569.

we should have been focusing on the states."[79]

Something of a national campaign did emerge, however, in a full-page ad in the *Washington Post* and *USA Today* in 1990, paid for by the Christian Coalition, that called for the elimination of taxpayer funded pornography. The reference here, of course, was to the government's support for the National Endowment for the Arts (a Lyndon Johnson Great Society project) that had funded the controversial works of Andres Serrano (*Piss Christ*, which displayed a crucifix of Christ immersed in a jar of urine) as well of Robert Mapplethorpe's offerings that exhibited human sexuality in ways that were deeply offensive.[80] Members of the Christian right, therefore, initiated a public debate and argued against federal tax dollars supporting works of art that degraded rather than elevated the human spirit. Again, why should public funds be used to mock and debase the Christian beliefs held by the overwhelming majority of Americans? And where was the protestation of separation of church and state when you needed it? With deepening hypocrisy in play, so conservatives argued, the government could apparently pay to have a crucifix placed in a jar of urine but not on a lawn.

The political left by this point was fully engaged—and angry. They feared that if the new Christian right were successful in their attempts to challenge or, worse yet, transform the moral life of the nation, then this could only result in a stifling and oppressive environment. Ralph Reed, for his part, attempted to allay some of these fears of the left by pointing out that if the people of the Christian Coalition, for example, as an important political interest group, came to power "they would not repeal the Constitution or attempt to impose their religion on others through the state."[81] What conservatives actually wanted, when all the smoke cleared, so to speak, was to pursue those goods that elevated the human spirit unfettered by government meddling.[82] To be sure, Reed vigorously maintained that the Christian right, as a political entity in a free and democratic society, had a right, indeed an obligation, to participate in the larger life of the

---

[79]Hankins, *American Evangelicals*, p. 155.
[80]*Piss Christ* was eventually destroyed on April 17, 2011 in Avignon, France, by Christians who were not convinced by the artistic and theological defenses offered for its creation and display.
[81]Reed, *Active Faith*, p. 25.
[82]Ibid., p. 189.

nation. In arguing along these lines Reed was of course utilizing the left's own platform against itself. That is, if diversity is so important, if difference does genuinely matter, then evangelical Christians as a minority in the United States must surely have a place at the table. To contend otherwise is not only contradictory but decidedly undemocratic.

The Christian Coalition exercised some of its political prowess in the 1992 presidential elections by circulating over 40 million voter guides among nearly a quarter of a million churches. These guides offered a side-by-side comparison of the three candidates (George H. W. Bush, Bill Clinton and Ross Perot) in terms of such issues as "abortion, school prayer, and homosexual rights."[83] Despite the setback of the election of Bill Clinton that year, the Christian right actually grew stronger in the days ahead, such that by the time of the mid-term elections two years later it was clearly a force to be reckoned with in American politics. Failing to notice that the political ground under her feet had already shifted, Governor Ann Richards of Texas, a Democrat, during her 1994 reelection campaign, made a huge gaffe by referring to conservative Christians as "mongers of hate."[84] Not surprisingly she suffered political defeat at the hands of none other than George W. Bush.

Getting behind Newt Gingrich's Contract with America, the Christian Coalition achieved the political success it so greatly desired in the off-year election of 1994, when President Clinton watched both the House of Representatives and the Senate slip away and turn Republican. This was not only the first time that Republicans held a majority in the House since 1954 but it was also the first occasion since Reconstruction that "a majority of members of Congress from the south [were] Republicans."[85] It was truly a historic election. But this was not to be a time for gloating simply because many of the leaders of the Christian right realized that despite this victory the Reagan and Gingrich revolutions had hardly "matched the shattering realignment of the New Deal."[86] In other words, all the major elements for the ongoing creation of a federal welfare state, that is, "the New Deal, the

---

[83]Erin Saberi, "From Moral Majority to Organized Minority," *Christian Century* 110, no. 23 (1993): 783.

[84]Reed, *Active Faith*, p. 70.

[85]Ibid., p. 71.

[86]Lichtman, *White Protestant Nation*, p. 437.

Great Society, and [even] Richard Nixon's liberal initiatives," remained very much in place.[87] In the eyes of many conservative Christians much more work needed to be done; they could celebrate later.

One of the first social issues that the Christian right addressed was abortion, a procedure accurately described in most cases as the killing of a fetus. At the national level the Democratic Party had not offered a pro-life candidate since the historic decision of *Roe v. Wade* in 1973. Both Bill Clinton and Al Gore earlier in their careers had actually supported pro-life initiatives, but by the time they sought national office, they had already embraced the pro-choice platform of their party. "Bill Clinton is another Jimmy Carter," Reed writes, "someone who accedes to a pro-abortion and liberal social agenda and promotes it beneath the veneer of Scripture."[88] Moreover, Reed describes the socially uncomfortable predicament of the president and the vice-president as they sat "stone-faced," as he put it, at the National Prayer Breakfast in 1994 listening to Mother Teresa denounce abortion as "the greatest destroyer of peace in the world today."[89] The following year the Christian Coalition joined forces with the National Right to Life Committee and announced their support for a ban of what has been called partial-birth abortion; that is, a procedure that entails the willful destruction of the infant as it "was partially delivered down the birth canal."[90]

By 1995 the Christian Coalition already had "1.6 million members, 50 state affiliates, and 1,600 local chapters."[91] Unlike the Moral Majority that had preceded it, the coalition utilized lay leadership from evangelical churches rather than pastors.[92] But like the Moral Majority the Coalition realized the importance of reaching out to Roman Catholics, many of whom would be natural allies on such social issues as abortion and homosexuality. Accordingly, during this same year the organization "launched

---

[87]Ibid.

[88]Reed, *Active* Faith, p. 96.

[89]Ibid., p. 84

[90]Ibid., p. 40. Putting social and political pressures aside, I want to be descriptively accurate. A being that is mature enough to make its way down the birth canal is suitably described as an infant. Anything less than this designation would be an unwarranted euphemism.

[91]Hankins, *American Evangelicals*, p. 154.

[92]Ibid.

the Catholic Alliance" in order to attract a new pool of members.[93] Two years later, however, in a surprising move, and while the Coalition was continuing to have influence in the national arena, Reed stepped down and channeled his energies elsewhere. "Organizationally, it's been tough-sledding for the coalition," as Leon Howell observes, "since Ralph Reed left as director."[94]

CULTURE WARS

With Reed gone, Pat Robertson stepped up the Clinton bashing and claimed that the White House had been turned into "the playpen for the sexual freedom of the poster child of the 1960s."[95] But the Clintons could give as well as they received. Hillary, for example, complained in very strident way on NBC's *Today* show that the political difficulties of her husband, even in terms of the Monica Lewinsky affair, were due to a "vast right wing conspiracy . . . led by people like Jerry Falwell."[96] *Wall Street Journal* columnist Harry Stein (who had shifted from political liberalism to conservatism upon the birth of his daughter) made sport of Clinton's claim in his trenchant and wildly humorous account *How I Accidently Joined the Vast Right Wing Conspiracy (and Found Inner Peace)*.[97] The tone of the national conversation was changing.

Noted professor of religion and culture James Davison Hunter had already employed the language of "culture wars" to describe many of the tensions that had been precipitated by the religious right during the 1980s in which the very identity of the nation, especially in terms of its cultural life and heritage, was in the offing.[98] Exploring the notion of a culture war in terms of different conceptions of moral authority, beliefs about truth, moral obligation, the good, as well as the nature of community, Hunter demonstrated that cultural conflict is largely about power, especially in

---

[93]Mary E. Bendyna, "Uneasy Alliance," *Sociology of Religion* 62, no. 1 (2001): 52.

[94]Leon Howell, "Ups and Downs of the Religious Right," *Christian Century* 117, no. 13 (2000): 462.

[95]Joseph Conn, "God, Guns and the GOP," *Church and State* 51, no. 10 (1998): 4-8.

[96]Thomas and Dobson, *Blinded by Might*, p. 30.

[97]Harry Stein, *How I Accidently Joined the Vast Right Wing Conspiracy (and Found Inner Peace)* (New York: Harper Paperbacks, 2001).

[98]See James Davison Hunter, *Culture Wars: The Struggle to Define America* (New York: Basic Books, 1991).

terms of the "struggle to achieve or maintain the power to define reality."[99]

As evidence of this ongoing cultural conflict Hunter took note of the speech to incoming freshmen in 1981 at Yale University in which its president, A. Bartlett Giamatti, cautioned against the "politically active evangelical Christians and their 'client groups' 'peddlers of coercion.'"[100] Since only a fraction of evangelical Christians would identify with the religious right, Giamatti also turned his attention to this particular movement and warned the freshmen that it was filled with angry, rigid, absolutistic, threatening and authoritarian people.[101] The following decade in 1993 Michael Weisskopf opined in a *Washington Post* article that evangelical Christians were "largely poor, uneducated, and easy to command," though the demographics tell a much different story.[102] In fact, as Christian Smith, a professor at the University of Notre Dame, points out, "self-identified evangelicals are among the best-educated Americans and have enjoyed the greatest intergeneration education mobility among all major American religious traditions."[103]

At the turn of the millennium, Stephen Carter, law professor at Yale University, discerned these same tensions playing out in society, and observed that on America's elite college campuses today "it is perfectly acceptable for professors to use their classrooms to attack religion, to mock it, to trivialize it, and to refer to those to whom faith truly matters as dupes."[104] Earlier he noted in his groundbreaking work *The Culture of Disbelief* that if people of faith express dissatisfaction with how the public schools talk about religion, or if they believe, worse yet, "that the school is inciting [their] children to abandon their religion," help is not on the way.[105] On the contrary, Carter notes, "you will probably find that the media will mock you, the liberal establishment will announce that you are engaged in censorship, and the courts will toss you out on your ear."[106]

---

[99]Ibid., pp. 49, 52.

[100]Ibid., p. 144.

[101]Ibid., p. 148.

[102]Mark A. Noll, *American Evangelical Christianity* (Malden, Mass.: Blackwell, 2001), p. 67.

[103]For a far more accurate assessment of evangelicalism see Christian Smith, *American Evangelicalism: Embattled and Thriving* (Chicago: University of Chicago Press, 1998).

[104]Carter, *God's Name in Vain*, p. 187.

[105]Stephen L. Carter, *The Culture of Disbelief* (New York: Basic Books, 1993), p. 52.

[106]Ibid.

Beyond this, Christian Smith explored the marginalization and alienation that evangelicals often experience at public institutions. A professor at an Ivy League graduate program, for example, used the words *evangelical, McCarthy* and *holocaust* in the same sentence, and "Not one student ... raised an eyebrow."[107] Seen as enemies of freedom and democracy (as defined by the left), activist conservative Christians are, according to Congressman Vic Fazio, "what the American people fear most."[108] Indeed, evangelicals remain one of the last groups in a postmodern, diverse society that is held up to ongoing scorn, and yet few cultural leaders will come to their defense. "Who among the well-educated is going to speak well of evangelicals?" Smith asks. "It's like standing up for the Crusades."[109] But are all American evangelicals being painted with the brush strokes that actually belong to the religious right?

WESLEYAN EVANGELICALS AND THE RELIGIOUS RIGHT

To the extent that the broad North American Wesleyan community, composed of many different denominations, is faithful to its theological founder, John Wesley, it will be marked by two key characteristics: first a no-nonsense emphasis on conversion, resulting in a distinctively holy life. In other words, "Conversion, regeneration [and] sanctification," as Olson puts it, will be the "meat and potatoes of Wesleyanism."[110] Second, Wesleyans will be characterized by a stress on social action that will be informed not only by the needs of the poor but also by a keen awareness of the danger of riches.[111] It is this second trait, especially in terms of the acquisition of wealth, that may make it difficult, though not impossible, for many Wesleyans to feel at home among the Christian right.

---

[107]Christian Smith, *Christian America? What Evangelicals Really Want* (Berkeley: University of California Press, 2000), p. 92.

[108]Ibid., p. 4.

[109]Ibid., p. 195.

[110]Roger E. Olson, "The World Its Parish: Wesleyan Theology in the Postmodern Global Village," *Asbury Theological Journal* 59, no. 1 (2004): 23.

[111]Wesley wrote a number on sermons warning about the corrupting power of wealth, such as "The Danger of Riches" and "The Danger of Increasing Riches" in *The Works of John Wesley*, vols. 1-4, *Sermons*, ed. Albert C. Outler (Nashville: Abingdon, 1986, 1987), 3:227-46; 4:177-86.

The Church of the Nazarene illustrates this dynamic remarkably well. On the one hand Nazarene pastors tend to be conservative, theologically speaking (aiming at conversion and entire sanctification). On the other hand they often express "more liberal views on social issues such as poverty, homelessness and discrimination."[112] Indeed, approximately 60 percent of these Holiness ministers, in an important study, agreed that "social justice is at the heart of the gospel."[113] Beyond this, Nazarene clergy repudiate a fundamentalist reading of the Bible "that prohibits women from positions of church leadership and ordination,[114] revealing, once again, their strong Wesleyan-Holiness roots. As William Kostlevy has pointed out: "Neo-fundamentalist historical categories distort the character of evangelicalism and, more significantly, obscure the important links between historic perfectionistic revivalism and . . . twentieth century reform movements."[115]

When these same Nazarene clergy, however, were polled specifically in terms of their politics, it became clear, surprisingly enough, that some of them would likely have little difficulty in identifying with the Christian right. For example, according to Smidt a full two-thirds of those surveyed indicated that they were opposed to big government and had no desire to see it "more actively engaged in solving social problems."[116] Beyond this, 87 percent of these same Holiness ministers identified themselves as politically conservative, 10 percent as moderate and only 4 percent as liberal. In fact, these pastors overwhelmingly supported the election of George W. Bush in 2000, to the tune of 90 percent![117] Such hard data suggest then that a vigorous concern for the poor does not necessarily entail leftist political policies or affiliation. That's a common mistake often made in the contem-

---

[112]Corwin E. Smidt, *Pulpit and Politics: Clergy in American Politics at the Advent of the Millennium* (Waco, Tex.: Baylor University Press, 2004), p. 167. Of course, the Church of the Nazarene is more complicated and diverse than Smidt's study suggests, since it focused simply on clergy. Professors and laity would constitute other important populations to be examined.

[113]Ibid., p. 173.

[114]Ibid., p. 172.

[115]William Kostlevy, *Holiness Manuscripts: A Guide to Sources Documenting the Wesleyan Holiness Movement in the United States and Canada* (Metuchen, N.J.: Scarecrow Press, 1994), p. 40. Kostlevy specifically mentions the Social Gospel movement, women's rights, temperance, and the civil rights movement as areas of interest.

[116]Smidt, *Pulpit and Politics*, p. 174.

[117]Ibid., p. 177.

porary political landscape. Indeed, social action can be expressed in more decentralized ways as in the Holiness involvement in Christians Supporting Community Organizing (CSCO) and in embracing what in effect are the major elements of compassionate conservatism.[118] Accordingly, given the concern of Nazarene pastors for social action *as well as* their political views, it is likely that many of them would have supported (if asked) such a balanced document as *The Villars Statement on Relief and Development*, drafted in the spring 1987 in Switzerland by forty evangelical Christians from around the world and signed by none other than the late Arminian scholar Clark Pinnock.[119]

Many Wesleyan evangelicals, of course, are not a part of small evangelical Holiness denominations but bear their witness, painful at times, in the midst of a large mainline denomination such as the United Methodist Church.[120] In this context the demographics are much different from the earlier example and more aptly mirror the political divisions of the American nation itself. For example, during the 2000 election 46 percent of United Methodist clergy voted for George W. Bush; 46 percent for Al Gore.[121] Again, among United Methodist ministers Democrats only outnumber Republicans 48 to 41 percent, and when this same population was asked to describe its theological identity, a surprising 49 percent classified themselves as "evangelical."[122] Despite these revealing statistics the United Methodist Church remains even today a politically left-leaning denomination in so many respects simply because its basic constituency, made up of so many evangelicals sitting in the pews, is largely ignored by the de-

---

[118]Mike Miller, "Community Organizing: Lost among Christians?," *Social Policy* 31, no. 1 (2000): 33. See Marvin Olasky, *Compassionate Conservatism: What It Is, What It Does, and How It Can Transform America* (New York: Free Press, 2000).

[119]Marvin Olasky et al., *Freedom, Justice, and Hope: Toward a Strategy for the Poor and the Oppressed* (Westchester, Ill.: Crossway Books, 1988), pp. 141-46.

[120]For a view from the theological right that has nevertheless repeatedly criticized Wesleyan evangelicalism ("evangelicalism collapses into 'an anthropomorphic vision of the Christian faith,'" and "Methodism [as well as Wesleyan theology] as a determined experiment . . . is over and gone") from the vantage point of an understanding of ecclesiology and theology that is virtually indistinguishable from Eastern Orthodoxy, see William J. Abraham, Jason E. Vickers and Natalie B. Van Kirk, eds., *Canonical Theism: A Proposal for Theology and the Church* (Grand Rapids: Eerdmans, 2008), p. 266, and William J. Abraham, "The End of Wesleyan Theology," *Wesleyan Theological Journal* 40, no. 1 (2005): 17.

[121]Smidt, *Pulpit and Politics*, p. 97.

[122]Ibid., pp. 96, 93.

nomination's administrative apparatus and key governing boards, such as the General Board of Global Ministries (GBGM) and the General Board of Church and Society (GBCS).

Earlier on April 7, 1980, David Jessup, a United Methodist layperson living in the outskirts of Washington, D.C., and a former Peace Corps volunteer, had issued a report that questioned the appropriateness of many of the contributions made by the GBGM and the GBCS to some political organizations. Among other things, he claimed that funds were going to "the totalitarian left as opposed to the democratic left."[123] Indeed, the Jessup Report linked United Methodist boards and agencies "to more than a hundred questionable political organizations."[124] Not liking the attention very much, these two boards financed a fifty-five-page document (known as the "Snoop Report") that questioned Jessup's findings as well as the founding of the Institute on Religion and Democracy in 1981 that emerged in the wake of this ongoing controversy.[125]

Composed at the time of evangelical Methodists (Ed Robb), Lutherans (Richard John Neuhaus) and Roman Catholics (Michael Novak), the Institute on Religion and Democracy (IRD) called for an "open church," one that would embrace full accountability to its *entire* membership, something that both the GBGM and the GBCS were apparently reluctant to do.[126] In other words, key religious leaders wanted nothing less than factual detail, not generalizations or spin. Beyond this the IRD celebrated the basic, historic orthodox teachings of the church, while at the same time it underscored the value of democracy and its many freedoms in a complex and troubled world.

Adept in both theology and political philosophy, Richard John Neuhaus composed the founding document of the IRD, which is simply titled "Christianity and Democracy."[127] In it, he argued against the *ideologues* (whether from the left or the right) and revealed the folly of

---

[123]Steven M. Tipton, *Public Pulpits: Methodists and Mainline Churches in the Moral Argument of Public Life* (Chicago: University of Chicago Press, 2007), p. 147.

[124]Ibid., p. 150.

[125]Michael Novak, "The Snoop Report," *National Review*, December 11 1981, p. 1488.

[126]Ibid.

[127]Richard John Neuhaus, "Christianity and Democracy," Institute on Religion and Democracy, www.theird.org/page.aspx?pid=215.

equating "the kingdom of God with *any* political, social, or economic order of this passing time."[128] Though the IRD was quickly labeled as the Christian right (and much worse) by its critics, the carefully written document by Neuhaus actually suggests otherwise. That is, in this work his nuanced political and theological thinking genuinely transcended the kind of partisanship that was so typical of mainline denominational agencies. "Our unity in Christ," Neuhaus reflected, "is greater than whatever may divide us."[129] And instead of calling for toe-the-line politics or for social justice issues to be ignored in the church, Neuhaus freely acknowledged that "disagreement about the meaning of social justice should not merely be tolerated; it should be celebrated."[130] Simply put, the truth of Jesus Christ, in Neuhaus's estimation, is far greater than whatever partisan cups can hold. The *universal* church then should not take the ideological turn.

EVANGELICALS AND CATHOLICS TOGETHER

Sensing a broad cultural shift, many Roman Catholics, like their evangelical cousins, were drifting from the Democratic Party. Richard Nixon, for example, won the Catholic vote in 1968 as did Reagan in 1980, George H. W. Bush in 1988 and George W. Bush in 2000 and 2004. In fact, George W. Bush actually increased his lead among Catholic voters in the 2004 election, especially in the key states of Ohio and Florida.[131] Earlier, in 1994, Catholics had voted Republican for the first time in an off-year election.[132] As the Democrats increasingly became the party of abortion and special rights for homosexuals, Catholics found themselves pulling a whole new set of levers in the voting booth.

In the early 1990s Neuhaus, with years of leadership in the IRD under his belt, fulfilled a long-held desire and became a Roman Catholic priest. As he and Charles Colson, convicted Watergate conspirator and born again Christian, looked out on Roman Catholic and evangelical relations

---

[128]Ibid. (emphasis added).
[129]Ibid.
[130]Ibid.
[131]Steve Waldman and John Green, "It Wasn't Just (or Even Mostly) the 'Religious Right,'" *Beliefnet*, www.beliefnet.com/News/Politics/2004/11/It-Wasnt-Just-Or-Even-Mostly-The-Religious-Right.aspx.
[132]Reed, *Active Faith*, p. 216.

in the Americas, they saw both significant problems and challenging possibilities. Tensions between evangelicals (mainly Pentecostals) and Catholics were especially troubling in Central and South America, where the number of people transferring from the Catholic church into an evangelical communion was simply staggering.[133] To illustrate, "over a half-million Brazilians [were] leaving the Catholic church for evangelical churches *each year.*"[134] This same pattern was being repeated elsewhere. Guatemala, for example, already had more Pentecostals than Roman Catholics, and in thirty years from now "half a dozen Latin American countries will have a Pentecostal majority."[135] Simply put, Latin America is becoming Protestant "more rapidly than central Europe did in the sixteenth century."[136]

Unfortunately, this ecclesiastical and social transition has not always been smooth, and at times it has actually turned violent, with charges of "sheep stealing" and "ecclesiastical imperialism" being lobbed back and forth.[137] Neither theological tradition, however, wanted the Americas to become another Northern Ireland.[138] And so in order to establish more peaceable relations between these two important communions of faith as well as a sound basis for ongoing discussions, Neuhaus and Colson began the project "Evangelicals and Catholics Together" in 1992. Such an ecumenical move expressed "common convictions about Christian faith and mission," and it held considerable promise for the North American context as well, though its leaders were careful to point out that their efforts "cannot speak officially for our communities."[139] The participants in this project suffered few illusions about the possibility of resolving "the deep

---

[133]Thomas P. Rausch, *Catholics and Evangelicals: Do They Share a Common Future?* (Downers Grove, Ill.: InterVarsity Press, 2000), p. 25.

[134]David Neff, ed., "Why Is Latin American Turning Protestant?" *Christianity Today* 36 (1992): 28-39.

[135]Steve Rabey, "Conversation or Competition? Pentecostals, Roman Catholics in Long-Standing Talks to Resolve Conflicts, Discover Some Commonalities," *Christianity Today* 42, no. 10 (1998): 22.

[136]Andres Tapia, "Why Is Latin America Turning Protestant?" *Christianity Today* 36, nos. 28-39 (1992): 28.

[137]Charles Colson and Richard John Neuhaus, eds., *Your Word Is Truth: A Project of Evangelicals and Catholics Together* (Grand Rapids: Eerdmans, 2002), p. viii.

[138]Mark Noll and Carolyn Nystrom, *Is the Reformation Over? An Evangelical Assessment of Contemporary Roman Catholicism* (Grand Rapids: Baker Academic, 2005), p. 152.

[139]Charles Colson and Richard John Neuhaus, eds., *Evangelicals and Catholics: Toward a Common Mission* (Dallas: Word, 1995), p. xv.

and long-standing differences between evangelicals and Catholics."[140] On the one hand, evangelicals maintained that "the Catholic Church has gone beyond Scripture, adding teachings and practices that detract from or compromise the Gospel of God's saving grace in Christ."[141] Indeed, J. I. Packer, British-born Canadian evangelical theologian, tersely observed, "the New Testament Church is not a sacramental and juridical organization sustained by priests channeling divine life through set rituals."[142] On the other hand, Cardinal Avery Dulles surmised that "It is hard to see how Catholics could consider themselves to be fully reconciled with churches that did not acknowledge the papacy as the bearer of a divinely instituted 'Petrine ministry.'"[143] The way forward, then, was that evangelicals and Catholics "must respect each other's identity"[144] and be careful "not to force anything on the other that would threaten the other's Christian identity."[145]

Operating from the Lund principle ("that ecclesiastically divided Christians should try not to do separately what their consciences allow them to do together"), the document "Evangelicals and Catholics Together" was finally published in the May 1994 issue of *First Things*.[146] Both theological traditions contended for the truth that "politics, law and culture must be secured by moral truth," a presupposition held by many of the founding fathers themselves.[147] On the one hand the signers of this document affirmed the separation of church and state (largely to protect the church from state interference); on the other hand they challenged the separation of religion from public life that many political liberals insisted—mistakenly we should add—was required by the Constitution itself.[148] Such an interpretation of the founding documents that had gained increasing momentum since the 1960s was viewed by both evangelicals and Catholics as an "assault upon the most elementary principles of demo-

---

[140]Ibid., p. xxi.
[141]Ibid., p. xxii.
[142]Ibid., p. 161.
[143]Avery Dulles, cited in ibid., pp. 122-23.
[144]Colson and Neuhaus, *Evangelicals and Catholics*, p. 139.
[145]Ibid.
[146]Ibid., p. 149.
[147]Ibid., p. xxiii.
[148]Ibid., p. xxiv.

cratic governance."[149] Signers of "Evangelicals and Catholics Together" maintained that it is necessary to transmit the cultural heritage of the American nation to succeeding generations, a heritage that is "inseparable from the formative influence of religion, especially Judaism and Christianity."[150] Beyond this, evangelicals and Catholics came together and criticized the antireligious bigotry that so often surfaced in the entertainment industry.[151] United in terms of several social and cultural values, evangelicals and Catholics were joining forces and becoming more powerful politically as they participated in what one author has called an "ecumenism of the trenches."[152] Evangelicals had found a new ally, so it seemed, in the ongoing cultural struggle.

Despite these successes, the publication of "Evangelicals and Catholics Together" (henceforth referred to as ECT I) was greeted by both "jeers and cheers."[153] Some evangelicals believed that the document glossed over evangelical and Catholic differences and in the end "betrayed the Reformation faith."[154] A clarifying statement was therefore published in *Christianity Today* on March 6, 1995, to address some concerns, but "fewer than half of the evangelicals who had signed the original document put their names on this clarification."[155] This subsequent statement made it clear that evangelical efforts to cooperate with Roman Catholics did not imply the acceptance of Catholic doctrinal distinctives. Pressure within the Southern Baptist Convention, however, was so strong that Richard Land, an original signer of ECT I, was forced to withdraw his name "from the document he had helped to write."[156] Feeling theologically threatened by this ecumenical effort, an Alliance of Confessing Evangelicals published "The Cambridge Declaration" on April 20, 1996, in which the five *soli* of the Reformation were reaffirmed (*sola scriptura, solus Christus, sola gratia, sola fide* and *soli Deo Gloria*).[157] Wesleyan evangelicals, however, did not have

---

[149]Ibid.
[150]Ibid., p. xxv.
[151]Ibid., p. xxvi.
[152]Dennis Hoover, "Ecumenism of the Trenches," *Journal of Ecumenical Studies* 41, no. 2 (2004): 270.
[153]Noll, *Is the Reformation Over?* p. 156.
[154]Ibid.
[155]Ibid., p. 158.
[156]Ibid., p. 157.
[157]Ibid., p. 189.

the same kind of difficulties as did their Reformed evangelical cousins. And Neuhaus's quip that "were John Wesley still with us, he would have signed ECT," is, in our judgment, accurate, especially in light of the father of Methodism's key sermon, the "Catholic Spirit."[158]

The following year a brief statement titled "The Gift of Salvation," or what became known as ECT II emerged. J. I. Packer's particular line of argument in defense of the earlier ECT I was dropped in terms of the second installment of this ecumenical project, in which it was now affirmed that the "partnership is in fact between 'Evangelicals who thank God for the heritage of the Reformation' and Catholics who are conscientiously faithful to the teaching of the Catholic Church.'"[159] Nevertheless, evangelical criticism of "The Gift of Salvation" was considerable and broadly based. The Alliance of Confessing Evangelicals, for example, contended that ECT II "really sells out the Reformation."[160] Other evangelicals were equally concerned and issued a separate counterstatement titled "The Gospel of Jesus Christ: An Evangelical Celebration," which was published in March 1999 and signed by over a hundred prominent evangelical leaders.[161] Neuhaus and Colson attempted to put the movement on more solid ground by focusing on Scripture in ECT III, "Your Word Is Truth," in which it was affirmed that "the books of Scripture must be acknowledged as teaching firmly, faithfully and without error that truth which God wanted put into the sacred writings for the sake of our salvation."[162] Catholic theologians, of course, continued to affirm the importance of sacred tradition whereby "the Holy Spirit himself guides the church into the fullness of truth and directs her in avoiding error,"[163] and so by the time that ECT IV, "The Communion of the Saints," was issued in 2003, both ecclesiastical traditions were by now, in some sense, ecumenically weary.[164]

---

[158]Albert C. Outler, *The Works of John Wesley*, vols. 1-4, *Sermons* (Nashville: Abingdon, 1985), 2:81-95.

[159]Iain H. Murray, *Evangelicalism Divided: A Record of Crucial Change in the Years 1950-2000* (Edinburgh: Banner of Truth Trust, 2000), p. 231.

[160]Rausch, *Catholics and Evangelicals*, p. 48.

[161]Noll, *Is the Reformation Over?* p. 189.

[162]Colson and Neuhaus, *Your Word Is Truth*, p. 48.

[163]Ibid., p. 94.

[164]Interestingly enough, the project of canonical theism is ecumenically weary as well in its repeated and trenchant criticism of Western Christianity. That is, canonical theism constitutes a decidedly anti-Western reading of the history of the church. Indeed, William Abraham freely admits that he "came to see that the life of the church was the reverse of what it had become in the West." Operat-

Their greatest strength perhaps lay not in articulating common, broad-based and widely accepted theological commitments, but in their promulgation of shared moral values and vision as they faced an increasingly hostile American state.

CONSERVATIVE EVANGELICALS AND THE REPUBLICAN PARTY

Emboldened by an alliance with key Roman Catholic leaders, such as Neuhaus, who maintained that "it was for all intents and purposes impossible to be a good Catholic and a member of the Democratic Party," many conservative evangelicals unreservedly made their way into the Grand Old Party.[165] Prior to the 1970s "conservative Protestants," as Kyle points out, "were more likely to be Democrats than Republicans."[166] Many political observers mark the evangelical shift into the Republican Party with the address of Ronald Reagan to the Religious Roundtable (called the "National Affairs Briefing") in August 1980.[167] By the 1990s evangelicals were decidedly Republican. For example, in 1972, according to the National Election Study, "42 percent of white Protestant evangelicals . . . identified as Republicans."[168] By 1996, however, that number had jumped to 57 percent, a clear majority. Earlier, in 1992, about one-fourth of the delegates to the Republican National Convention regarded themselves as "'members' or 'supporters' of the Christian Right."[169] And the 1994 sweep of the House and Senate revealed that conservative evangelicals contributed much to those victories.[170]

With the election of George W. Bush in 2000, which proved to be one of the closest political contests in U.S. history, the evangelical vote had

---

ing within the confines of his own scholarly constructions, Abraham complains that "Both Protestantism and Roman Catholicism work with a radically epistemic conception of canon," in violation of his own more limited view of the term *canon*. Thus, in a way that neglects the basic understanding of canon as a "reed," so evident in the early church, Abraham engages in special pleading for his own terminology and maintains that canon should be viewed *not* as a norm or standard (the epistemic view) but for the most part as a means of grace. See Abraham, Vicker, and Van Kirk, *Canonical Theism*, pp. 151, 4, and Kenneth J. Collins, "Is 'Canonical Theism' a Viable Option for Wesleyans?" *Wesleyan Theological Journal* 45, no. 2 (2010): 82-107.

[165]Linker, *Theocons*, p. 169.
[166]Kyle, *Evangelicalism*, p. 168.
[167]Reed, *Active Faith*, p. 111.
[168]Lichtman, *White Protestant Nation*, p. 399.
[169]John Green, "Evangelical Realignment," *Christian Century* 112, no. 2 (1995): 676.
[170]Ibid.

become as important to the Republican Party as the labor union vote had been for the Democratic Party.[171] Put another way, it was impossible for a Republican candidate to win a national election without conservative evangelical support. In fact, Green observed in 2003 that "high church-at-tending white evangelicals . . . gave three quarters of their votes to the GOP across the country."[172] And during the 2004 election conservative Protestants preferred Bush over Kerry to the tune of 78 to 21 percent.[173]

For their support many evangelical leaders naturally expected President George W. Bush to govern in a way favorable to their interests. And initially at least they were not disappointed. Cabinet meetings were opened with prayer; weekly Bible studies were conducted at the White House ("attended by roughly fifty White House officials and staff");[174] the tradition of a National Prayer Breakfast (that had begun under Eisenhower) continued, and the National Day of Prayer (going back to the Truman administration) was observed. Evangelicals especially liked how Bush cut off funds for groups that provided abortions overseas.[175] They also appreciated his announcement on his ninth day in office of a Faith-Based and Community Initiative that would end "a legacy of discrimination against faith-based charities."[176] This was to be a key element in Bush's compassionate conservatism, and John Dilulio, a Harvard-trained political scientist, was appointed the head of the Office of Faith-Based and Community Initiatives (OFBCI) though the program faltered later on.[177]

Also welcomed by the evangelical community were the new guidelines enacted by Bush in terms of student free speech in the public schools that were a part of his No Child Left Behind Act.[178] The guidelines required that schools "under the threat of losing their federal aid must allow students their right to free expression, including religious expression."[179] Such

[171]John Green, "The Undetected Tide," *Religion in the News* 6, no. 1 (2003): 6.
[172]Ibid., p. 4.
[173]Kyle, *Evangelicalism*, p. 168.
[174]Monique El-Faizy, *God and Country: How Evangelicals Have Become America's New Mainstream* (New York: Bloomsbury, 2006), pp. 203-4.
[175]Ibid., p. 205.
[176]Lindsay, *Faith in the Halls of Power*, p. 49.
[177]Ibid.
[178]David Limbaugh, *Persecution: How Liberals Are Waging War Against Christianity* (Washington, D.C.: Regnery, 2003), p. 47.
[179]Ibid.

action was deemed necessary because the freedom of students to express their own views had been restricted by the state in an important case in Tennessee. To illustrate, Brittney Settle, a fifteen-year-old student, had submitted an essay for her sophomore English class on the life of Jesus Christ, since the topic clearly expressed her own interest and preference. Failing to understand the proper intent of the First Amendment, her teacher gave Brittney a failing grade because of the religious flavor of the essay. To make matters worse, a federal court "upheld the right of the school to flunk Britney," precisely because of the religious nature of the work, content that could not be tolerated in the context of public, government supported, education.[180] The need for the new guidelines by Bush was therefore warranted and much appreciated by the evangelical community.

Shortly after Bush won the 2004 election, members of his own Republican Party began to complain of the undue influence of conservative Christians within their ranks. John C. Danforth, for example, former Senator from Missouri and ambassador to the United Nations, warned the following year, "By a series of initiatives, Republicans have transformed our party into the political arm of conservative Christians."[181] Earlier Ralph Reed had reminded his Republican critics that "the Republican party was born in revival, was nurtured in the cradle of the Second Great Awakening, and was founded . . . to oppose slavery as a vast social evil."[182] And a couple of years after the Danforth op-ed piece, Rob Boston pointed out that the religious right's role in the Republican Party is "now secure," such that members of the GOP can only ignore this power base at their own peril.[183] And even the supposed political maverick John McCain, who earlier during a campaign in 2000 had referred to Pat Robertson and Jerry Falwell as "agents of intolerance," eventually had to face political reality such that by 2006 he appeared as the commencement speaker at Falwell's Liberty University![184] McCain was rewarded for this change of heart because during the 2008 election, of the 26 percent of Americans who con-

---

[180]Reed, *Active Faith*, p. 118.
[181]"Religious Right Holds Too Much Power in the GOP," *Church and State* 58, no. 5 (2005): 16.
[182]Reed, *Active Faith*, p. 34.
[183]Rob Boston, "The Religious Right After Falwell," *Church and State* 60, no. 7 (2007): 5.
[184]Ibid.

sidered themselves evangelical, "74 percent voted for McCain, with 25 percent voting for Obama."[185]

The greatest critics of this Republican and conservative Christian alliance were prominent Christians themselves who believed that evangelicalism's bold grasp for political power, especially during the administration of George W. Bush, resulted in the undermining of the faith as it was often intermixed with the quotidian policies of the Republican administration. In this religious and political flux it was difficult at times to determine where Jesus left off and where George W. Bush began. One especially sore point was the Iraq War, which was vigorously supported by several prominent evangelicals. Richard Land, for example, the president of the Ethics and Religious Liberty Commission of the Southern Baptist Convention, had gone so far as to compose a letter to President Bush on October 3, 2002, "that outlined a theological justification for preemptive war."[186] This letter was signed by such prominent evangelicals as Bill Bright (1921-2003), founder of Campus Crusade for Christ, Chuck Colson (1931-), head of Prison Fellowship Ministries, D. James Kennedy (1930-2007), head of Coral Ridge Ministries, and Carl D. Herbster, president of the American Association of Christian Schools.[187] Beyond the offer of daily prayers for the president, the letter concluded in the following words: "Mr. President, we make that stand with you. In so doing, while we cannot speak for all of our constituents, we are supremely confident that we are voicing the convictions and concerns of the great preponderance of those we are privileged to serve."[188]

Charles Marsh, professor of religion at the University of Virginia, cried foul and issued a lengthy jeremiad in his book *Wayward Christian Soldiers: Freeing the Gospel from Political Captivity*, published in 2007. In this work he criticized the conservative Christian and Republican alliance in support of the Iraq War and maintained that such a cultural accommodation of the faith had "unwittingly taken the word of God captive and incarcerated it in partisan gulags."[189] Put another way, American evangelicals

---

[185]http://blog.christianitytoday.com/ctpolitics/2008/11/the_evangelical.html.
[186]Lichtman, *White Protestant Nation*, p. 442.
[187]"Land Letter," *Wikisource*, http://en.wikisource.org/wiki/Land_Letter.
[188]Ibid.
[189]Marsh, *Wayward Christian Soldiers*, p. 27.

have resolved "to serve a political agenda with the passion we once gave to personal soul-winning."[190] The result of this partisan captivity of the gospel, according to Marsh, constituted nothing less than "the gravest theological crisis of the Christian faith in our time."[191] Other critics added their voices to Marsh's jeremiad. The centrist David Gushee, for example, charged that the evangelical right in aligning itself tightly with the Republican Party "has given up its fundamental allegiance to Jesus Christ."[192] And the left-leaning Randall Balmer, for his part, contended that the Christian right's dalliance with the Republican Party means that evangelicalism itself now "stands in need of renewal."[193]

The Republican influence on evangelicals and fundamentalists, some of whom make up the Christian right, was not simply in matters of foreign policy but also in terms of domestic politics in general and economics in particular. During the Reagan administration, for example, James Davison Hunter observed that "58 percent of [evangelical] seminarians agreed that 'economic growth is a better way to improve the lot of the poor than redistributing existing wealth.'"[194] Confusing the liberty of the gospel with the logic of the free enterprise system, Jerry Falwell maintained that "God is in favor of freedom, private property ownership, competition, diligence, work and acquisition."[195]

By being closely tied to the Republican Party during the Reagan era and beyond, many evangelicals ended up championing the economic principles of the political right with its emphasis on liberty, equality of opportunity (though not results), and the idea that people are entitled to the fruits of their achievements unfettered by the state. Indeed, this particular political and economic philosophy was cast in a Christian, evangelical glow in Pat Robertson's book *The Secret Kingdom*, though his law of reciprocity outlined in the book clearly emphasized the im-

---

[190]Ibid.

[191]Ibid., p. 76.

[192]David P. Gushee, *The Future of Faith in American Politics: The Public Witness of the Evangelical Center* (Waco, Tex.: Baylor University Press, 2008), p. 49.

[193]Balmer, *Making of Evangelicalism*, pp. 74-75.

[194]James Davison Hunter, *Evangelicalism: The Coming Generation* (Chicago: University of Chicago Press, 1987), p. 135.

[195]Jerry Falwell, cited in Kyle, *Evangelicalism*, p. 183.

portance of giving (so that one would *receive* in return).[196] As one author put it, evangelicals have baptized America's political and economic systems in terms of promulgating a "Christian nation, the free enterprise system, and limited government."[197]

One of the consequences of the influence of Republican economics on evangelical thinking is that it led to a particular conception of social justice. Drawing from Alasdair MacIntyre's work *After Virtue*, we observe that evangelical reasoning with respect to economic fair play was in many ways (though not all) similar to what MacIntyre had termed "A" (as opposed to "B") in this ground-breaking work.[198] That is, persons A stress the importance of just acquisition and saving, and therefore resent when the state interferes with their projects by means of raising taxes.[199] In this context, *freedom* to achieve as well as to fail are emphasized, and whatever inequalities emerge between the haves and have-nots is simply the price that has to be paid for justice so understood.

Contrary to the claims of the political and evangelical left, the conception of social justice offered in the reasoning of persons A, as MacIntyre has amply demonstrated, is after all a viable way of thinking about social justice in a modern democratic state. That is, the emphases on just acquisition and liberty found among the Christian right represent a *particular* social and economic philosophy that has numerous articulate and rational adherents. Nevertheless, it must also be borne in mind that other equally viable ways of thinking about social and economic justice exist. To illustrate the reasoning of persons B, to continue MacIntyre's analogy, will underscore the "arbitrariness of the inequalities in the distribution of wealth," and they therefore will call for the state in the name of *equality* to redistribute social and economic goods in order to help those who in-

---

[196]Pat Robertson and Bob Slosser, *The Secret Kingdom: Your Path to Peace, Love and Financial Security* (Nashville: W Publishing, 1992).

[197]Kyle, *Evangelicalism*, p. 187.

[198]Alasdair MacIntyre, *After Virtue*, 3rd ed. (Notre Dame, Ind.: University of Notre Dame Press, 2007), p. 244. My use of the argument with respect to "A" and "B" is somewhat different than that offered by MacIntyre in that I have underscored the libertarian aspects of just acquisition with respect to "A" in a way that MacIntyre has not. I also consider MacIntyre's typology to be for the most part noncontroversial. In other words, it is simply a way, and by no means the only way, of thinking about social justice issues. Such a typology, precisely because of its heuristic value, clearly warrants a place at the table, so to speak.

[199]Ibid.

variably fall through the cracks in economic systems that simply stress lib-erty.[200] In other words, the argument of persons B consists, at least in part, in holding that "principles of just distribution set limits to legitimate ac-quisition and entitlement,"[201] especially when it is realized that "the richest 1 percent of Americans [many of whom by the way vote Republican] possess over a third of the country's wealth, more than the combined wealth of the bottom *90 percent* of American families."[202]

MacIntyre argues that in a pluralist culture such as the United States there is no overarching reasoning that can resolve the dispute between persons A and B, no set of standards that can adjudicate the preference of one for just acquisition or liberty, and the other for equality. That is, each preference is legitimate; however, taken together these same preferences may prove to be incommensurable. Given this understanding, problems will quickly emerge for the evangelical right (and even for some mod-erates) when their favored and well-worn approach to social justice is uni-versalized by their leaders in the pulpit and the classroom by being asso-ciated with the very will of God, the teachings of Jesus in particular. When this move occurs, when the evangelical ethos is confused on some level with what can be called American free enterprise, then other Christian be-lievers who hold quite different views on social and economic justice will only feel alienated in evangelical churches. So understood, a particular po-litical and economic ideology, albeit a popular and socially validated one (supported by both evangelicals and conservative Catholics alike) has edged out the universal nature of the gospel. Simply put, the good news of Jesus Christ is far greater than any political ideology; its vision is far more extensive than the insights of the Republican Party.

---

[200]Ibid., p. 245.
[201]Ibid., pp. 245-46.
[202]Michael J. Sandel, *Justice: What's the Right Thing to Do?* (New York: Farrar, Straus & Giroux, 2009), p. 58.

4

Evolution, Intelligent Design and
the Transformation of Culture?

F ROM THE DEFEAT OF THE SCOPES TRIAL TO winning the presidency, from the seclusion of small-town Bible colleges to lobbying for legislation in the halls of Congress, and from the insularity of anti-Catholicism to the generosity of evangelicals and Catholics working together in common moral and social causes, American evangelicals had increased their political power by leaps and bounds during the 1980s and beyond, so much so that they sparked measures of fear among the American left.

Though the political stock of evangelicals was clearly on the rise through the administration of George W. Bush, such that social and religious critics were now warning of strange, new admixtures of the Christian faith and Republican politics, evangelicals yet lacked a significant cultural footprint largely because the movement as a whole was still trapped in the shadows of Dayton, Tennessee. Indeed, the study of American evangelicalism is fascinating precisely because it reveals that a movement can have considerable political clout and yet, surprisingly enough, remain something of a social and cultural pariah, shunned by a knowledge class that comforts itself with the vain notion that it always knows better. Accordingly, if the cultural power of evangelicals were ever to increase, then it would have to arise out of a considerable intellectual effort as evangelical thinkers emerged from beyond the shadows and began to tackle the unfinished business going back to 1925. Since some of the intellectual structures of that period were held in placed by a number of social and cultural constraints, challenging the current ideas and worldview of someone like a modern-day Clarence Darrow would likely evoke not merely a considerable intellectual response but a visceral one as well.

THE SCOPES TRIAL REVISITED?

As H. L. Mencken headed back east to Baltimore, after having witnessed the drubbing that Clarence Darrow gave William Jennings Bryan at the Scopes Trial of 1925, he surely thought that the intellectual capital spent in Dayton was simply unrecoverable, especially on the topic of evolution. He failed to discern, however, that the intellectual roots of fundamentalism were actually very deep and considerable. Such a heritage went back to the Princeton theologians, Charles Hodge and B. B. Warfield among them, and it was infused with an energetic and creative Puritan/Reformed sensibility that took responsibility, in some sense, for the cultural life of the nation, especially in terms of its intellectual life. In its farthest reach this heritage went back to John Witherspoon and even Jonathan Edwards, early presidents of Princeton, and on to the Puritans. One of its more notable goals, of course, was to take every thought captive to Jesus Christ, to develop, in other words, the life of the mind. Indeed, even today Wheaton College, with its fundamentalist and evangelical roots, requires that all of its faculty members write a lengthy theology of culture paper that grapples seriously with the intellectual life of the nation.

With this background in mind it becomes much easier to comprehend not only why the issue of evolution as an intellectual and cultural phenomenon would not simply go away, as Mencken and Darrow had hoped, but also why a national discussion erupted once more during the Reagan presidency. Actually, the early work that launched the intelligent design movement was not written by a North American but by an Australian. As a medical doctor and scientist who lived much of the time in Sydney, Michael Denton produced a book in 1985, *Evolution: A Theory in Crisis*, that employed critical reasoning and carefully gathered scientific facts to call into question some of the reigning shibboleths of neo-Darwinism.[1] It was

---

[1]See Michael Denton, *Evolution: A Theory in Crisis: New Developments in Science Are Challenging Orthodox Darwinism* (Bethesda, Md.: Adler & Adler, 1986).

apparently a word spoken in due season, for a few years later a flurry of similar works appeared. In 1989, for example, Dean H. Kenyon and Charles B. Thaxton published in Texas what was soon to become the basic textbook of creationism and later on of intelligent design, namely, *Of Pandas and People: The Central Question of Biological Origins.*[2] In 1991, Phillip Johnson, a Presbyterian lawyer who had become increasingly interested in the topic of evolution during a sabbatical in England, published his ground-breaking work *Darwin on Trial,* which gave encouragement to those who were not at all content with the cultural consequences of the reigning Darwinian paradigm as they played out in American society.[3] The following year Thaxton penned his *Mystery of Life's Origin: Reassessing Current Theories,* which continued the themes of his earlier textbook but this time in a more philosophical way.[4] A movement had been born, and both fundamentalists and evangelicals, in particular, realized just how much was at stake.

It would be a serious error, however, as is sometimes done, to view the rise of the intelligent design movement simply as a continuation of the arguments that played out in Dayton, Tennessee. While there is some similarity, to be sure, much had changed in the span of sixty or seventy years of American intellectual life. Not only had the criticism of evolution become much more sophisticated over time but also the theory of evolution itself was a moving target, as it was redefined during the 1930s and thereafter to take into account the latest scientific advances in the field of biology. It is therefore imperative that evolution and intelligent design be explored in some detail so that their intellectual orientation as well as their cultural contribution in American life, especially in terms of configurations of power, can be properly assessed.

EVOLUTION AS NEO-DARWINISM

In exploring considerable amounts of literature on this topic, we must observe at the outset the surprising lack of definitional precision with respect

---

[2]See Dean H. Kenyon and Charles B. Thaxton, *Of Pandas and People* (Dallas: Haughton, 1989).
[3]Phillip E Johnson, *Darwin on Trial* (Downers Grover, Ill.: InterVarsity Press, 1991).
[4]Charles B. Thaxton, *The Mystery of Life's Origin: Reassessing Current Theories* (New York: Lewis & Stanley, 1992).

to the term *evolution* in contemporary North American culture.[5] This has been something of a surprise. Indeed, the term *evolution* as it is employed today is actually made up of a constellation of related ideas, no one of which can bear the full weight of the meaning of the term. Helpful in this regard is the work of Jerry Coyne, who highlights six major components: "evolution, gradualism, speciation, common ancestry, natural selection, and nonselective mechanisms of evolutionary change."[6] Moreover, Alvin Plantinga, the gifted evangelical philosopher, has in a similar fashion underscored five basic elements of what is currently being taught today under the banner of evolutionary theory, broadly conceived: the claim that the earth is very old, that life has progressed from relatively simple to complex forms, that life evidences common ancestry, that this last process is best understood in naturalistic terms, and that life itself developed at some point from nonliving matter without any special creative activity of God.[7]

Given the problematic nature of a suitable definition, a favorite form of argument of some contemporary Darwinists is to criticize theists (who affirm that God is, after all, the Creator) by lifting up a particular aspect of evolution that is actually uncontested by many in this community (that life is old for instance) and suggesting on the contrary that it is. Such a practice naturally makes the theist's position appear to be unreasonable. However, many in the intelligent design movement—the evangelical William Dembski and the Roman Catholic Michael Behe, for example—clearly affirm that the earth, and life itself, is very old. Therefore, to suggest otherwise (in which the terminology is used in a loose and imprecise way and elements of the definition of evolution are switched in and out as

---

[5]If we define *evolution* most basically as change through time with development, the idea is not original to the nineteenth century but goes back to ancient Greece in the fifth century B.C. and thereafter. For his part, Democritus, who hailed from Thrace, articulated the idea clearly in his own century (4th B.C.) in terms of a social and cultural evolution. Moreover, in the nineteenth century the idea does not seem to have been original to Charles Darwin (1809-1882), even in terms of biology, for Erasmus Darwin (1731-1802), Charles's grandfather, had expressed the idea in his *Zoonomia*, and Alfred Russell Wallace (1823-1913), a competing naturalist, explored the notion in considerable biological detail in his own works. Because of these concurrent developments Darwin and Wallace were led to issue a joint announcement of the discovery a year before Darwin published his *Origin of Species* in 1859.

[6]Jerry A. Coyne, *Why Evolution Is True* (New York: Penguin, 2009), p. 3.

[7]Alvin Plantinga, "Evolution and Design," in *For Faith and Clarity: Philosophical Contributions to Christian Theology*, ed. James Beilby (Grand Rapids: Baker Academic, 2006), p. 202.

needed) is to confuse the matter at hand very badly and never face the heart of Dembski's and Behe's principal objections. Similar problems emerge in the definition of *creationist* as well, a term once again that actually represents a number of variegated meanings.

Darwin, in his nineteenth-century setting, was well aware of the operations of artificial selection as employed, for example, by dog breeders. Joining this insight with the fruit of his numerous and careful observations in the Galapagos islands, Darwin postulated a theory of evolution that gave a leading role to what he called "natural selection." That is, nature itself (in many instances simply the environment) plays the role of the breeder and "selects" those traits or characteristics that will continue in the species. Over the course of time, so Darwin maintained, all sorts of helpful transformations (survival of the fittest) occur and progress is clearly evident. Looking to the scientific method itself, which put aside the old Aristotelian formal and final causes so that he could focus simply on material and instrumental ones, Darwin propounded a theory that offered an explanation for the complexity of life, though he may have crossed the methodological bounds of empiricism in some of his more general and expansive conclusions that seemed invariably to touch upon a particular philosophical outlook.

One of the things that Darwin could not have seen in his nineteenth-century context was the revolution in biology that occurred in the early twentieth century due to the impact that Mendelian genetics had on the whole matter of mutation and change. With the source of the variability of species now more clearly understood, an insight that in turn was wedded to natural selection as Darwin had originally envisioned it, scientists began to talk of neo-Darwinism. In other words, genetic mutation provides the variability that is then selected by nature. Or as Coyne put it, "it is the filtering of that variation by natural selection that produces adaptations."[8] More recently, Francis Collins, an acknowledged Christian believer, has not only helped to map the human genome in his own research but he has also written extensively on the importance of DNA as a factor that helps to illustrate several of the truths of the larger theory of

---

[8]Coyne, *Why Evolution Is True*, p. 119.

neo-Darwinism. Citing Theodosius Dobzhansky, a prominent twentieth-century biologist and Eastern Orthodox Christian, Collins exclaims, "Nothing in biology makes sense except in light of evolution."[9]

Not only have changes in understanding been embraced by the scientific community in terms of the engine of mutation, but also Darwin's earlier notion of natural selection has been modified as well. Chafing (or perhaps *annoyed* is a better term) under the ongoing criticism of creationists and intelligent design advocates (such as Phillip Johnson and Jonathan Wells), Richard Dawkins, Oxford professor and champion of neo-Darwinism, has attempted to take the sting out of the claim that randomness plays far too great a role in the theory of evolution as it is taught today. In response to this objection Dawkins has argued that natural selection must be seen as a cumulative process, in other words, that the problem of improbability posed by randomness must be broken up into smaller, more manageable pieces. Employing the image of climbing a steep mountain, what Dawkins refers to as "climbing mount improbable," the ascent is not made on the steep side of the summit in one great leap; instead, the climber turns to the backside of the mountain and creeps up the gentle slope by a series of steps. Dawkins concludes that this process (which supposedly can make an eye, for example) is "easy," though his critics are not convinced.[10]

In light of this illustration or model, Dawkins contends that natural selection itself is therefore best described as a *nonrandom* process in which a number of possibilities have been excluded (delimited, if you will) at each step along the way. But in his oft-cited example Dawkins may have assumed far too much. Though neo-Darwinism should have dropped the notion of teleology (goal-directedness) in its focus on instrumental and material causation, Dawkins has apparently slipped it back in. That is, the summit of the mountain clearly functions as the goal, the telos, of the journey at *every* step along the way. Other critics, such as the British evan-

---

[9]Francis S. Collins, *The Language of God* (New York: Free Press, 2006), p. 141. See also Francis S. Collins, "Can an Evangelical Believe in Evolution?" *International Journal of Frontier Missions* 20, no. 4 (2003): 109-12., in which he makes the claim that "Arguments against macroevolution, based on so-called gaps in the fossil records, are also profoundly weakened by the much more detailed and digital information revealed from the study of genomes" (ibid., p. 111).

[10]Richard Dawkins, *The God Delusion* (London: Black Swan, 2006), p. 9.

gelical Alister McGrath, observed that "Darwin clearly did not intend his readers to understand that nature acted *purposefully* and rationally in 'selecting' variants," even by increments.[11] And Antony Flew, for his part, argued that "natural selection does not positively produce anything. It only eliminates, or tends to eliminate, whatever is not competitive."[12]

Equipped with the two elements of genetic mutation and natural selection, as well as with a distinct methodology, prominent neo-Darwinists during the latter part of the twentieth century began to overstep the bounds of their discipline and make broad, sweeping statements in terms of philosophy in general (especially relating to the issues of meaning and reality) and anthropology in particular. The late paleontologist and biologist Stephen Jay Gould, for instance, who spent much of his career at Harvard, concluded that "biology took away our status as paragons created in the image of God. . . . Before Darwin, we thought that a benevolent God had created us."[13] In the twenty-first century, Viktor Stenger, a well-published physicist, observed that "Evolution implies humanity was an accident and not the special creature of traditional doctrine."[14] And even Coyne concluded from his own biological observations: "If humans are just one of many outcomes of natural selection, maybe we aren't so special after all."[15]

In light of the conclusions that several neo-Darwinists are drawing with respect to humanity, it is eminently reasonable to ask if such forays into philosophy and the nature of a human being are warranted by the scientific methodology employed by these thinkers, a methodology that in its most ambitious attempts looks not like a hard science at all (physics or chemistry, for example) but appears to be methodologically loose and "spongy," a particular way of thinking by which one feels emboldened, even entitled, to fill in the gaps with an eager imagination. Viewed another

---

[11]Alister E McGrath, *Science and Religion: An Introduction* (Malden, Mass.: Blackwell, 1999), p. 159 (emphasis added).

[12]Antony Flew, *There Is a God: How the World's Most Notorious Atheist Changed His Mind* (New York HarperOne, 2007), p. 78.

[13]Stephen Jay Gould, cited in William Dembski, *Intelligent Design Uncensored: An Easy-to-Understand Guide to the Controversy* (Downers Grove, Ill.: IVP Books, 2010), p. 38.

[14]Victor J. Stenger, *God: The Failed Hypothesis: How Science Shows That God Does Not Exist* (Amherst, N.Y.: Prometheus, 2008), p. 52.

[15]Coyne, *Why Evolution Is True*, p. xvii.

way, the error of Stephen Jay Gould and others in this context is one of reductionism, that is, the mistake of thinking that the fullness and multidimensional nature of human beings is exhausted or even adequately ex-
plained by an analysis of its constituent biological parts. Part of the
difficulty here, no doubt, is that the mantle of scientific authority has been
placed on top of a wide range of pronouncements, ranging from tight empirical observations to amorphous personal beliefs or worldviews. Steven
Weinberg, for instance, American physicist and Nobel laureate, hoped that
one of the consequences of contemporary science would be the destruction of religious belief.[16] "I personally feel that the teaching of science
is corrosive of religious belief," he exclaimed, "and I am all for that!"[17]

Complicating this picture is that the cultural power of the scientific
community in North America is considerable, and authority readily bleeds
from one discipline to another. Freud becomes an authority on religion
(though he was too bored to read the literature of the field), and the late
Carl Sagan was free to tuck his own personal philosophy in the midst of
his astronomical pronouncements: "The cosmos is all there is, or was, or
ever will be."[18]

THEISTIC EVOLUTION

Some of the critics of Darwinism (creationists and intelligent design advocates among them) have sensed the significant cultural power of this way
of thinking and have surmised that it may be one of the reasons why a
number of prominent theists such as Francis Collins have championed the
cause of theistic evolution as if belief in God as a Creator and Darwinism
could be easily reconciled. For example, "Freeing God from the burden of
special acts of creation does not remove Him as the source of the things
that make humanity special, and of the universe itself," Collins affirms. "It
merely shows us something of how he operates."[19] And in his proffered definition of theistic evolution, Collins adds, "Once evolution got under way,

---

[16]Dembski, *Understanding Religious Belief*, p. 97.
[17]Steven Weinberg, cited in David DeWolf et al., *Traipsing into Evolution: Intelligent Design and the
    Kitzmiller vs. Dover Decision* (Seattle: Discovery Institute Press, 2006), p. 67.
[18]Carl Sagan, *Cosmos* (New York: Random House, 1980), p. 1.
[19]Collins, *Language of God*, p. 141.

no special supernatural intervention was required."[20] In William Dembski's judgment, however, "Theistic evolution takes the Darwinian picture of the biological world and baptizes it."[21] In other words, a divine role is somehow added to the elements of genetic mutation and natural selection, though it is difficult to figure out just what that role is. Such a move is expressed in the oft-asserted claim that "evolution is God's way of creating," a statement that in its attempt to soft pedal any possible conflict between religion and science may have given up far too much in the bargain. Granted it is best to avoid the warfare model of the relation between religion and science that had played out in American culture in the wake of Darwin's discovery, especially in the writings of John William Draper (*History of the Conflict Between Religion and Science*) in 1874 and of Andrew Dickson White (*History of the Warfare of Science with Theology in Christendom*) in 1876, as noted earlier. Nevertheless a better, more sophisticated, approach to the relation of these two disciplines appears warranted in light of subsequent history.

LEADING WESLEYAN EVANGELICALS (AND OTHERS) DEBATE THEISTIC EVOLUTION

Other considerations (and motives), however, may have led to the eager embrace of Darwinism by theists—especially among some in the evangelical community. For example, Karl Giberson, physics professor at Eastern Nazarene University, wrote a book titled *Saving Darwin*, though Giberson obviously uses the word *save* in his title in a way far different from his fellow evangelicals.[22] This does not suggest, however, that Giberson hasn't identified a genuine problem; he clearly has. According to Michael Shermer, "70 percent of evangelical Christians believe that living beings have always existed in their present form, compared with 32 percent of Protestants and 31 percent of Catholics."[23]

More recently, Giberson has teamed up with Francis Collins to es-

---

[20]Ibid., p. 200.

[21]William Dembski, *Intelligent Design: The Bridge Between Science and Theology* (Downers Grove, Ill.: InterVarsity Press, 1999), p. 110.

[22]See Karl W. Giberson, *Saving Darwin: How to Be a Christian and Believe in Evolution* (New York: HarperOne, 2008).

[23]Michael Shermer, "Darwin on the Right," *Scientific American* 295, no. 4 (2006): 38.

tablish BioLogos, a foundation whose main purpose is to articulate a new form of theistic (Logos) evolution (Bio) that not only is "biblically based and scientifically sound" but also challenges the "linkage between evolution and atheism."[24] Such an approach is also reflected in Giberson's new book *The Language of Science and Faith*, which he coauthored with Collins. Remarkably enough, the tone of this latest apologetic work is much better, far more irenic, than Giberson's earlier account, *Saving Darwin*, and the two books clearly warrant comparison. In the earlier work, for example, Giberson repeatedly criticizes intelligent design, finding hardly anything of value in the movement. In their latest offering, however, both Giberson and Collins are now willing to admit that ID has several good points after all, as is evident in their following observations:

- "We enthusiastically endorse the idea that the universe is intelligently designed."

- "We think it is important to acknowledge the real similarities between fine-tuning arguments and arguments made by ID."

- "In our opinion these similarities are such that we might think of ID and BioLogos as two ends of the same spectrum."

- "Despite these concerns we are quite willing to embrace ID in its central affirmation that the universe is best understood when we allow that there is a mind behind it all."[25]

Clearly, Giberson and Collins are both gifted scientists: the one is a physicist; the other a world-class geneticist. The problem, however, is that *The Language of Science and Faith* is not simply a book about science; it is also very theological. And this is precisely where some difficulties quickly emerge. We will note two.

First, Giberson and Collins contend that evolution is able to issue in a theodicy (a defense of a good and omnipotent God in the face of evil) such that "evolution makes the problem of evil less serious."[26] Drawing an analogy between "the gift of creativity that God bestowed on creation" and

---

[24]Karl W. Giberson and Francis S. Collins, *The Language of Science and Faith* (Downers Grove, Ill.: InterVarsity Press, 2011), pp. 72, 23-24.

[25]Ibid., pp. 190, 195.

[26]Ibid., p. 139.

"the gift of freedom God bestowed on us," the authors maintain that "when nature's freedom leads to the evolution of a pernicious killing machine like the black plague, God is off the hook. Unless God micromanages nature so as to destroy its autonomy."[27] But if God is off the hook, so to speak, in terms of the evil that nature spawns (given its apparent autonomy), then it follows that God is also off the hook in terms of what good nature produces. In such a view, we believe, God could become irrelevant.[28]

Second, an equally serious problem in this line of *theological* reasoning emerges in the use of the term *freedom* in the diverse contexts of both nature and the moral realm of human action. In other words, they employ the one word *freedom* to refer to the *indeterminacy* (the randomness of mutation) of nature on the one hand, and to the *liberty* associated with moral agency on the other.[29] Such usage, in our judgment, will likely result in remarkably different theodicies. To illustrate, in terms of moral evil, theodicy often takes the following form: The greater good of love requires the freedom of the moral dimension, a freedom that can be abused to commit evil. Here, in other words, there seems to be no other way around this predicament; the goal of love itself poses a number of constraints. That is, not even an omnipotent and good God can create a universe that is fashioned to aim at love without running the risk of moral evil, given that the freedom necessary for love may be employed in evil ways.[30] But what is the corresponding lofty goal, the great end, of nature that God is aiming at that runs the risk of natural evil? And could not God have created nature differently? Again, are there constraints in nature akin to the moral realm that even an omnipotent God must take into account? If so, how is the autonomy of nature to be understood in terms of such omnipotence? Perhaps Giberson and Collins will answer such pertinent theological questions in future installments of the BioLogos project, but so far evolution has not

---

[27]Ibid., pp. 136-37.

[28]As Giberson and Collins underscore the "autonomy" of nature, "that once evolution got under way, no special supernatural intervention was required" (ibid., p. 115), their thought begins to move not in a theistic direction but in a deistic one, a problem that they both apparently recognize as well: "we acknowledge that the BioLogos perspective can slip too easily into *deism*—the view that God starts things off and then leaves them to run on their own" (ibid., p. 191).

[29]I am dependent on the thinking of Jerry Walls, in part, for the development of this argument.

[30]The classic theodicy on this score has been offered by C. S. Lewis, *The Problem of Pain* (New York: Macmillan, 1962), pp. 55ff.

made the problem of natural evil any less serious.

Though Giberson's work has been well received at his own Wesleyan institution, that is, Eastern Nazarene University, the same cannot be said for his fellow Nazarene biologist Richard Colling, who holds a Ph.D. in microbiology and immunology from the University of Kansas. Upsetting several board members (and many donors to boot!) at Olivet Nazarene University in Illinois, where he once taught, Colling made some statements about the relation between evolution and theism in his controversial book *Random Designer*, published in 2004. Reasoning in a way not very different from Giberson, Colling contends that evolution "is fully compatible with . . . contemporary religious beliefs," as if the heated disputes along these lines were in the end all about nothing. Several constituencies of the university, however, were dissatisfied with key aspects of Colling's views. Indeed, the controversy became so great, at least in the minds of some, that Colling was eventually forced out in 2009.

Writing in a gracious and irenic spirit, Colling attempted to reconcile his evangelical faith with neo-Darwinism. However, his work, despite his numerous good intentions, is long on claims (made on behalf of theistic evolution) but very short on augments to substantiate such claims or even to render them philosophically intelligible. This may have been part of his trouble at Olivet. Indeed, according to Colling, once a single replicating cell (eukaryote) is on the scene, "it is relatively *easy* for scientists to construct a coherent paradigm for the formation of all living organisms from this one cell."[31] The platform chosen by the "Random Designer" (one of Colling's favorite ways of referring to God) "appears to be random mutation and subsequent selection." However, if a coherent paradigm does indeed exist among neo-Darwinists that can chart the course from a replicating cell to all living things, as Colling has claimed, then what is left for God to do? And how is a Random Designer different from simple randomness or from no designer at all?

Sharon Begley, in a *Wall Street Journal* article in 2004, stoked the fires of the controversy by portraying the debate as one between the forces of reason and moderation on the one hand, and unyielding fundamentalism

---

[31]Richard G. Colling, *Random Designer: Created from Chaos to Connect with the Creator* (Bourbonnais, Ill.: Browning Press, 2004), p. 2 (emphasis added).

on the other. Apparently knowing little of the nature and ethos of Wesleyan educational institutions, she mistakenly referred to Olivet Nazarene University at the outset as a "fundamentalist Christian college," though Olivet is hardly fundamentalist.[32] Nazarene ministers in Caro, Missouri, soon expressed deep concern about what was being taught at Olivet and they threatened to withhold financial support.[33] A meeting was held with Colling and Nazarene District Superintendents in May 2006, and during the spring of that year, Mark Quanstrom, professor of religion, composed a confidential internal document critiquing not so much the biology but the *theology* of *Random Designer*.[34] In an effort "to get the bull's eye off Colling and let the storm die down," John Bowling, the president of the university, banned the curricular use of the book *Random Designer* and relieved Colling of his responsibilities for teaching general biology in 2007.[35] Not surprisingly, Colling filed a formal grievance against President Bowling in August of that year.

In 2009 the American Association of University Professors weighed in and published a report on the controversy at Olivet and made two determinations: first, that President Bowling had violated policies of shared governance (in removing Colling from general biology courses); second, that ONU had violated professor Colling's academic freedom.[36] Beyond this, the AAUP claimed, giving life to a well-worked stereotype, that the university had to "placate fundamentalist critics" among its constituency.[37]

Though in placing so much of this case under the banner of "academic freedom," the AAUP report is open to the criticism that it never grappled seriously with the specific *constellation* of issues that administrators and board members had to face at Olivet. Consider these facts: the entire biology department at Olivet supported Colling, though not one of *its* scien-

---

[32]Sharon Begley, "Tough Assignment: Teaching Evolution to Fundamentalists," *Wall Street Journal*, December 3, 2004, p. A15.

[33]Sharon Begley, "Can God Love Darwin, Too?" *Newsweek*, September 17, 2007, p. 45.

[34]Upon request I received this document but am not at liberty to reveal its contents. It is clear, however, from a careful reading of both Colling's book and Quanstrom's document that the theology of *Random Designer* would likely be judged deficient by the diverse constituencies that make up the Church of the Nazarene.

[35]Ibid.

[36]Gregory Scholtz and Ruth Caldwell, "Academic Freedom and Tenure: Olivet Nazarene University," *Academe: Bulletin of the AAUP* 95, no. 1 (2009): 54-55.

[37]Ibid., p. 53.

tific views was ever questioned by Bowling.[38] In fact, the president insisted, "We will still teach science."[39] Again, the biology department taught evolution as a science at the university in virtually the same way as Colling. Why then was Colling censured and the biology faculty not? The answer to this question quickly emerges from a careful reading of *Random Designer*, which is *not* a biology text, pure and simple, but is a theological work as well, one that mixes biology and theology, and is therefore open to ongoing theological criticism from many corners of the church. It is precisely this and other issues that an administrator like John Bowling and board members, such as Ted R. Lee and Stephen Anthony, in their wisdom, in their attempt to embrace the larger horizon and promise of a genuine Christian liberal arts education, saw so clearly. The drafters of the AAUP report, in contrast, had missed so much of the context at Olivet perhaps because they, like so many others in our secular age, thought that theological matters are of so little concern.

NEO-DARWINISM AS A SUFFICIENT EXPLANATION

If the basic premise of neo-Darwinism is true—that genetic mutation and natural selection is a *sufficient* explanation and therefore adequately elucidates the development of life without any appeal to a deity—then the addition of God by others, the appeal to anything beyond natural causation, such as a Random Designer, is contrary to the focused methodological preferences of Darwinism. From this perspective, it is outright contradictory, a nonstarter if you will, to combine neo-Darwinism, as embraced by contemporary scientists, with theism simply because the former excludes *any* appeal to God by eliminating the very notion of first and final cuases (design and purpose). Thus, adding God to the evolutionary mix is *not* what most scientists mean by this term. Employing Occam's razor, many scientists will no doubt argue that the *simplest* explanation (mutation and natural selection understood in terms of natural causes apart from God) is to be preferred in the field of biology. Hence, a Random Designer, no matter how graciously conceived, is precluded.[40]

---

[38]Ibid., p. 47.
[39]Ibid.
[40]The difficulty that theistic evolution faces as it seeks to understand not the origin of life but its de-

Bruce Waltke, then professor of Old Testament at Reformed Theological Seminary, entered the fray by appearing in a video that "addressed the barriers evangelicals face in considering the possibility of evolution."[41] Waltke chided the evangelical community for its views on science and declared that "if the data is overwhelmingly in favor of evolution [and Waltke believes that it is] to deny that reality will make us a cult."[42] But just what sense of evolution does Professor Waltke have in mind? If it is neo-Darwinism in all the senses outlined previously, then he, like those theistic evolutionists who have preceded him, will have to demonstrate how the addition of God to a theory that excludes the Most High as a presupposition of its method is rationally coherent and even workable. It appears, once again, that the neo-Darwinism to which evolutionary theists add their theism is something far different from what many scientists have in mind in their methodological rigor. There remains, of course, the possibility that *the assumption or belief that mutation and natural selection, apart from God, can actually get the whole job done, so to speak, is false.* And this is an assumption that the members of BioLogos and other theistic evolutionists are working on. However, Richard Dawkins, the atheistic neo-Darwinist, has mocked such attempts in his observation drawn from Peter Atkins that the God of theistic evolution is remarkably lazy: "Atkins' lazy God [in criticizing theistic evolution] is even lazier than the deist God of the eighteenth-century Enlightenment: *deus otiosus.*"[43] Not content with this barb, Dawkins then adds, "Atkins succeeds in reducing the amount of work the lazy God has to do until he finally ends up doing nothing at all: he might as well not bother to exist."[44]

---

velopment, its outworking, can be expressed in the following two considerations: (1) If the mechanism of evolution (mutation plus natural selection) is understood as a *sufficient* explanation for the development of all life, then the appeal to God is unnecessary. Here, in other words, theology suffers. (2) If, however, God is yet appealed to as somehow or other "working within the system" (of mutation plus natural selection), then such a system is *not* what scientists have in mind in their methodological rigor, since it calls into question the important characteristic of sufficiency. Here science suffers. The deist option (rejected by theists) avoids this dilemma by having God set things up, so to speak, in the creation of the first living cell. An "autonomous" nature then takes its course in the development of life, a development that can be understood simply in terms of the processes of mutation, natural selection and such things as genetic drift.

[41]Charles Honey, "Adamant on Adam," *Christianity Today* 54, no. 6 (2010): 14.
[42]Bruce Waltke, cited in ibid.
[43]Dawkins, *God Delusion*, p. 144.
[44]Ibid.

INTELLIGENT DESIGN

One of the more significant reasons why the intelligent design movement began to emerge during the mid-1980s, largely in North America, was the overwhelming sense of dissatisfaction with how leading educators viewed the fit of the discipline of biology in general and evolutionary theory in particular with the *remainder* of human knowledge. Not content with the claims of the theistic evolutionists and dissatisfied with the methodological assumptions of evolutionists themselves, intelligent design burst onto the scene in a challenging—and some would add iconoclastic—manner. Its voice, whether represented by Behe, Johnson or Dembski, was therefore hardly welcomed in cultural discussions about biology, the nature of humanity or even life in general.

After exploring the major primary literature of intelligent design and comparing it to the movement's current cultural image, we can only conclude that relatively few North Americans actually understand what intelligent design is. Part of the problem here, no doubt, is the barrage of misinformation leveled against the movement by its eager critics. Liz Craig, for example, a member of the Kansas Citizens for Science, reveals that her strategy is to portray ID adherents in the "harshest light possible, as political opportunists, evangelical activists, ignoramuses, breakers of rules, unprincipled bullies, etc."[45] Moreover, Michael Ruse, in an article published in *The Chronicle of Higher Education*, aims in a misdirected way at the target of what he considers to be the silly statements made by creationists (a class that would include all sorts of views if the term were broadly understood) and argues that as a writer the pronouncements of someone like Pat Robertson "means more work for me: bread on my table."[46] Ruse is so happy about his prospects, given the supposed stupidity of evangelicals, that he wistfully opines, "I see steak in my future."[47] Such "arguments by contempt," for want of a better designation, are even found among some of the most articulate defenders of Darwinism who declare that any appeal to something higher or different from natural causation to

---

[45]Dembski, *Intelligent Design Uncensored*, p. 136.
[46]Michael Ruse, "What Darwin's Doubters Get Wrong," *Chronicle of Higher Education* 56, no. 26 (2010): 6-9.
[47]Ibid.

explain life is simply beyond the pale and therefore more than suitable for ridicule. Coyne, for example, writes: "Now, science cannot completely exclude the possibility of supernatural explanation. It is possible though very unlikely—that our whole world is controlled by elves."[48]

A WORKING DEFINITION OF INTELLIGENT DESIGN

Properly understood, intelligent design works with the basic sense of most people that the universe in general and life in particular gives abundant evidence of having been designed. "Given such powerful design intuitions," Dembski observes, "it seems only reasonable that the burden of proof is on those who reject design."[49] In contrast, Richard Dawkins, one of the chief champions of scientism (human knowledge is limited to what science can know), contends that "the *illusion* of design makes so much intuitive sense that it becomes a positive effort to put critical thinking into gear and overcome the seductions of naïve intuition."[50] It is difficult, however, to comprehend what Dawkins could possibly mean by critical thinking in this context. For one thing, since he, like Darwin who preceded him, has bracketed out any appeal to first causes in his preferred methodology, and since first causes themselves treat the questions of design one way or the other, it appears that Dawkins is unwarranted in answering such a question in an unremittingly negative way, a question that his own methodology has precluded.

Not surprisingly, then, many neo-Darwinists fail to understand precisely what ID is and what challenge it actually poses to several of their presuppositions simply because they set up the wrong contrast from the beginning. Thus, for example, the opposite of a naturalistic explanation for life (which the neo-Darwinists favor) is not a supernatural one, as is so often claimed, but something else, properly speaking. Once again, Dembski is to the point: "The proper contrast is between *natural causes* on the one hand and *intelligent causes* on the other."[51] Indeed, it is precisely ID's focus on intelligent causation that makes information theory and mathematical probability so integral to its

---

[48]Coyne, *Why Evolution Is True*, pp. 224-25.

[49]William A. Dembski and Sean McDowell, *Understanding Intelligent Design: Everything You Need to Know in Plain Language* (Eugene, Ore.: Harvest House, 2008), p. 26.

[50]Richard Dawkins, *The Greatest Show on Earth: The Evidence for Evolution* (New York: Free Press, 2009), p. 371 (emphasis added).

[51]Dembski, *Intelligent Design*, p. 105.

overall approach. Like the science of forensics or the search for extraterrestrial life, ID seeks to discern patterns that bespeak of intelligence by exploring vast amounts of empirical data.

Though many evangelicals are a part of the intelligent design movement (Dembski and Johnson, for example) and though many evangelical publishing houses have taken the lead in propounding this view (InterVarsity Press and Baker Publishing Group), it would be a mistake to label ID simply as a form of theism (a popular and well-worked misunderstanding) because this way of reasoning, this intellectual strategy, leaves the whole question of the nature of the designer open and not closed, as the critics contend. To be sure, the ID movement is not only made up of theists (Protestants, Roman Catholics, Jews and Muslims, for instance) but it also embraces agnostics (Michael Denton) and even secular Jews (David Berlinski) and atheists (Bradley Monton). Put another way, "design-theoretic reasoning does not warrant bringing up God," because the question of the existence of God, one way or the other, entails not a particular research project but a *belief*.[52] Simply put, "there's no inferential chain that leads from such finite design-conducing patterns in nature to the . . . God of the world's major theistic faiths."[53] Unlike theistic evolution, ID is *not* necessarily a form of theism, for it depends on how the designer is understood.[54] To argue otherwise, therefore, is simply misleading. Accordingly, to Yong's helpful typology of young earth creationism, old earth or progressive creationism, and theistic evolution as the principal options playing out in the evangelical community today, we must tease out a fourth, namely, ID evolution, which, once again, unlike the other three options, does not necessarily raise the question of God.

It should be evident by now that ID, properly defined, does not reject evolution in toto. For one thing this intellectual approach is quite compatible with a very old earth, a common ancestor for humans and apes,[55]

---

[52]William Dembski, *The Design Revolution: Answering the Toughest Questions About Intelligent Design* (Downers Grove, Ill.: InterVarsity Press, 2004), p. 26.

[53]Ibid., p. 26.

[54]Since the nature of the designer is left open, theists are free, of course, to understand such agency in a theistic way but agnostics are likewise free to consider such a designer in terms of a great intelligence that does not imply the existence of God.

[55]Mano Singham, *God vs. Darwin: The War Between Evolution and Creationism in the Classroom* (New York: Rowman & Littlefield Education, 2009), p. 111.

organisms evolving over time (descent with modification) and life pro-
gressing from relatively simple to complex forms. ID can even embrace a
limited form of neo-Darwinism in the sense that natural selection "might
work on variations that are not truly random."[56] It is therefore grossly inappropriate, a genuine caricature, to consider ID in the same breath as young
earth creationism as proffered by Eugenie Scott (1945-), the director of the
National Center for Science Education, in her video on the website of none
other than Richard Dawkins.[57] The likely intention of this video, among
other things, is to present ID advocates as lacking in intelligence and good
sense. However, the Finkelstein Institute found that "some 60 percent of
U.S. medical doctors think that intelligent design played some role in the
origin of humans."[58] Such a population, educationally privileged in so
many ways, is hardly lacking in intellectual acuity! Nevertheless, the negative cultural campaign continues.

THE INTELLECTUAL STRATEGY OF INTELLIGENT DESIGN

Since the intelligent design movement represents a small, though growing,
voice in North American life today, it is best perhaps to categorize its attempts to come to greater acceptance in terms of two principal strategies:
first, an intellectual one in which rational arguments are laid out in order
to make a convincing case for intelligent design, and second, a cultural one
in which the societal pathways to plausibility and acceptance (painting a
picture of reality and an associated worldview) become open to this way of
thinking. It is to this first strategy that we now turn.

When many people think of intelligent design today they envision a
counterpoise to Darwinism, a discipline, in other words, limited by and
large to biological concerns. Once again, this is a mistake in terms of an accurate definition. Intelligent design as an intellectual project is by no
means limited to the field of biology but is open to the examination of any
kind of empirical evidence (whether physical, chemical, astronomical,

---

[56]William Dembski and Michael Ruse, eds., *Debating Design: From Darwin to DNA* (New York:
Cambridge University Press, 2004), p. 3.

[57]"Eugenie Scott on Intelligent Design and Young Earth Creationism," Richard Dawkins Foundation, May 5, 2010, http://richarddawkins.net/videos/1777-eugenie-scott-on-intelligent-design-and-
young-earth-creationism.

[58]Dembski, *Intelligent Design Uncensored*, p. 36.

etc.) in order to discern patterns of information and mathematical probabilities that would at the very least be highly suggestive of, if not outright
prove, design. As such ID has taken note of the anthropic principle,
"named by the mathematician Brandon Carter in 1974 and expanded by
the physicists John Barrow and Frank Tipler," that maintains, among other
things, many of the variables that make the universe observable have been
fine-tuned to allow for life.[59] Peter Ward, a professor of geological sciences
at the University of Washington in Seattle, and Donald Brownlee, a faculty
member at the same institution in the area of astronomy (neither of whom,
by the way, is an ID advocate), list a host of factors in their book *Rare Earth*
that in a Goldilocks sort of way have all been set just right:

- right distance from star
- right mass of star
- stable planetary orbits
- right planetary mass
- Jupiter-like neighbor
- a Mars
- plate tectonics
- ocean
- large moon
- the right tilt
- giant impacts
- the right amount of carbon
- atmospheric properties
- biological evolution
- evolution of oxygen
- right kind of galaxy
- right position in galaxy[60]

[59]Dawkins, *God Delusion*, p. 162.
[60]Peter D. Ward and Donald Brownlee, *Rare Earth: Why Complex Life Is Uncommon in the Universe*

Given his methodological commitments and worldview, it is not surprising that Richard Dawkins explains the fine-tuning here in terms of chance, that is, by a vigorous appeal to a numbers game in which many universes exist (a multiverse)[61] and ours just so happens to allow for life and the observations that are based on it due to the luck of the draw. The problem with this view, of course, is that there is not a shred of empirical evidence that demonstrates the existence of any universe other than our own. Dawkins, as with an increasing number of scientists today, subtly (and sometimes not so subtly!) interlaces his philosophy of life into what he offers the public as the fruit of nothing but his scientific reasoning. In contrast, Guillermo Gonzalez, professor at Grove City College, and Jay W. Richards, senior fellow at the Discovery Institute, both of whom are champions of intelligent design (and are well aware of the anthropic principle), marvel that the myriad conditions, the fine-tuning if you will, that make the earth habitable are also "the ones that make the best overall places for discovering the universe in its smallest and largest expressions."[62] In other words, the precise setting of a number of variables renders the universe remarkably knowable, and for Gonzalez and Richards, at least, this results in a rich sense of wonder. Moreover, how is it that at the origin of the universe, during the big bang, so much that mattered in terms of the subsequent formation of a cosmos that allowed for human life was not only precisely set but also occurred in an instant, a time frame that is anathema to any Darwinist thinker?

INTELLIGENT DESIGN'S CRITIQUE OF MUTATION AND NATURAL SELECTION

Intelligent design's challenge to Darwinism today is remarkably focused on the mechanism of evolution, that is, mutation understood in the context of natural selection. It is not that ID contends that natural selection cannot explain anything, for it does indeed illuminate much, but that "it doesn't explain *everything*."[63] In other words, ID rejects the notion

---

(New York: Copernicus Books, 2000), pp. xxxi-xxxii.

[61]Fred Adams, *Our Living Multiverse* (New York: Pi Press, 2004).

[62]Guillermo Gonzalez and Jay W. Richards, *The Privileged Planet: How Our Place in the Cosmos Is Designed for Discovery* (Washington, D.C.: Regnery, 2004), p. 334.

[63]Dembski and Ruse, *Debating Design*, p. 356 (emphasis added).

that mutation and natural selection, apart from any other considerations, is able to offer an adequate explanation for the development of life. As Michael Behe, ID champion, points out, "Although it clearly can explain relatively small changes, the *sufficiency* of Darwin's mechanism to account for larger, more complex changes in organisms remains in question."[64]

Though Darwinists like to attribute many forms of action and agency to natural selection (choosing, selecting, preferring, eliminating, etc.), Dembski argues that nature in fact has no such power to choose. "All natural selection does," he points out, "is narrow the variability of incidental change by weeding out the less fit."[65] In a similar fashion, Phillip Johnson contends that natural selection hardly has all the power that Darwinists attribute to it (in what looks like a category mistake, philosophically speaking), but that it "merely preserves or destroys something that already exists."[66] And Stephen Meyer, for his part, suggests that natural selection can do nothing "to help *generate* new functional sequences, but rather can only preserve such sequences once they have arisen."[67]

The real action, then, in a certain sense is in the change, the transformation of living entities from one form to another due to mutations in DNA. Darwin, of course, understood virtually nothing of the complex life of a cell, which for him was little more than a glob of jelly. But mutations of genetic materials according to neo-Darwinists in conjunction with natural selection (determining what survives) must result in a host of accumulated favorable traits to account for the variety and complexity of life. The problem, however, as Johnson observes, is that "mutations having a favorable effect on the organism are extremely rare."[68] Indeed, most mutations in DNA sequencing are in fact quite harmful.

To avoid the difficulty of damaging mutations Darwinists make an appeal to broad swaths of time. Given enough time, so the argument runs,

---

[64]Michael J. Behe's "Darwin's Breakdown: Irreducible Complexity and Design at the Foundation of Life," in *Signs of Intelligence: Understanding Intelligent Design*, ed. William Dembski and James M. Kushiner (Grand Rapids: Brazos, 2004), p. 91 (emphasis added).

[65]Dembski, *Design Revolution*, p. 263.

[66]Johnson, *Darwin on Trial*, p. 31.

[67]Steven C. Meyer, "The Cambrian Information Explosion: Evidence for Intelligent Design," in Dembski, *Debating Design*, p. 378.

[68]Phillip E. Johnson, *Reason in the Balance: The Case Against Naturalism in Science, Law and Education* (Downers Grove, Ill.: InterVarsity Press, 1995), p. 80.

the proper mutations will eventually occur that will in turn be selected by nature to survive. Here time appears to be functioning as a "magic bullet," so to speak, and Dawkins is well known for his claim, by way of analogy, that with enough time monkeys at a keyboard could type out the complete works of Shakespeare.[69] Antony Flew, however, the world-renowned philosopher was so taken aback by the shoddy reasoning entailed in the monkey theorem that it constituted one of the key reasons that led him to renounce atheism in favor of a designer.[70] And though Darwinists often like to bedazzle the public with appeals to billions of years, actually until about five hundred million years ago, in what is called the Cambrian explosion, all that existed were "simple or single celled organisms such as bacteria and algae."[71] Even more troubling for Darwinist theory is the observation made by several scientists that most of the changes that took place during this remarkable period occurred over a relatively brief span of time, that is, within ten million years. As Ward and Brownlee note, "In a relatively short interval of time, all of the phyla still on Earth appeared. Since the end of the Cambrian [period], no new phyla have evolved."[72] Not surprisingly, Peter Medawar, well known for his work in the philosophy of science, has expressed some skepticism in terms of the role that chance plays in evolution: "something is missing from orthodox theory," he surmises.[73] Might there even be room for mystery?

MICHAEL BEHE AND IRREDUCIBLE COMPLEXITY

In the *Origin of Species* Darwin wrote that "If it could be demonstrated that any complex organ existed, which could not possibly have been formed by numerous, successive, slight modifications, my theory would absolutely

---

[69]Dembski, *Understanding Intelligent Design*, p. 109.

[70]Ibid., p. 110. In a symposium held at New York University in 2004 Flew responded to the question whether recent work on the origin of life pointed to a creative intelligence: "Yes, I now think it does . . . almost entirely because of the DNA investigations. What I think the DNA material has done is that it has shown, by the almost unbelievable complexity of the arrangements which are needed to produce (life), that intelligence must have been involved in getting these extraordinarily diverse elements to work together" (Flew, *There Is a God*, pp. 74-75).

[71]Dembski, *Understanding Intelligent Design*, p. 80.

[72]Ward and Brownlee, *Rare Earth*, p. 178.

[73]Peter Medawar, cited in Denton, *Evolution*, p. 328. See also Peter Medawar, *The Limits of Science* (Oxford: Oxford University Press, 1984).

break down."[74] Such a statement is an important window on the very focused critique of ID. It is precisely this issue of gradualism, that all change must occur as slight, accumulated modifications of degree, that is called into question, for example, in the work of Michael Behe, professor of biochemistry at Lehigh University. In his seminal work *Darwin's Black Box*, Behe postulated that many examples exist in the biological realm of what he calls an "irreducibly complex structure," that is, "a single system composed of several well-matched, interacting parts that contribute to the basic function wherein the removal of any one of the parts causes the system to effectively cease functioning."[75] In other words, function is only achieved when all the components of a system are simultaneously in place. Remove any one of the parts and the function of the *system* disappears and with it anything that natural selection could possibly "choose." Take a mouse trap, for example. All the components of this mechanism (spring, hammer, holding bar, platform or catch) must be in place *at once* in order for the specific function of trapping mice to occur. Remove any component of the device and you no longer have a trap.

Professor Behe has applied this line of reasoning to the blood-clotting cascade and to other biological phenomena, but his most celebrated and controversial example (depending on one's perspective) can be found in the complexity of the bacterial flagellum. This ambulatory device (by means of which the bacterium swims) is actually quite remarkable and is composed of bushings, a stator, studs, a drive shaft, a universal joint and a rotor. If, however, one of the protein parts is removed from the flagellum motor, "you don't end up with a slower, clunkier motor. You end up with a pile of junk," and therefore with nothing for natural selection to prefer.[76]

Kenneth Miller, professor of biology at Brown University and a theist, has challenged Behe's notion of irreducible complexity with respect to the bacterial flagellum in particular and has developed a form of argument that has become so typical of Darwinists of late. According to Miller, extensive homologies (similarities often attributed to a common origin) exist between

---

[74]Charles Darwin, *The Origin of Species* (New York: Penguin, 1958), p. 171.
[75]Michael J. Behe, *Darwin's Black Box: The Biochemical Challenge to Evolution* (New York: Simon & Schuster, 1996), p. 39.
[76]Dembski, *Intelligent Design Uncensored*, p. 19.

type III secretory proteins (that make up a microsyringe) and the proteins involved "in export in the basal region of the bacterial flagellum."[77] However, it is not sufficient to point out that "that some genes for the bacterial flagellum are the same as those for a type III secretory system (a type of pump)."[78] The mere observation of the similarity of some of the genes (and the assumption of a homology) between the two structures neither establishes any causal relation between them (or even that one structure could be degraded into the other), nor does it articulate a detailed incremental process by which the one structure could have evolved into the other.

Surprisingly enough, very little evidence is necessary in this type of reasoning for the specific matter at hand in terms of the bacterial flagellum itself or for the additional claim made by Miller that irreducible complexity has now been refuted. However, the best available evidence today actually suggests that "the microsyringe appeared after the bacterial flagellum motor and not the other way around."[79] At any rate, Ford Doolittle and Olga Zhaxybayeva, fellow Darwinists, contend that "Evolutionists need not take on the impossible challenge of pinning down every detail of flagellar evolution. We need only show that such a development . . . is feasible."[80] Imagination, not empiricism, in other words, can fill in the gaps. Or as Coyne puts it, the onus is not on evolutionary biologists "to sketch out a precise step-by-step scenario"; the burden rather is on the critics of any such a claim.[81] In his research Miller had only identified about ten (in the secretory structure) out of the thirty or so proteins that make up the bacterial flagellum.[82] Thirty-three is not a very high percentage, but it is evidently good enough for the Darwinists. Declare victory early and often; announce that irreducible complexity has been forever refuted. Several others then will simply repeat the claim (arguments based on authority) in their peer-reviewed journals without hardly ever taking into account other considerations. Little wonder then that many in the intelligent design movement are crying foul!

---

[77]Kenneth R. Miller, "The Flagellum Unspun: The Collapse of 'Irreducible Complexity,'" in *Debating Design: From Darwin to DNA*, ed. William Dembski and Michael Ruse (New York: Cambridge University Press, 2004), p. 86.

[78]Dembski and Ruse, *Debating Design*, p. 326.

[79]Dembski, *Intelligent Design Uncensored*, p. 56.

[80]Ford Doolittle and Olga Zhaxybayeva, cited in Coyne, *Why Evolution Is True*, p. 138.

[81]Ibid.

[82]Dembski and Ruse, *Debating Design*, p. 90.

WILLIAM DEMBSKI AND COMPLEX SPECIFIED INFORMATION

With two doctoral degrees in the areas of philosophy and mathematics, Dembski is remarkably well equipped to point out some of the more ponderous claims made by neo-Darwinists in terms of the specific mechanisms of evolution. Drawing from the fields of statistics and information theory, Dembski has created a universal probability bound[83] such that for something to exhibit specified complexity (and therefore giving evidence of design) it must match a "conditionally independent pattern that corresponds to an event" having a probability of less than one in 10^{150}—a very rare event indeed![84] With the universal probability bound in hand, coupled with his explanatory filter (contingency → complexity → specification = design) Dembski takes a careful look at the odds entailed in many of the claims made by Darwinists as they attempt to apply their particular way of thinking to questions such as the origin of life. Take a simple cell for example. It contains at least 250 genes and their corresponding proteins.[85] "The odds of the early Earth's chemical soup randomly burping up such a microminiaturized factory," Dembski claims, "are unimaginably longer than 1 chance in 10^{150}." In other words, "the universe isn't big enough, fast enough or old enough to roll the proverbial dice often enough to tame an improbability that big."[86]

The key to understanding intelligent design, then, is not theology or evangelical belief, but mathematics and information theory.[87] Intelligent design examines the reality of the "vast databases of informational stuff in DNA, RNA, and proteins," that give evidence of complex, specified information.[88] In particular, DNA employs a four-letter alphabet "to build the bigger alphabet of twenty amino acids that are used for 'writing proteins.'"[89] Even a primitive cell would require "more than 300,000 bits of information

---

[83]A universal probability bound refers to a degree of improbability that is so low for a particular event (carefully defined) that it cannot reasonably be assigned to chance regardless of what probabilistic resources are considered. See Dembski and Ruse, *Debating Design,* pp. 319-20.

[84]Ibid., p. 319.

[85]Dembski, *Intelligent Design Uncensored,* p. 71.

[86]Ibid.

[87]Dembski, *Understanding Intelligent Design,* p. 131.

[88]Thomas Woodward, *Darwin Strikes Back: Defending the Science of Intelligent Design* (Grand Rapids: Baker, 2006), p. 138.

[89]Dembski, *Intelligent Design Uncensored,* p. 70.

coded in correct order" to get the job done.[90] This is equivalent to the amount of information contained in the average book. Given such truths, "is there any evidence that the mechanism of mutation-selection touted as the 'generator of complexity' [by Darwinists] can create body plans and new files of genetic information?"[91] For his part, Dembski obviously thinks not. And even the University of Chicago biologist James Shapiro admits that "there are no detailed Darwinian accounts for the evolution of any fundamental biochemical or cellular system, only a variety of wishful speculations."[92] In an essay titled "Not Necessarily a Wing," Stephen Jay Gould weighed in on this issue and observed: "Our technical literature contains many facile verbal arguments—little more than plausible 'just-so' stories."[93] And it was after all Darwin himself who in a letter to Asa Gray observed, "one's imagination must fill up very wide blanks."[94]

To be sure, when Darwinists are asked empirical and mathematical questions in terms of the specific operations of the mechanism of evolution (mutation plus natural selection), they often respond out of a virtually limitless fund of imagination, concocting answers that are more akin to poetry than to the rigors of hard science. This form of response has been offered so often by Darwinists that it has become virtually formulaic. The structure of the reply is ably expressed in the following:

> I [insert your name] am personally unable to think of any way in which [insert biological phenomenon] could have been built up step by step. Indeed, I am not required to substantiate this specific, gradual process at all in my preferred way of reasoning. I will therefore instead construct a vague "just so story" out of my own imagination. Upon this basis I will once again affirm that the mechanisms of evolution have been unassailably confirmed. To doubt such mechanisms, therefore, is ignorance of the highest order.[95]

---

[90]Woodward, *Darwin Strikes Back*, p. 177.

[91]Ibid., p. 173.

[92]James Shapiro, cited in Dembski, *Understanding Intelligent Design*, p. 98.

[93]Stephen Jay Gould, "Not Necessarily a Wing," SJG Archive, www.stephenjaygould.org/library/gould_functionalshift.html.

[94]Denton, *Evolution*, p. 103.

[95]I am giving a new twist to an old argument (in a much different form) used by Dawkins. See Dawkins, *God Delusion*, p. 155.

MAKING WAY FOR DOUBT AND AMBIGUITY: LAUGHLIN, ANDERSON, HIMMELFARB AND BERLINSKI

No one less than Robert Laughlin, professor of physics at Stanford University and Nobel Prize winner, has expressed both dismay and frustration with the specious reasoning of Darwinists in his book *A Different Universe: Reinventing Physics from the Bottom Down*. He writes:

> Evolution by natural selection, for instance, which Charles Darwin originally conceived as a great theory, has lately come to function more as an antitheory, called upon to cover up embarrassing experimental shortcomings and legitimize findings that are at best questionable and at worst not even wrong. Your protein defies the laws of mass action? Evolution did it! Your complicated mess of chemical reactions turns into a chicken? Evolution! The human brain works on logical principles no computer can emulate? Evolution is the cause![96]

And Chris Anderson, editor-in-chief of *Wired* magazine, has begun to express a few doubts: "The Intelligent Design movement has opened my eyes," he writes. "I realize that although I believe that evolution explains why the living world is the way it is, I can't actually prove it."[97] In a more trenchant manner, Gertrude Himmelfarb observed much earlier in her classic essay on Darwinism, "Natural selection, in fact, has become the *Deus ex machina* [of biology] rescuing nature from the impossible situation in which the Darwinians had put her."[98] And if evolution is an underdetermined theory in which many details are missing, as everyone agrees, would it not be best to be more modest in one's claims in terms of the mechanism of evolution instead of continuing along the lines such that "As possibilities were promoted into probabilities, and probabilities into certainties, so ignorance itself was raised to a position only once removed from certain knowledge"?[99]

Beyond this, when the Jewish intellectual and ID champion David Ber-

---

[96]Chris Anderson, cited in Robert B. Laughlin, *A Different Universe: Reinventing Physics from the Bottom Down* (New York: Basic Books, 2005), pp. 168-69.

[97]John Brockman, ed., *What We Believe but Cannot Prove: Today's Leading Thinkers on Science in Age of Certainty* (New York: Harper Perennial, 2006), p. 10.

[98]Gertrude Himmelfarb, *Darwin and the Darwinian Revolution* (Chicago: Elephant Paperbacks, 1959), p. 335.

[99]Ibid.

linski called into question the mathematical rigor of macroevolutionary theory as propounded by Darwinists in a famous essay in *Commentary*, the magazine quickly received "a deluge of indignant letters to the editor, including howls of pain from several of the world's most prominent Darwinists," although no one saw fit to offer an empirical answer to what originally had been an empirical and mathematical question.[100] Indeed, the response to Berlinski was little more than the usual string of "just so stories" with a few ad hominem arguments thrown in all gussied up for public consumption.

Perhaps no one has faced the issue of doubt more forthrightly than Berlinski, who in his most recent book, *The Devil's Delusion*, points out that not only is Western science "saturated in faith" but also scientists themselves remain incapable of comprehending "that faith itself, whether religious *or* scientific, is inherently vulnerable to doubt."[101] Why is it then when a college junior struggles with her Christian faith her elders refer to her as "weighty, a serious Christian, a genuinely solid person," but if this same young woman dares to express some of her nagging doubts about aspects of Darwinism, her professors immediately call her "a yahoo," "a dolt" or the most misused label of all, "a fundamentalist"?

Methodological Naturalism and the Wedge

Contemporary Darwinists insist that the scientific method (as it arose in the sixteenth and seventeenth centuries and was later passed down) necessarily takes the perspective of methodological naturalism in its approach to any subject in general and to biology in particular.[102] With the elimination of teleology and final causes in place, the scientific method as practiced by modern biologists simply focuses on nature itself as well as material causation in its proffered explanations. And it is precisely at this

---

[100]Woodward, *Darwin Strikes Back*, p. 153. See also David Berlinski, *The Deniable Darwin*, ed. David Klinghoffer (Seattle: Discovery Institute Press, 2009).

[101]David Berlinski, *The Devil's Delusion: Atheism and Its Scientific Pretensions* (New York: Basic Books, 2009), p. 46.

[102]It may be the case that the seventeenth century's understanding of "nature" was very different from that of a modern neo-Darwinist. In other words, the term *nature* itself has a history, and we should therefore not read back into the past what are in reality contemporary judgments and worldviews. This no doubt has been the position of Phillip Johnson and others in the ID movement. See Johnson, *Reason in the Balance*.

point that the argument from intelligent design appears to be somewhat confused. On the one hand ID wants to present itself as science. The problem here, of course, is that with ID's inclusion of first causes (matters pertaining to design) in its own approach it is actually practicing a discipline that has not been defined as science (by the community of scientists themselves) either in the sixteenth century or the twenty-first. On the other hand, though ID likes to consider itself a science, it actually offers a thoroughgoing critique of the discipline as it is understood today. In other words, ID, methodologically speaking, challenges some of the basic presuppositions of science that go all the way back to the sixteenth century. Such a move is clearly evident in the so-called wedge strategy of Phillip Johnson in his call to drive a wedge "between empirical scientific practice and methodological naturalism."[103] The advocates of intelligent design, then, must be frank enough to admit that what they are actually calling for is nothing less than a *redefinition* of science at its most basic level. There may be very good reasons for doing this, but it does little to advance their cause, especially in the broader cultural arena, when the champions of ID do not fully acknowledge that their project is nothing less than *revolutionary*.

From our perspective ID is at its best when, like a Socratic gadfly, it challenges the short-sightedness and the reductionism that is so often a consequence of the scientific method, especially when it is applied to complicated, multidimensional entities such as a human being. Not only evangelicals and conservatives but also our postmodern twenty-first-century culture in general has grown increasingly weary of scientific pronouncements in the form "a human being is *nothing but* chemical, physical operations" or "a human being is *nothing but* a repertoire of behaviors" (B. F. Skinner) and so on. Moreover, information and matter are indeed much different things, as ID has claimed, and perhaps then a more generous scientific method can emerge in the future that can adequately take into account both.

Methodological Discipline?

Viewed in another way, ID's criticism of the procedures in science in the form of methodological naturalism may be appropriate in the sense that

---

[103]Phillip Johnson, cited in Dembski and Ruse, *Debating Design*, p. 33.

science repeatedly fails to exercise *methodological discipline*, and it often therefore pontificates with all the conviction it can muster in areas well beyond its competence. For example, since the scientific method supposedly eliminates questions of metaphysics and teleology (of first and final causes, for example) in its method, then it should therefore have nothing to say on the topic of God, one way or the other. As Medawar points out, "It is not therefore to science, but to metaphysics, imaginative literature or religion that we must turn for answers to questions having to do with first and last things. Because these answers neither arise out of nor require validation by empirical evidence."[104] Accordingly, on such broad-based, philosophical questions science is supposed to remain open and neutral. Stephen Jay Gould, however, had to remind his fellow Darwinists to exercise considerable restraint, for they were apparently all too eager to make philosophical judgments on the existence and activity of God on the basis of little more than their naturalistic method. With evident exasperation Gould cautioned, "To say it for all my colleagues and for the umpteenth millionth time: Science simply cannot by its legitimate methods adjudicate the issue of God's possible superintendence of nature. We neither affirm nor deny it."[105]

Unfortunately, Gould's caution has not stopped other American scientists from making unwarranted judgments in an area beyond their competence. Victor Stenger for example, concludes that "God should be detectable by scientific means," demonstrating not only methodological confusion but also a glaring failure to comprehend just what theologians mean by the terminology of God.[106] And Darwin himself may be part of the problem in that although *The Origin of Species* does not contain the specific language of first causes in the form of design (indeed the words *intelligent* and *intelligence* are not used in the book), he nevertheless speculates at points on the role of the Creator in a negative and indirect way, especially in terms of agency.

This larger problem, significant as it is, nevertheless is compounded

---

[104]Medawar, *Limits of Science*, p. 60.
[105]Stephen Jay Gould, "Impeaching a Self-Appointed Judge," a review of Phillip Johnson's *Darwin on Trial, Scientific American* 267 (1992): 166-67.
[106]Stenger, *God*, pp. 11-13.

by the cultural perception in America and elsewhere (in our judgment the myth) that scientists are always objective, eager to receive criticism and that they are ever fair-minded critical thinkers who are humble before the vast and mysterious arena of human knowing. However, to the claim that biologists as members of the scientific community positively welcome criticism, Berlinski replies, "Nonsense. Like everyone else, biologists loathe criticism and arrange their lives so as to avoid it."[107] Wrapping their discipline in an objectivity drawn in some sense from the Age of Reason, scientists maintain that they ever pursue truth in a dispassionate, even-handed way. Of course, this would all be quite wonderful if it were true, but the actual *practice* of scientists (and their pronouncements), especially in the field of biology (and in terms of neo-Darwinism in particular), gives more than enough evidence of people with agendas, biases, vested interests, personal prejudices and even just downright sloppy reasoning. Simply put, scientists, despite the well-worked claims to the contrary, are hardly saints. Participating in the rigors of science does not by itself issue in sanctification.

METAPHYSICAL NATURALISM

The key leaders in ID, such as Phillip Johnson and William Dembski, have contended that the methodological naturalism of scientists so often issues in metaphysical naturalism (which is quite a different thing) in which an all-encompassing worldview, a distinct philosophy, is spun out of a method that in its elimination of design and purpose, first and final causes, nevertheless is offered as a total explanation for life. Such a shift is clearly evident in the ruminations of A. N. Wilson, a member of the Royal Society of Literature, especially when he observes, "Darwinism removes not merely the necessity of supposing a Designer, but its very plausibility."[108] Others have made what is called "the Darwinian jump" to metaphysical naturalism by affirming a variation of Carl Sagan's earlier statement now in the form, "Nature is all there is, ever was, or ever will be."[109] And so when Darwinists declare there is absolutely (the form of a dogmatic statement) no

---

[107]Berlinski, *Deniable Darwin*, p. 61.
[108]A. N. Wilson, *God's Funeral* (New York: W. W. Norton, 1999), p. 310.
[109]Dembski, *Intelligent Design Uncensored*, p. 111.

evidence for teleological forces, they are actually telling us far more about their own method (and its exclusions) than about the nature of reality itself, a matter that remains, despite the protests of Darwinists, a philosophical one.[110] So then, if Intelligent Design advocates are methodologically inappropriate when they appeal to first (design) and final (purpose) causes that go beyond the scientific method, then so too are those scientists who likewise transgress these limits by intermixing science and particular philosophical views. No one less than Stephen Hawking, the celebrated Lucasian Professor of Mathematics at the University of Cambridge, along with another scientist, claimed in a recent book: ". . . philosophy is dead. Philosophy has not kept up with modern developments in science, particularly physics. Scientists have become the bearers of the torch of discovery in our quest for knowledge."[111]

Phillip Johnson may be correct in his claim that philosophical commitments are already embedded in the scientific method itself (demonstrating once again that ID is a revolutionary project); in other words, that an approach that was supposed to be neutral and objective, may already contain factors that skew its vision from the start. "The doctrine that only purposeless forces played a role in biological history," Johnson cautions, "is not an empirical finding but a metaphysical assumption built into the definition of science."[112] Dembski, for his part, declares that Darwinists should keep "whatever philosophical biases they may have from invading their public presentations of evolutionary science."[113] However, Darwinists often feel compelled, even entitled, to propound a worldview "that attempts to explain *everything* often on the basis of a single principle."[114] Indeed, Daniel C. Dennett, a cognitive scientist at Tufts University, considers natural selection to be a universal acid. "Once you accept the theory of evolution by natural selection as applying in *any* area of life," he opines, "there is no way to prevent it being used to explain *every* aspect of life."[115] Such a view,

---

[110]Coyne, *Why Evolution Is True*, p. 14.

[111]Stephen Hawking and Leonard Mlodinow, *The Grand Design* (New York: Bantam Books, 2010), p. 5. It deserves noting that these authors deny the ongoing viability of philosophy in what is clearly a philosophical judgment touching on the area of epistemology!

[112]Johnson, *Reason in the Balance*, p. 190.

[113]Dembski and Ruse, *Debating Design*, p. 234.

[114]Dembski, *Understanding Intelligent Design*, p. 22 (emphasis added).

[115]Daniel C. Dennett, cited in Singham, *God vs. Darwin*, p. 17.

however, constitutes not science but an *ideology*.[116] Indeed, the situation has become so problematic that Johnson points out that for Christians to be regarded as rational (in the eyes of Ruse and Gould, for example), they must first of all "cede to science the authority to determine what is real and what is not."[117]

It is precisely on this point of the Darwinian jump from methodological naturalism to metaphysical naturalism that some of the judgments of the theistic evolutionists appear to be problematic. For one thing they fail to recognize how science is actually *practiced* within a larger cultural arena in all its messiness, and that methodological naturalism, which may be appropriate within certain limits, all too often oversteps those boundaries to issue in a thoroughgoing metaphysical naturalism, that is, a worldview that so long as it is touted simply as science improperly makes judgments with respect to God, the good and the beautiful. So then is the claim of the advocates of ID that methodological naturalism so readily issues in metaphysical naturalism plausible or are they mistaken on this point, as is claimed by so many theistic evolutionists? To answer this question one must get beyond the rhetoric of the debate and grapple with the hard data.

A survey of the religious views of scientists was conducted as far back as 1916. The results were considered shocking at the time, for they revealed that only a minority of scientists, 40 percent to be exact, held personal religious beliefs including belief in God.[118] Interestingly enough, this percentage has remained stable throughout the twentieth century, for when this study was repeated in 1996 it showed "no significant reduction in the proportion of scientists holding such beliefs."[119] Another important study of the religious attitudes and practices of scientists (*Connecticut Mutual Life Report on American Values*) was conducted in the 1980s. It revealed lower levels of religiosity for scientists (as compared with the broader American public) across a wide range of scales: from the percentage of scientists who believed that God loved them (31 percent of scientists versus 73 percent of the general public) to those who

---

[116]Ibid.

[117]Phillip E. Johnson, "Should a Darwinist Bother to Be a Christian?" *Philosophia Christi* 4, no. 1 (2002): 185.

[118]Alister E. McGrath, *The Twilight of Atheism* (New York: Doubleday, 2006), p. 111.

[119]Ibid.

had religious experiences (8 versus 25), from the percentage of scientists who have ever read the Bible (64 versus 75) to the number of those who attend church often (28 versus 44).[120]

Perhaps the most telling statistic of all, however, emerged in a much discussed research project undertaken by Edward J. Larson and Larry Witham in 1998 for the journal *Nature*. They examined the religious beliefs of a highly select group of scientists, namely, those whose achievements and prestige were significant enough to gain entrance to the elite group the National Academy of Sciences. Here a number of social, professional, cultural and even political pressures would naturally come into play among such a population. Of this membership only about 7 percent believed in a personal God![121] Additional evidence suggests that the percentage would be even lower among biologists.[122] So much for the notion that science is simply objective and that it leaves the question of the existence of God open. In so many instances the practice of science invariably leads to a myth-making, worldview-creating philosophy or way of life that is inimical to the faith of theists in general and evangelicals in particular. Not to recognize this fact in a forthright way is once again to mistake the ideals of science for its actual practice. The numbers simply do not lie. As William Provine, the Cornell University evolutionist, put it, "Evolution is the greatest engine of atheism ever invented."[123]

THE CULTURAL STRATEGY OF INTELLIGENT DESIGN

If intelligent design has fared somewhat better than expected in terms of its intellectual strategy, though not without its problems, it has faltered badly in terms of its cultural one. Two key factors have led to this unenviable situation. First, in trying to amass as much cultural power as possible ID has made an appeal to groups that would rightly fall outside its focused definition. Dembski, for example, championed the merits of ID "not

---

[120]Robert Wuthnow, *The Struggle for America's Soul: Evangelicals, Liberals and Secularism* (Grand Rapids: Eerdmans, 1989), pp. 144-45.

[121]Dawkins, *God Delusion*, p. 126.

[122]Dawkins argues (citing the work of R. Elisabeth Cornwell and Michael Stirrat) that there is a "small but significant tendency for biological scientists to be even more atheistic than physical scientists" (Dawkins, *God Delusion*, p. 128).

[123]William Provine, cited in DeWolf, *Traipsing into Evolution*, p. 61.

only with regard to young earth creationists on the right but also with regard to theistic evolutionists on the left of the evangelical spectrum."[124] Such a move has resulted in an uneasy coalition, and members of local school boards who are actually young earth creationists have spoken out incautiously at times. Not surprisingly, the media was quick to classify such ill-conceived pronouncements as yet another variation of "intelligent design." But then again this is the same media for whom the distinction between a fundamentalist and an evangelical floats by them like a blur.

Second, a far more serious problem emerged because it appeared that some of the leaders of the intelligent design movement were not ready for the cultural mine field that is more commonly known as the U.S. public school system. Indeed, such a network is chock full of vested interests ranging from the liberal democratic teacher's unions to the legal pressures of an ever hovering ACLU waiving the banner of separation of church and state like a sword. This highly contested environment is further complicated in that what was once considered the cultural space of public education (in the nineteenth century, for example) has now become simply government space and therefore the politics of the state as well as the declarations of the Supreme Court rule of the day. And though the Court had nothing to say on the topic of evolution and the public schools in 1925, letting the lower courts do the heavy lifting, all of that changed, once again, in the massive cultural shift of the 1960s.

THE SUPREME COURT AND EVOLUTION

The issues that played out in the Scopes Trial in 1925 did not reach the Supreme Court until as late as 1968 in the case *Epperson v. Arkansas*. Here the court ruled unanimously that an Arkansas law that prohibited the teaching of evolution in the classroom was unconstitutional. Though Justice Hugo Black (1886-1971) affirmed this decision, he was nevertheless troubled by a line of reasoning offered by the defendants that suggested the teaching of evolution was antireligious (in other words in our language methodological naturalism was issuing in metaphysical naturalism) and therefore the state (in terms of its schools) should be neutral

---

[124]Amos Yong, "God and the Evangelical Laboratory: Recent Conservative Protestant Thinking About Theology and Science," *Theology and Science* 5, no. 2 (2007): 209.

on this question in line with the freedom of the First Amendment.[125] This specific issue was addressed three years later in another case that came before the Supreme Court, that is, *Lemon v. Kurtzman,* in which guidelines were set down "for judging whether any law violated the Establishment Clause."[126] For a state law to pass constitutional muster, then, it must meet three criteria: First, the statute must have a secular legislative purpose; second, its principal effect must neither advance nor inhibit religion; and third, the statute must not foster "an excessive government entanglement with religion."[127]

In light of what has become known as "the Lemon test," if the teaching of evolution in the public schools does indeed undermine the religious beliefs of children such that they feel alienated and marginalized in holding the worldviews that they do, that's simply an unfortunate though unintended consequence of the teaching of science. In other words, such instruction, in this line of reasoning, does *not* violate the neutrality requirement of the Establishment Clause simply because "teaching science has a clearly secular purpose."[128] As Singham points out, "the goal of teaching science is to advance scientific knowledge and not to undermine religion."[129] The deck, however, may have already been stacked, so to speak, in the Lemon test in terms of how secularity was defined. To illustrate, the term *secular* can communicate a host of meanings, ranging from the fleeting and ephemeral (as opposed to the eternal) to the religiously indifferent or neutral. Moreover, the terminology of secularism may mistake what is actually a lively and debatable cultural issue for a governmental one (under the purview of the state) by framing the discussion as a "religious" matter (and the freedom from such) rather than as the more basic philosophical issue (suggesting different worldviews) that it actually is.

Second, in distinguishing between the primary effect of teaching the science of evolution (and neo-Darwinism) in the classroom and its incidental (not directly intended) consequences, the Court once again considered science unswervingly in an idealistic fashion and not how it is ac-

---

[125]Singham, *God vs. Darwin,* p. 84.
[126]Ibid., p. 87.
[127]Ibid., p. 84.
[128]Ibid., p. 88.
[129]Ibid.

tually carried out by flesh and blood scientists who are never as objective (part of the Enlightenment myth that is being deconstructed by postmodernism) as they have supposed. Clearly, the transition from methodological naturalism to metaphysical naturalism occurs all too often in the scientific community, as the hard data reveal. Therefore to be oblivious to this *very same dynamic* as it plays out in numerous classrooms across the nation is blindsided and exceedingly problematic as intelligent design advocates have maintained all along. To use the language of John Rawls (1921-2002), the late Harvard political theorist, the Court, in setting up the issue in this way, has preferred the particular "comprehensive doctrine" of some, and it has therefore invariably marginalized that of others.[130] In effect, the Court has rendered these "others" second-class citizens. This is hardly a very liberal democratic thing to do, even if it is done in the touted name of science.

THE JUDICIARY DECLARES INTELLIGENT DESIGN
A RELIGION AND DEFINES SCIENCE

Whereas in the Epperson case the Supreme Court ruled in 1968 against a state statute in Arkansas that prohibited the teaching of evolution (which was what the Scopes Trial was all about), in the *Edwards v. Aguillard* case in 1987 the Court ruled by a seven to two vote (Chief Justice William Rehnquist and Justice Antonin Scalia dissented) that Louisiana's attempt to mandate the teaching of creationism as a counterbalance to evolution was likewise unconstitutional.[131] A Gallup poll about a decade later, however, revealed that most Americans disagreed with the Court's decision. In fact, a whopping 69 percent favored teaching creationism in the public schools along with evolution.[132] Such a statistic suggests that though Darwinists clearly have a cultural hold on the knowledge class of university professors, journalists and judges (where the numbers would be much different), that reach does not extend to the average American. According to Johnson, this difference in cultural power helps to explain, in

---

[130]John Rawls, *Justice as Fairness: A Restatement* (Cambridge, Mass.: Belknap Press, 2001), p. 9.
[131]Ted Jelen, "American Clergy on Evolution and Creationism," *Review of Religious Research* 51, no. 3 (2010): 277.
[132]Phillip E. Johnson, *The Wedge of Truth: Splitting the Foundations of Naturalism* (Downers Grove, Ill.: InterVarsity Press, 2000), p. 78.

part, why Darwinists do not take challenges in stride but "react in panic even to a narrow vote by a board of education in a minor state."[133]

The court case that was to rock the whole evolution versus intelligent design debate was not, however, heard by the Supreme Court but by a District Court in Dover, Pennsylvania. Members of the local school board who eventually became the defendants in this case (*Kitzmiller v. Dover Area School District*) mandated that a statement describing a different view, that of intelligent design, be read aloud in all ninth grade biology classes when Darwinism was taught. The plaintiffs in the case, represented by Tammy Kitzmiller, filed suit in District Court against such a requirement and they were assisted in this effort by none other than the ACLU.

A number of irregularities quickly emerged in the bench trial (no jury was involved) surrounding the way the plaintiffs and even the judge had framed the case. According to the distinguished University of Chicago law professor Albert Alschuler, in the eyes of Judge Jones "Dover is simply [the] Scopes trial redux."[134] Or as David Dewolf has put it, "The proponents of intelligent design are guilty by association, and today's yahoos are merely yesterday's reincarnated."[135] In fact, the judge, in tipping his own hand early on in the trial, enthusiastically related to a reporter that he was going to watch *Inherit the Wind*, that mishmash of historical fact and fiction in order to get, as he put it, the proper "historical context!"[136] Additional problems in framing the issue were also evident in both the plaintiff's and the judge's insistence that intelligent design, contrary to what its own advocates had maintained all along, was a theological view pure and simple, and therefore on the basis of a certain reading of the First Amendment, ID could rightfully be excluded from any schools run by the state, not simply the one in Dover. This was a bold and decisive move, for with these understandings in place from the very beginning, the trial was already over even before it began. Such a tactic demonstrates once more that the one who gets to frame the issue at the outset inevitably wins the day. The trial in Dover then simply became the outworking of a script that

---

[133]Ibid., p. 161.
[134]DeWolf, *Traipsing into Evolution*, p. 10.
[135]Ibid.
[136]Ibid., p. 16.

never permitted ID to have or find its proper voice. Henceforth the burden of proof would be on those who oppose evolution in any sense, "to prove that they do not have religious reasons for doing so."[137]

Remarkably enough, the intelligent design movement itself did not support the policy of the Dover school board. It knew that such an approach was ill-conceived, and the Discovery Institute, for example, rejected the requirement that ID be mentioned in the classroom.[138] In fact, the Institute repeatedly urged "repeal of the Dover policy well before any lawsuit was filed—to no avail."[139] Once again the intelligent design movement was defined by elements of its loose and amorphous coalition (upon which the media quickly focused), elements that were clearly not up to snuff either on a proper definition of ID or on the difficult and perplexing nature of the legal environment that they were about to enter.

Not content with defining intelligent design, Judge Jones thought he would try his hand at defining science as well. Once the judge's intent was clear, a group of eighty-five scientists immediately filed an amicus brief with the court requesting that the judge refrain from such an ill-advised action: "Amici strenuously object to appeals to the judiciary to rule on the scope of science in a manner that might exclude certain scientific theories from science."[140] The brief went on to note that "such questions should be decided by scientists, not lawyers."[141] Not only did the court reject this counsel and proceed to pencil in its own understanding of science, but it also declared that "ID's negative attacks on evolution have been refuted by the scientific community," despite considerable evidence to the contrary.[142] At any rate, on December 20, 2005, the U.S. District Court, with Judge John E. Jones III presiding, ruled in favor of the plaintiffs and against the Dover school board.

The cultural consequences of this celebrated trial were just as disturbing as those that emerged in the wake of the earlier Scopes debacle. Clearly, the decision at Dover had a chilling effect on critical thinking in

---

[137]Singham, *God vs. Darwin*, p. 133.
[138]DeWolf, *Traipsing into* Evolution, p. 8.
[139]Ibid.
[140]Ibid., p. 27.
[141]Ibid.
[142]Ibid., p. 29.

the area of evolution and intelligent design across the curriculum, not simply in science classes. For example, an elective *philosophy* course at a school in El Tejon, California, was abruptly cancelled on January 17, 2006, out of *fear* that some of the ideas to be considered in the course (such as the plausibility of intelligent design) would be ruled unconstitutional.[143] Is this what the founding fathers had in mind as they framed the First Amendment? And is it really best to make curricular decisions out of fear? Such are the results when education, through the intervention of the government, has become overly politicized. The coercive powers of the state should not be employed to settle an argument that in the end is largely philosophical.[144]

In light of these court cases the cultural pathways in America seem as closed as ever to several elements that make up the worldview of many in the intelligent design movement. Given this perplexing situation, if evangelicals want to make headway along these lines in the broader cultural arena, especially in terms of their own intellectual life and power, no easy solution is in the offing. For one thing evangelical leaders cannot skirt the scientific community and then seek to gain entrance to the classroom through political maneuvers and machinations, for a veritable legal fortress awaits. Instead, they must raise up a new generation of well-educated evangelical youth, those who can rightly balance both heart and mind, theology and science, and continue to ask the tough and at times embarrassing questions that their ancestors have been asking for decades. This will not be easy, and such a vocation in life is clearly not for the faint of heart or for the thin-skinned. These younger scholars must develop the life of the mind in an exemplary way and seek degrees at the highest level in physics, biology, chemistry, mathematics, theology, law and philosophy. They must learn to think critically and fairly, following the hard evidence wherever it leads, comforted by the basic intuition that all truth is God's truth. But even then a new generation of scholars may make little headway in terms of the intellectual and cultural powers already well chiseled into

---

[143]Singham, *God vs. Darwin*, p. 137.
[144]As one of the advocates of ID puts it, "The boundaries of science are not established by science itself but by philosophy, and the fascinating question of what constitutes science has vexed philosophers of science for many years" (DeWolf, *Traipsing into* Evolution, p. 25).

the American cultural edifice. And yet their gifts and graces will still be needed, even if only to mediate between the ongoing plausibility of evangelical life as a cherished worldview and an increasingly complex and challenging American culture.

5

The Resurgence of the Evangelical Left

Enough evangelicals were caught up in the development of intelligent design, either as key leaders or as supporters, that some critics began to warn of a reactionary movement, a genuine juggernaut, that was not content with political gains but sought more broadly based cultural ones as well.[1] Adding to these concerns was the resilience of the alignment between evangelicals and Republicans, which proved to be a shock to some cultural observers who missed the ongoing evangelical preoccupation with an entire range of *values*. The sexual revolution of the 1960s, along with *Roe v. Wade* in 1973, represented a tectonic shift in American ethics in the eyes of evangelicals, with the result that the sexual practices touted by cultural elites left many evangelicals with a gnawing and deepening sense of alienation. By the 1990s and the turn of the millennium these refashioned cultural values were held in place not by an appeal to objective or transcendent moral criteria—the acids of postmodern relativism were already well at work—but by an identity politics that viewed the question of homosexuality, for example, not in any sense as a moral issue but as the preference of a particular *interest group*.

Though Democrats often appealed to the significant resources of religion during the civil rights movement of the 1960s, with the black church leading the way, *Roe v. Wade* caused many Democrats to drop such appeals

---

[1]See Eugenie C. Scott and Glen Branch, eds., *Not in Our Classrooms: Why Intelligent Design Is Wrong for Our Schools* (Boston: Beacon, 2006), pp. 1-27.

and take on the older liberal rhetoric that religion is, after all, a private matter. The fear among many Democrats was simply that if religious arguments were seriously entertained on the leading issues of the day, this influence could only prove to be disruptive. Such a judgment highlights once again the differences in moral reasoning and values between evangelicals and the Democratic leadership of late. Indeed, according to Ralph Reed, former head of the Christian Coalition, one of the chief reasons for the political strength of religious conservatives is simply that "liberals and Democrats have abandoned religion as the basis of their own political activity."[2] This last element helps to explain, at least in part, why "a growing majority of people who do not profess faith or attend church support the Democratic party."[3]

Fear of American evangelicals participating in the democratic process, with their politically incorrect views on abortion and homosexuality, has resulted in pointed critiques by cultural elites, whose arguments at times look more like an expression of disdain than anything else. For example, Chris Hedges, a noted author, labeled the evangelicals who make up the Christian right as "American fascists."[4] Not surprisingly, the reluctance to hear evangelical voices on the national level by many cultural leaders today has resulted in a steeled determination on the part of evangelicals to become increasingly politically active, especially when their cherished values, many of them related to the family, appear to be threatened. As Michael Cromartie has pointed out in a new take on an old quip from H. L. Mencken: "Heave an egg out a window anywhere on Capitol Hill today and you will likely hit an evangelical political activist."[5] However, from the evangelical point of view, it is not so much that they would like to enforce their will on other Americans (that's how it is often presented in the American media) but that they would prefer to shrink the encroaching power of government so that "the left can no longer impose its secular values on churches and families."[6]

---

[2]Ralph Reed, *Active Faith: How Christians Are Changing the Soul of American Politics* (New York: Free Press, 1996), p. 26.
[3]George G. Hunter, *Christian, Evangelical and Democrat?* (Nashville: Abingdon, 2006), p. 27.
[4]Barry N. Hankins, *American Evangelicals: A Contemporary History of a Mainstream Religious Movement* (Lanham, Md.: Rowman & Littlefield, 2008), p. 1.
[5]Michael Cromartie, "Fixing the World: From Nonplayers to Radicals to New Right Conservatives: The Saga of Evangelical Social Actions," *Christianity Today* 36, no. 5 (1992): 23.
[6]Reed, *Active Faith*, p. 189.

THE EVANGELICAL LEFT FINDS ITS VOICE

It is well known that conservative evangelicals have been repeatedly criticized by mainline liberals. It is therefore something of a surprise to learn that some of the most vocal detractors of conservative and even moderate evangelicals are found not merely among denominational liberals but among the evangelical left as well. As Gushee has pointed out, "'When the evangelical left turns to what (and who) it is against, the primary target is clearly the evangelical right."[7]

To be sure, not all evangelicals were pleased with the rising political power of the Christian Coalition, a group that they continued to refer to as the religious right. To illustrate, writing in 2008, Jim Wallis of *Sojourners* fame repeatedly excoriated this movement as having "discredited the role of faith in politics."[8] Moreover, in an article in *Tikkun* Glen Stassen complained that "the Religious Right is giving evangelicals a bad name. It is even giving Christians a bad name."[9] And Charles Marsh, for his part, criticized the rise of an evangelical empire that has produced "a world bereft of moral accountability, intellectual curiosity, trustworthiness, and honesty."[10] Beyond this, Dan Stiver grossly underestimated the systemic and wrenching critique of American religion by the neo-atheists and actually thought that they might be pleased to learn of the rise of the evangelical left. "Those on the anti-religious reactionary left like Dawkins and Harris," he observes, "can come to be familiar with the 'shocking and awful news' about a confessional Christian stance that makes people think positively rather than negatively about Christ."[11]

The reawakening of the evangelical left, whose roots go back to the progressive movement of the early twentieth century and beyond, can be seen in the publication of the magazine *The Other Side* in 1965, whose pages championed economic and social values in general and the plight of the poor in particular. A few years later, in 1971, Jim Wallis launched the pe-

---

[7]David P. Gushee, *The Future of Faith in American Politics: The Public Witness of the Evangelical Center* (Waco, Tex.: Baylor University Press, 2008), p. 76.

[8]Jim Wallis, *The Great Awakening: Reviving Faith and Politics in a Post-Religious Right America* (New York: HarperOne, 2008), p. 3.

[9]Glen Stassen, "The New Evangelicals," *Tikkun* 21, no. 5 (2006): 35-37.

[10]Charles Marsh, *Wayward Christian Soldiers: Freeing the Gospel from Political Captivity* (Oxford: Oxford University Press, 2007), p. 197.

[11]Dan R. Stiver, "A Word About Evangelicals on the Left," *Review and Expositor* 104, no. 4 (2007): 715.

riodical the *Post American*, which later became known simply as *Sojourners*. The original title is remarkably suggestive of the politics and the countercultural revolution of the 1960s, a decade that appears to have shaped much of Wallis's thought. Recalling this early period, Wallis confesses, "I felt I had lost my faith. I found my home instead in the civil rights and antiwar movements of the late sixties."[12] Perhaps even more telling in terms of his value judgments at the time is his further observation, "I had left the church in order to become involved in what I saw as the *real issues* of my time."[13]

Evangelicals from all over the United States met in Chicago in 1973 and expressed their burgeoning social concern in the document titled "A Declaration of Evangelical Social Concern." This groundbreaking meeting eventually led to the founding of Evangelicals for Social Action five years later, a group that some cultural observers mark as the true beginning of the evangelical left. By the following year concern for social justice among evangelicals had grown so considerably that it cut across denomination lines to embrace "Calvinists, Wesleyans and Mennonites."[14] For example, Leon Hynson, a leading evangelical Wesleyan, was already grappling with ecclesiology and social transformation in an important work in 1976.[15] Much later, in 1995, several evangelical leaders came together to establish Call to Renewal (CTR), a national network of individuals, churches and faith-based organizations to undertake social action more effectively. In addition, the Evangelical Environment Network was founded in 1993 in order to educate, inspire and mobilize Christians in their effort to care for God's creation.

THE POLITICS OF THE EVANGELICAL LEFT

Jim Wallis. Born in Detroit in humble surroundings, Jim Wallis launched a career as a political activist in his youth. Deeply concerned about social

---

[12]Jim Wallis, *The Call to Conversion: Why Faith Is Always Personal but Never Private* (San Francisco: HarperSanFrancisco, 2005), p. xvii.

[13]Ibid., p. xviii (emphasis added).

[14]Richard Kyle, *Evangelicalism: An Americanized Christianity* (New Brunswick, N.J.: Transaction, 2006), p. 206.

[15]Leon Hynson, "The Church and Social Transformation," *Wesleyan Theological Journal* 11 (1976): 49-61.

justice, Wallis has often made the claim that he seeks nonpartisan solutions to the problems of the nation, and Stan Guthrie has pointed out that just prior to the 2004 presidential campaign *Sojourners* released an ad that touted the line, "God is not a Republican or a Democrat."[16] However, just below the claim that "we are not single-issue voters" was a series of "black and white questions," Guthrie continues, "seemingly pulled directly from John Kerry's briefing book."[17] Indeed, the most recent publications of Wallis not only give every indication of moving decidedly in a Democratic, leftist direction but also the tone of his commentary has taken a sharp turn. This was not at all how *Sojourners* began. To illustrate, Wallis is now maintaining, in what looks like a species of triumphalism, that "the Religious Right is over" and "the Religious Right is being replaced with Jesus."[18] However, the demographics of American religion, the hard data, tell a much different story. In 2006, for example, a study conducted by the Pew Research Center revealed that approximately three times as many white evangelicals considered themselves a part of the religious right as opposed to the religious left.[19] And in a study conducted two years earlier, James Penning and Corwin Smidt determined that "today's evangelical college students identify with the Republican Party far more than with the Democratic Party."[20] Put another way, "Liberals continue to be a rare species among evangelical students," despite the hype from the left.[21] Moreover, the (sub)cultural and political power of the Christian right in America far exceeds that of the religious left. To illustrate, in 2006 John Coleman observed that an inventory of the *New York Times* since 1981 reveals that "1,689 stories [referred] to the religious right and only 29 about [were] about the religious left.[22]

Beyond this, the evangelical left faces a problem hardly encountered by

---

[16]Stan Guthrie, "When Red Is Blue," *Christianity Today* 51, no. 10 (2007): 100.

[17]Ibid.

[18]Wallis, *Great Awakening*, pp. 25, 43.

[19]Hankins, *American Evangelicals*, p. 159. The ratios here are 20 percent for the Religious Right as opposed to a mere 7 percent for the Religious Left.

[20]James M. Penning and Corwin E. Smidt, *Evangelicalism: The Next Generation* (Grand Rapids: Baker Academic, 2002), p. 140.

[21]Ibid., p. 127.

[22]John Coleman, "Left Behind: Who and Where Is the Religious Left in the United States," *America* 194, no. 15 (2006): 11.

the Christian right, and one that weakens its influence. While it is almost a truism in American religion that conservative evangelicals have become, at least to some extent, culturally accommodated to a welcoming Republican Party with win-win power configurations in the offing, the evangelical left is by no means embraced with open arms by the Democratic Party. Not only is the religious left "badly outgunned by the secular left" but many leaders in the Democratic Party are resolutely secular.[23] As the editor of the *Economist* put it recently, "Appalled by the religious right, most [Democrats] have been indifferent to or unaware of the religious left."[24] Undeterred, Wallis wistfully opines, "Democrats have done some soul-searching (and some political math) and are again becoming a party more friendly to faith."[25] But if Democrats have moved in the direction of faith due to math, then they may have grossly miscalculated once again the broader evangelical concern with a full array of human *values*, some of them having to do with *holiness*.

Several evangelical left leaders, Jim Wallis and Tony Campolo among them, have accused their evangelical brothers and sisters from both the right and center of being obsessed with the two hot-button issues of abortion and homosexuality. Wallis, for his part, recounts the story of a woman who claimed that she would have aborted her child (who eventually graduated from Harvard) if she had not received economic support from the government. The woman continued to recount the story and then made a request, "I want you to tell people that if they want to prevent abortions they need to support low-income women like me."[26] Wallis took this plea as one that should galvanize American evangelicals to "social justice," that is, to demand that the government should spend more money to alleviate social ills. While not failing to appreciate the poignancy and human emotion of this account, and while we wish the young graduate well, we offer a slightly different interpretation of the request, one that is focused, to be sure, and unswervingly honest, "Pay up or we will abort our babies."

Though Wallis likes to employ the label of being "biblical" for his social

[23]"American Theocracy," *Economist* 379, no. 8479 (2006): 32.
[24]Ibid., p. 26.
[25]Wallis, *Great Awakening*, pp. 44-45.
[26]Ibid., p. 189.

and political policies, upon closer examination there is actually little that distinguishes such policies from the judgments of the left wing of the Democratic Party.[27] First of all, for example, Wallis draws a moral equivalence between the disruptive, life-threatening and violent looting by the poor in American cities with the normal, ongoing practices of American capitalism: "The spirit of pillage in our inner cities is a crude and desperate reflection of an entire economic order whose basic premise is looting," he warns.[28] This is a claim, however, that is never carefully sustained by a well thought out and reasonable argument. Instead what is offered is a distorted generalization of the complexities of American free enterprise.[29]

Second, Wallis was opposed to Bill Clinton's 1996 Welfare Reform Act, which would have required greater accountability, more responsible action, on the part of the recipients of aid such that they would not be left wards of the state.[30] Beyond this, Wallis intends to use the power of the state both on a national and local level to bring "the blessings of good housing down the economic ladder, including making home ownership possible for poor families."[31] Never once does Wallis entertain whether the poor will actually be able to make the mortgage payments for this housing. Moreover, to fall back on government housing subsidies to bring about this particular vision may in the end just be another way of fostering the ongoing dependency of an entire class of people. Emboldened by the motto "God hates inequality and we should, too," Wallis argues vigorously against a free market in housing and instead prefers that the coercive arm of local governments should be used to place poor people in the middle of neighborhoods whose housing they cannot afford.[32] "So why keep all the poor people in poor neighborhoods?" he asks. "Why not let them live in all

---

[27]Gushee, *Future of Faith*, p. 58.

[28]Wallis, *Call to Conversion*, p. 40.

[29]For a far more balanced assessment of economics and politics, see Ronald J. Sider, "Developing an Evangelical Political Framework: Moving Toward Consensus," *Evangelical Review of Theology* 32, no. 2 (April 2008): pp. 103-17; *Just Generosity: A New Vision for Overcoming Poverty in America* (Grand Rapids: Baker Book House, 1999), and most recently, *Fixing the Moral Deficit* (Downers Grove, Ill.: InterVarsity Press, 2012).

[30]Michelle Cottle, "Prayer Center: Let's Not Talk About Sex," *New Republic* 232, no. 9 (2005): 25.

[31]Wallis, *Great Awakening*, p. 122.

[32]Ibid., p. 125.

kinds of neighborhoods, go to better schools?"[33] Unfortunately Wallis never seriously entertains the thought that there might be a tradeoff here between equality and freedom such that as the one goes up, the other goes down. On the way to a radically egalitarian society, where differences are forcefully leveled out, it may be important after all to consider the consequences of empowering the state in this way. To claim glibly that God hates inequality may just be another way of saying that God hates freedom.

Rejecting at least in some sense the precept of Dr. Martin Luther King Jr. that persons should be judged not on the color of their skin but on the content of their character, some in the evangelical left take on the ersatz morality of the 1960s radicals and champion affirmative action, a policy that some argue is more accurately labeled reverse discrimination in philosophical circles. As Judge Bork points out, the 1964 Civil Rights Act "explicitly forbade *all* forms of discrimination on the basis of race or sex."[34] However, the promise of equal rights for all under this Act was quickly shunted aside by a zealous Johnson administration and its courts, who were more than determined to substitute equality of results for that of opportunity and in a way that has been favored by the evangelical left. In a recent book, however, Wallis parts company with his comrades in a very reasonable and reflective way and admits that *justice*, so understood, actively discriminates against one group (whose basic characteristics like race and gender are no fault of its own) in order to socially advance another preferred group.[35] Such a policy transforms the American nation from a society whose "rewards may be achieved by individual merit to one whose rewards are handed out according to group identity."[36] The means-ends calculus here in which one group is simply used as a *means* to the ends of another is incapable of being rationally justified but is nevertheless held in place by considerable social and political force. As Charles Sykes argued more than a decade ago, "It is no longer necessary to engage in

---

[33]Ibid., p. 122.

[34]Robert H. Bork, *Slouching Towards Gomorrah: Modern Liberalism and American Decline* (New York: Regan Books, 1996), p. 231 (emphasis added).

[35]Jim Wallis, *The Great Awakening: Reviving Faith and Politics in a Post-Religious Right America* (New York: HarperOne, 2008), p. 165.

[36]Bork, *Slouching Towards Gomorrah*, p. 249.

lengthy and detailed debate over such issues as affirmative action; it is far easier and more effective to simply brand a critic as insensitive."[37]

One of the more egregious problems of this political policy (and there are several) championed by the evangelical left is that formal equality before the law is in conflict with and may actually be undermined by the activity of the government as it aims at the substantive equality of politically favored groups.[38] This discriminatory practice in which the rights of people of nonfavored groups are ignored, if not outright repudiated, was amply illustrated most recently in *Ricci v. DeStafano* of New Haven, Connecticut, a case on which Judge Sotomayor had ruled. At issue was the claim of Frank Ricci and seventeen other white firefighters that though they had scored high enough on a civil service exam to be promoted, they were nevertheless passed over simply due to the color of their skin. The city of New Haven feared a lawsuit if the white members were accorded the fruits of what their scores had actually warranted since no African Americans were being promoted. In the estimation of the evangelical left this is precisely how things should be. And though this movement often claims that this sort of racial discrimination constitutes social justice informed by a biblical ethic (it even calls for white people "to make restitutions" to blacks), it actually looks more like the evangelical left is exegeting the op-ed page of the *New York Times* than anything from the Bible.[39]

Tony Campolo. Growing up in difficult economic conditions in Philadelphia, Tony Campolo, professor emeritus of sociology at Eastern University in St. Davids, Pennsylvania, is an evangelical, an engaging speaker and a political activist. Aligned with both the evangelical left and the Democratic Party, Campolo has written numerous books and has lectured throughout the country. Like Jim Wallis, Campolo directs so much of his criticism toward the Christian right, attacking, for example, "Christian talk radio . . . [and] the emergence of conservative Christians as a bloc within the Republican Party."[40] Fearful that many Americans, the secular left among them, will fail to understand evangelicalism properly, Campolo

---

[37]Charles J. Sykes, *A Nation of Victims: The Decay of the American Character* (New York: St. Martin's Press, 1992), p. 17.

[38]F. A. Hayek, *The Road to Serfdom* (Chicago: University of Chicago Press, 2007), p. 117.

[39]Wallis, *Great Awakening*, p. 161.

[40]Gushee, *Future of Faith*, p. 63.

confesses that "One of my biggest concerns about American evangelicalism today is that, in the minds of many, it has become synonymous with the Religious Right."[41]

Campolo and other leaders have recently championed the term "Red Letter Christians" to express their theological and political emphasis and to distinguish themselves from other evangelicals, especially the Christian right. The terminology itself, interestingly enough, was suggested by a Jewish country and western disc jockey in Nashville, Tennessee, who quipped on one occasion, "So you're one of those Red Letter Christians—you know—who's really into those verses in the New Testament that are in red letters."[42] Campolo, however, is quick to point out that he and other Red Letter Christians affirm the authority of the whole Bible, a claim that is credible for the most part, and that "we have no particular political agenda," which, from our perspective, is not.[43] For although Campolo insists that Red Letter Christians are conservative on some issues and liberal on others, his most recent writings—in several key places—read more like the party platform espoused at the Democratic Convention in 2008 than anything else. Red Letter Christians, it seems to us, bleed blue—as in blue state.

Maintaining that Red Letter Christians are passionately committed to social justice, Campolo contends that this group of believers is "unwilling to become single-issue voters whose politics are determined by abortion."[44] Campolo insists that Red Letter Christians will *not* "solely focus on the hot-button issues of abortion *and* gay marriage."[45] Moreover, though Campolo is apparently opposed to abortion, his description of the views of Red Letter Christians on this topic has left many conservative and moderate evangelicals scratching their heads. Employing an argument similar to the left wing of the Democratic Party, Campolo informs us that "To vote against abortion is, to some Red Letter Christians, a vote against the right of women to make decisions that determine their own biological

---

[41]Tony Campolo, *Letters to a Young Evangelical* (New York: Basic Books, 2006), p. 3.
[42]Tony Campolo, *Red Letter Christians: A Citizen's Guide to Faith and Politics* (Ventura, Calif.: Regal, 2008), p. 21.
[43]Ibid., p. 11.
[44]Ibid., p. 121.
[45]Ibid., p. 47.

destinies," a declaration that ignores a host of so many other considerations that should be factored into the mix.[46]

Even more troubling, Campolo considers how some, though clearly not
all, Red Letter Christians want to sever the moral and spiritual connection
between pro-choice views on abortion and being a Christian. "Red Letter
Christians," he notes, "must face the reality that there are good Christians
on both sides of the debate."[47] Accordingly, Campolo points out that some
evangelicals "will not use one's opinions or convictions on the issue of
abortion or homosexuality to define who is, or who is not, a Christian."[48]
Ignoring the teaching of the early church fathers, who in many of their
writings equated abortion with murder (Clement of Alexandria, Ter-
tullian, Basil the Great, Ambrose, Chrysostom and Jerome), Campolo ex-
plores a line of reasoning (which he, himself, no doubt rejects) whose
moral community must clearly be beyond that of the church, though he
identifies it as "evangelical." He writes:

> Some [evangelicals] have even adopted an ideological justification for
> abortion, making a case that abortion is not murder if performed in the ear-
> liest weeks of a pregnancy. They contend that what makes homo sapiens
> human is interaction with one or more humans. The traits that differentiate
> humans from other animals—language, self awareness, conscience, and
> even a sense of the sacred—are all traits that are imparted to a developing
> person though socialization.[49]

But such an argument surely "proves" too much: for not only would
abortion be permitted according to this logic but infanticide as well.

On the topic of homosexuality, Campolo gives every evidence of
thinking with the church and its rich tradition, and consequently he affirms that "same gender eroticism cannot be reconciled with Scripture."[50]
He does, however, freely admit that his own wife, Peggy, believes that the
church should legitimize homosexual "marriages." "She thinks," Campolo
observes, "that lifelong commitments by people who love each other en-

---

[46]Ibid., p. 124.
[47]Ibid., pp. 125-26.
[48]Tony Campolo, *Speaking My Mind: The Radical Evangelical Prophet Tackles the Tough Issues Christians Are Afraid to Face* (Nashville: W Publishing, 2004), p. 224.
[49]Campolo, *Letters to a Young Evangelical*, pp. 152-53.
[50]Campolo, *Speaking My Mind*, p. 55.

hance their humanity."[51] In describing this view, Campolo expresses the judgment of Lewis Smedes, Reformed Christian and professor of theology and ethics at Fuller Theological Seminary for over twenty-five years, who believed that a "committed, lifelong, monogamous relationship between homosexuals may be what he would call the 'circumstantial will of God.'"[52]

Like Jim Wallis, Tony Campolo's left-leaning views emerge most strongly as he tackles the question of poverty in America. After setting up the polarizing notion of his own "*avant garde* of progressive politics" on the one hand and the supposed stilted approach of right-wing conservatives on the other, Campolo attempts to link the political activity of current Red Letter Christians with the heydays of evangelical, progressive social action back in the nineteenth century, a time when Charles Finney was center stage.[53] The problem, of course, is that Campolo fails to realize that the progressivism of nineteenth-century evangelicalism was markedly different from the progressivism being offered to evangelicals today, simply because the decade of the 1960s marks a watershed in American social and political life whereby some of the very foundations of society were shaken and displaced.

In an attempt to bring about the "common good," as he envisions it, Campolo calls for collectivist solutions that enhance the power of the federal government in the areas of Medicare, Medicaid, Social Security and public assistance for poor children.[54] "And we have no problem with tax dollars from all Americans," Campolo continues, "being used to such Kingdom ends."[55] But how have American evangelicals come to the state of affairs in which one of its key leaders is describing the ongoing advance of the American welfare state (which has weakened both the family and the church) as nothing less than the emergence of the kingdom of God? How has Campolo moved so rapidly from the red letters of the pages of the New Testament to the black ink of public policy without articulating in considerable detail a normative framework and the political philosophy that will help bring it into being?

---

[51]Ibid., p. 55.
[52]Ibid., p. 64.
[53]Campolo, *Red Letter Christians*, p. 15.
[54]Ibid., p. 157.
[55]Ibid.

A careful reading of Campolo's writings reveals that he has an unacknowledged internal contradiction in some areas of his social and political thinking. Thus, on the one hand, he repeatedly turns to the state to rectify what social ills are identified, not envisioning a role for the church in any significant way. "And if churches are not ready to meet the needs of the poor," Campolo complains, "then ought we not turn to the government, managing our tax dollars, to care for them?"[56] On the other hand Campolo also contends throughout that "the church is Christ's primary instrument for bringing about social change and transforming the institutions of society to conform with his will."[57] So what is it? Is the government the primary instrument for social change or is it the church? And just how will the church transform the institutions of society, weak as it is in the larger cultural scheme of things, to conform to the very will of Christ? Will the church in the end employ the coercive political power of the state to achieve what ends it cannot realize itself? This does not appear to be a prescription for the kingdom of God but for a much different kind of kingdom.

Some might argue that the political judgment of Campolo is also evidenced as he moves from the pages of the book of James, "The wages of the laborers who mowed your fields, which you kept back by fraud, cry out, and the cries of the harvesters have reached the ears of the Lord of hosts" (Jas 5:4), to the pungent observation, "These verses are a warning against those who embrace *lasissez-faire* capitalism without question and declare that workers should be paid whatever the market value of labor establishes."[58] However, James, as a first-century leader, had little understanding of how complex capitalist economies function and so they could hardly have been the object of his censure. In a real sense what takes place in Campolo's hermeneutic, here as elsewhere, is that key Scripture passages are lifted from their historical context in support of social and political views that are actually arrived at through other means. And sometimes this trumped up "Thus saith the Lord" approach actually *harms* the poor. Take for example the incident in which Campolo in the name of a supposed "Kingdom ethic" protested along with others against the Disney

---

[56]Ibid., pp. 156-57.
[57]Campolo, *Letters to a Young Evangelical,* p. 73.
[58]Campolo, *Red Letter Christians,* p. 167.

Corporation, which was producing T-shirts in Haiti and failing to give the local workers a fair share of the profits. What did the corporation do in the face of such opposition? It shut down the plant in Haiti and thereby threw hundreds of Haitians out of work.[59] So much for the coming of the kingdom.

Brian McLaren. Brian McLaren, who is a member of the *Sojourners* board, made something of a splash in evangelical circles with his controversial book *A Generous Orthodoxy*. After expressing dissatisfaction with understanding the terminology of orthodoxy as "getting it right" or "getting it straight," McLaren offered his own postmodern, allegedly culturally savvy option of "curvy orthodoxy," a designation that will hardly be satisfactory to mainstream evangelicals.[60] He explains:

> If, for you, *orthodox*, means finally "getting it right" or "getting it straight," mine is a pretty disappointing, curvy orthodoxy. But if, for you, orthodoxy isn't a list of correct doctrines, but rather the *doxa* in orthodoxy, which means "thinking" or "opinion," then the lifelong pursuit of expanding thinking and deepening, broadening opinions about God sounds like a delight, a joy.[61]

Denying any significant training or background in theology, McLaren proceeds methodologically like much of the evangelical liberalism of the early twentieth century; that is, he develops his novel theology, for the most part, out of human *experience*. "I have become convinced that a generous orthodoxy appropriate for our postmodern world," McLaren proclaims, "will have to grow out of the experience of the post-Christian, post-secular people of the cities of the twenty-first century."[62] Such an approach privileges the current experience and social location of the populations that McLaren prefers, but it neglects, in significant ways, the larger voice of the past in terms of church tradition. And even McLaren's touted image (which supposedly typifies the emergent church) of a growing, expanding tree does not help matters much but only serves to give inordinate attention to the present, almost in a myopic way: "But some thought seeks

---

[59]Campolo, *Speaking My Mind*, p. 174. Even Campolo admits, "It is amazing how much damage has been done by good, well-meaning people who are trying to help the poor" (ibid., p. 123).
[60]Brian McLaren, *A Generous Orthodoxy* (Grand Rapids: Zondervan, 2004), p. 334.
[61]Ibid.
[62]Ibid., p. 100.

to embrace what has come before—like a new ring on a tree—in something bigger."[63] Observe that in this proffered image not only is the "bigger" identified with the present (the supposedly cutting-edge experience of postmoderns, which McLaren prefers), but it also presupposes unending progress in which each successive ring incorporates and is an advance on the former.

With these theological commitments in place, McLaren repeatedly criticizes conservative Protestants, some of whom are a part of the Christian right, though the evangelical left remains unscathed.[64] "I am consistently over-sympathetic to . . . dreaded liberals," he writes, "while I keep elbowing my conservative brethren in the ribs in the most annoying—some would say *ungenerous*—way."[65] One area in particular in which McLaren does indeed make common cause with liberals is in terms of a particular conception of social and political justice. However, lacking a significant background in first-century Christianity, and the broader Judaic and Roman cultures, McLaren ends up reading much of North American leftist political thought of the past fifty years back into the first century, where it simply does not belong. Indeed, the problem of anachronism (confusing time frames) is an ongoing one for McLaren as he envisions a politically active Jesus confronting the Roman state with all the concerns of a modern liberation theologian. First, "Jesus confronts the Roman Empire, which many Jews identify as the source or focal point of all evil and trouble among them."[66] And second, McLaren observes elsewhere, "the Jesus of liberation theology, firmly rooted in the struggles of the first century, inspires Christians to continue his work and mission in all centuries throughout history."[67] However, it is difficult, if not impossible, to make the case that Jesus was a political messiah sticking it to the Roman state or that he shared the materialist presuppositions of Marxism, with their undue emphasis on the maintenance needs of people that has informed some theologies of late.

---

[63]Ibid., p. 316.
[64]Ibid., p. 40.
[65]Ibid.
[66]Brian McLaren, *The Secret Message of Jesus: Uncovering the Truth That Could Change Everything* (Nashville: Thomas Nelson, 2006), p. 66.
[67]McLaren, *Generous Orthodoxy*, p. 71.

Equally disturbing in McLaren's political and theological mix is the gnostic motif that he develops in postulating that the "core message of Jesus has been unintentionally misunderstood or intentionally distorted," with the implication that the key to unlock "the secret message of Jesus" (the actual title of McLaren's book) has somehow been provided to *him* and other select leaders in the emergent movement, though it was not apparently available to centuries of the history of the church.[68] Indeed, McLaren exclaims with all the gnostic fervor he can muster: "The Christian religion has downplayed, misconstrued, or forgotten the secret message of Jesus entirely."[69] And though he insists that "this carpenter's son from Galilee challenges every existing political movement to a radical rethinking," such a rethinking at McLaren's interpretive hands is not reminiscent of first-century realities but once again of twentieth-first-century ones.[70] The secret here, if there is one, is that Jesus is a postmodern, North American leftist. This is hardly new.

Jimmy Carter. During his presidential campaigns Jimmy Carter was harried by fundamentalists. Jerry Falwell, for example, criticized Carter repeatedly and noted among other things that the candidate "'claimed' to be a Christian."[71] Nevertheless, many evangelicals were eager to embrace this Southern Baptist, though some were troubled by the numerous gaffes Carter made during one of his campaigns, such as his claim that in the eyes of God America is no better than any other nation (think of Hitler's Germany or Stalin's Soviet Union) in history.[72] Upon taking office, Carter also proved to be puzzling, at least initially, to many Washington insiders (some of whom were thoroughly secular and had little understanding of religious faith). On the one hand Carter believed that religion was a private matter, adhering firmly to a *particular* understanding of the separation of church and state.[73] On the other hand one of his first acts in office was to admonish his staff members to stop living in sin and get married in

---

[68]McLaren, *Secret Message of Jesus*, p. 3.

[69]Ibid., p. 78.

[70]Ibid., p. 17.

[71]Jimmy Carter, *Living Faith* (New York: Three Rivers Press, 2001), p. 33.

[72]Ronald B. Flowers, "President Jimmy Carter, Evangelicalism, Church-State Relations, and Civil Religion," *Journal of Church and State* 25, no. 1 (1983): 130.

[73]Carter, *Living Faith*, p. 5.

order "to make their relationships legal."[74]

Failing to develop a proper working relationship with the Democratic Congress, Carter ruled more by fiat more than anything else. He issued more executive orders, for instance, than any other president since Eisenhower, and he employed the veto more often "than any Democratic president who had a Democratic Congress."[75] The religious right quickly turned on this go-it-alone president once Paul Weyrich and other leaders realized that Carter had reneged on his promise to appoint evangelicals to his administration.[76] A particular bone of contention was Carter's handling of the federal bench. At least one study has demonstrated that the judges appointed during this administration were even more liberal in their rulings "than their Johnson appointed colleagues."[77] Add to this Carter's creation of the federal Department of Education in 1979, which was viewed by conservative Christians as a social engineering project that would target their schools, and it is easy to understand why many evangelicals were alienated during the Carter presidency.

Though evangelicals, as with other Americans, were genuinely appreciative of the many good works undertaken by Carter *after* he left office, in particular the Carter Center and Habitat for Humanity, they did not look favorably on his ongoing criticism of conservative Christians, especially fundamentalists. Indeed, in perusing the president's writings after he left office, one quickly realizes that the word *fundamentalist* is often employed in a nearly stereotypical way; that is, it epitomizes all that is supposedly wrong with the Christian religion. To illustrate, according to Carter, fundamentalists "condemn those who differ from them";[78] they change the subtleties of historic debate "into black and white rigidities"; and they take up "narrowly defined theological beliefs" into a rigid agenda.[79] In fact,

---

[74]James M. Wall, "Jimmy Carter, Religion and Public Service," *Christian Century* 102, no. 16 (1985): 460.

[75]D. Jason Berggren, "I Had a Different Way of Governing: The Living Faith of President Carter," *Journal of Church and State* 47, no. 1 (2005): 52.

[76]Robert Freedman, "The Religious Right and the Carter Administration," *The Historical Journal* 48, no. 1 (2005): 238. This observation is not to deny the partisan nature of the religious right that it might have preferred, for instance, a go-it-alone president if he or she governed in *its* favor.

[77]Sue Davis, "President Carter's Selection Reforms and Judicial Policymaking," *American Politics Quarterly* 14, no. 4 (1986): 334.

[78]Carter, "Living Faith," p. 36.

[79]Jimmy Carter, *Our Endangered Values: America's Moral Crisis* (New York: Simon & Schuster, 2005), p. 3.

Carter believes that three words aptly characterize activist fundamentalists: *rigidity, domination* and *exclusion*.[80] To be sure, things had gotten so out of hand earlier that when Carter was running for reelection in 1980, a Democratic television ad claimed that "if Reagan goes on to the White House, Falwell will come with him, and they'll purify the land as someone else did years ago."[81] The Moral Majority filed a lawsuit and the ad was quickly withdrawn.[82]

Criticizing those "'inerrantists,' who think that every word in the Bible, preferably the King James, is literally true," Carter turned his attention toward his own Southern Baptist Convention in the year 2000.[83] He especially disliked the new "Baptist Faith and Message" statement issued that year,[84] since in his judgment it opened the way for the ongoing rise of fundamentalists within the denomination that had been occurring since 1979 when the leadership of the SBC had changed significantly.[85] Naturally, there had been disagreements between the president and his denomination throughout the years, but the last straw for Carter came when these same Southern Baptist leaders in 2000 made a decision, in the estimation of the former president, not only "to remove Jesus Christ, through his words, deeds and personal inspiration, as the ultimate interpreter of the Holy Scriptures,"[86] a move that he claimed left pastors or church officials as the ultimate authority, but also, to use his own words, "to increase prejudicial attitudes based on gender."[87] Deeply annoyed on both counts, Carter bolted from the denomination in October of that year, severing a relationship that had existed for over seventy years.

Free from his SBC denominational ties, Carter spoke out more acerbically, not simply in terms of conservative Christians but also with respect to the church in general. Holding up Washington politicians as exemplars of conscience and social justice, the former president observed, "the ma-

---

[80]Ibid., p. 35.
[81]Freedman, "The Religious Right," p. 257.
[82]Ibid.
[83]Carter, *Living Faith*, p. 197.
[84]Carter, *Our Endangered Values*, p. 41.
[85]Carter, *Living Faith*, p. 34.
[86]Jimmy Carter, cited in Greg Warner, "Jimmy Carter Says He Can 'No Longer Be Associated' with the SBC," *Baptist Standard*, www.baptiststandard.com/2000/10_23/pages/carter.html.
[87]Carter, *Our Endangered Values*, p. 90.

jority of church members are more self-satisfied, more committed to the status quo, and more exclusive of non-similar people than are most political office holders I have known."[88] Again, in a comparison between politicians of the day and members of the body of Christ, in Carter's estimation the office holders always came out on top: "it is often government, and not the Christian churches, that is in the forefront of the struggle to 'bring good news to the poor, to proclaim freedom for the prisoners, recovery of sight for the blind, and to release the oppressed.'"[89] And yet when Carter considered these very same politicians and what they had done to combat poverty and disease around the world, he could only conclude that America is "the stingiest country on earth."[90]

Three of Carter's strongly held views led to ongoing difficulties with conservative Christians. First, though many evangelicals, Southern Baptists in particular, favor the notion of separation of church and state, they do so principally in order to protect the integrity of the church. Such a view has a rich heritage going back to the teaching of Roger Williams (c. 1603-1683) in early America. The problem, however, is that many evangelicals view Carter as adhering to this teaching not so much to protect the church as to safeguard the state. Indeed, though many of Carter's predecessors had extended an invitation to Billy Graham to conduct worship services in the White House as a courtesy in light of the overwhelming majority of Christians in the United States, Carter declined to offer this gesture, claiming it "would violate our concept of the church and state being kept separate."[91] With such a view in place, Carter naturally opposed prayer in schools (though most Americans favor this); he rejected the Packwood-Moynihan bill to provide tax credits for Americans to attend the schools of their own choice," and he even championed (during his first presidential election campaign) the taxation of church properties other than the church building itself.[92] For his part, President Ford rejected this last item as an unnecessary intrusion of the state. It "would place an undue financial hardship," he argued, "on al-

[88]Carter, *Living Faith*, p. 108.
[89]Ibid., pp. 107-8.
[90]Berggren, "I Had a Different Way," p. 55.
[91]Carter, *Living Faith*, pp. 129-30.
[92]Flowers, "President Jimmy Carter," p. 119.

ready hard-pressed church-sponsored institutions."[93]

Second, though Carter was personally opposed to abortion in most instances, he nevertheless took his obligation seriously as required by the oath of his office to support and defend the Constitution of the United States, an obligation that included, of course, enforcement of the decision of *Roe v. Wade*. Looking back on his tenure in office, Carter maintained that he "accepted [his] obligation to enforce the *Roe v. Wade* Supreme Court ruling, and at the same time attempted in every way possible to minimize the number of abortions."[94] The last part of that claim, however, was doubted by conservative Christians who noted not only the kind of federal appointments to the judiciary that Carter had made, as noted earlier, but also his elevation of Margaret "Midge" Costanza (1932-2010) to the office of special assistant for women's affairs, a well known pro-choice advocate. Here once again evangelicals and Roman Catholics were united around a salient social issue, for the complaints heard among the latter group often took the form that Costanza was "raucously pro-abortion."[95] Overall such policies and procedures enacted during the Carter administration were hardly the way to minimize the number of abortions.

Third, in a way similar to other evangelical-left leaders such as Wallis, Campolo and McLaren, Carter believes that conservative and moderate Christians have simply made too much of the issue of homosexuality. Admonishing, once again, the leadership of the SBC, Carter writes: "Leaders of the Southern Baptist Convention, for instance, have elevated homosexuality to a pinnacle of great importance among deviations from their increasingly narrow and rigid definition of the Christian faith."[96] And Carter referred to those in the 2004 presidential campaign who wanted to amend the U.S. Constitution to define marriage in terms of one man and one woman as "shrewd political demagogues."[97] Earlier he attempted to soften the sexual ethic of Jesus of Nazareth (no doubt attempting to make it more palpable to modern tastes and sensibilities) by employing an argument from silence, one of the weakest forms of reasoning: "homosexuality," he

---

[93]Ibid.
[94]Carter, *Our Endangered Values*, p. 72.
[95]Freedman, "Religious Right and Carter," p. 238.
[96]Carter, *Our Endangered Values*, p. 66.
[97]Ibid., p. 68.

writes, "was never mentioned by Jesus."[98] Setting up a tension between the Old Testament and the New that some biblical scholars would certainly find troubling, Carter adds, "It is much easier and more convenient for heterosexual Christians to attack homosexuals, based primarily on selected verses in the Old Testament."[99] But perhaps Carter should have recalled from his own experience (and interviews!) that the sexual ethic of Jesus was both lofty and challenging in its radical holiness, for even to look upon a woman with lust constituted adultery (Mt 5:28). Does anyone really doubt, then, the rigor of the sexual ethic of Jesus?

THE HOUSING CRISIS AS A CASE STUDY IN POLITICAL MISCHIEF AND CONFUSION

The recent housing boom and bust in the United States is a good window on some of the political policies advocated by the evangelical left in the name of social justice. For although this movement often defines itself in opposition to the Christian right, and sometimes in a very polarizing way, such a mindset is in reality a hindrance to a perceptive, factual and even-handed analysis of American social problems in general and the mortgage crisis in particular. For one thing, both Democrats and Republicans, liberals and conservatives, played important roles in disrupting the economic health of the nation. Therefore, partisan interpretations, whether from the left or the right, are only possible if one focuses on a particular time period (for example, the greed of Wall Street brokers at the turn of the millennium and afterward), and ignores significant contrary evidence.

During the early 1970s many cities in the United States developed more restrictive zoning laws to preserve open space and to keep their communities green. Galvanized by the arguments of Charles Reich in his book *The Greening of America*, several politicians in California, for instance, severely restricted the amount of land that could be used for home construction. The unintended consequence of this policy was to drive up home prices in the state to some of the highest in the nation. This scenario was repeated in several other states until finally Congress declared that a national housing crisis existed. But members of the House and Senate put a new spin on the

---

[98]Carter, *Living Faith*, p. 187.
[99]Ibid.

story and contended that the free market had failed to produce affordable housing. Such a claim became the grounds for government intervention, and the Community Reinvestment Act was passed in 1977, during the Carter administration. This Act, championed by the president, effectively made the housing problem a political matter, and the identity politics of the day soon became the major script to deal with the "crisis."

In the hands of federal bureaucrats the Community Reinvestment Act eventually became a prescription for all sorts of political and economic mischief. To illustrate, the Act stipulated that federal supervisory agencies should encourage banks to meet the credit needs of the communities in which they serve, especially in terms of low and moderate income borrowers, a policy that the evangelical left has favored. Over the course of decades, however, into the 1980s and 1990s these same federal agencies began to pressure the banks to make loans (with all sorts of incentives and disincentives) that were not economically sound. "Members of Congress from both political parties," Thomas Sowell points out, "have urged federal regulatory agencies to press banks and other lenders to lower mortgage loan requirements."[100] In other words, not financial viability but compliance with the CRA itself was the standard that federal officials used to determine whether a bank could open a new branch or even add ATM machines. This leverage as well as the political pressure faced by the banks were enormous, and many of them simply caved in and started to make risky subprime loans. In short, a government initiated policy of forcing financial institutions to meet arbitrary quotas based on the low income status of perspective borrowers (a financial affirmative action program, if you will) eroded "traditional mortgage lending safeguards," with inevitable results.[101]

The problem with playing politics in terms of the housing industry is that the rules of the game, so to speak, remain in force despite the quotas or the determination on the part of the government to bring about *equality* of results. Thus, in terms of all the subprime loans that were made in the past three decades, the borrowers still faced the normal rules of making monthly payments and forfeiting the house if those payments stopped

---

[100]Thomas Sowell, *The Housing Boom and Bust* (New York: Basic Books, 2009), p. 30.
[101]Ibid., p. 44.

coming. Given this ongoing reality, it may have been a cruel injustice to these borrowers to be offered these loans in the first place. Sowell, an African American, considers the damage that was done to his own people by well-meaning though misguided politicians:

> How much any of this actually helped blacks is another question entirely. Being granted loans because the bank needs to meet statistical targets— quotas—in order to keep federal agencies off their backs, rather than because you are likely to be able to repay the loans, is not unequivocally a benefit to the borrower.[102]

Well-to-do speculators added to the mortgage crisis once Alan Greenspan, chairman of the Federal Reserve Bank, reduced interest rates to near record lows in 2004. Not only did investors buy up housing with the hopes of selling it a few years later in order to turn a handsome profit (flipping), but they also invested in risky financial instruments that were being marketed internationally but whose value was tied to American subprime mortgages. This was the Wall Street phase of the housing boom and bust, and it had much to do with the financial collapse in 2008. In other words, not simply misguided financial policy, driven by the identity politics so favored by the left, but also good old-fashioned greed had precipitated the crisis. Therefore, polarizing or partisan accounts, here as elsewhere, do not even begin to grapple with the depth of the disorder that runs through several American institutions, many of which touch upon the topic of poverty.[103]

LEFTIST POLITICAL PHILOSOPHY AND THE MODERN DEMOCRATIC STATE

One of the principal difficulties with the approach of the evangelical left with respect to many of the leading issues of the day, whether it be housing, education or health care, is that it has failed to consider in a forth-

---

[102]Ibid., pp. 107-8.

[103]The political and governmental policies (especially the Community Reinvestment Act) have received the lion's share of attention here quite simply because they provided the wherewithal in terms of extremely risky mortgages that were subsequently packaged in various financial products once the Wall Street phase of this malaise set in. In other words, Wall Street was not the source of these unstable mortgages, though it intended to profit from them in speculative ways and thereby compound an *already* difficult problem.

right manner the nature of liberal democracies and how such governments can readily undermine the values of the faithful community. The historic liberal approach to governance, broadly speaking (not to be confused with the specific political ideology of liberalism as found for example in the Democratic Party), emerged in the eighteenth century in the philosophies of John Locke (1632-1704) and Adam Smith (1723-1790). Locke in particular was well aware of the strife in the civil order that can easily emerge in the wake of animated religious adherence, as all of this played out in the English Civil War (1642-1651). Seeking peace and good order in society, Locke articulated a political philosophy that not only underscored individual liberty but also attempted to avoid religious disputes on the national level. Indeed, it is something of a trick of political history that the classical term *liberal*, with its strong associations with freedom, has now come to mean "advocacy of almost every kind of government control."[104] This is to turn Locke or Thomas Jefferson, for that matter, on his head.

A newly developed expression of the nature of liberal democracies can be found in the writings of John Rawls (1921-2002), the late Harvard professor. Well aware of the challenge of pluralism to modern democracies, Rawls propounded a political philosophy in which no comprehensive doctrine (whether religious, philosophical or moral) would be allowed to emerge. In other words, at the level of national discussions citizens must set aside their moral and religious convictions and instead take on a "political conception of the person," that is, a standpoint "independent of any particular loyalties, attachments, or conception of the good life."[105] Only in this way Rawls reasoned can ongoing strife be avoided given the radically plural nature of modern democracies. Observe, however, that Rawls is not denying that comprehensive doctrines exist or that people hold them (belief in God, for example) but only that pluralistic democracies "cannot expect to reach a workable political agreement as to what it [a comprehensive doctrine] is."[106]

Though the work of Rawls aptly describes how American liberal de-

---

[104]Hayek, *Road to Serfdom*, p. 45.
[105]Michael J. Sandel, *Justice: What's the Right Thing to Do?* (New York: Farrar, Straus & Giroux, 2009), p. 248. Sandel's work includes one of the clearest expressions of the political philosophy of Rawls.
[106]John Rawls, *Justice as Fairness: A Restatement* (Cambridge, Mass.: Belknap, 2001), p. 84.

mocracy has come to be understood at least in modern times, it has unfortunately set limits to public reasoning, especially in the areas of morality and religion. Indeed, some cultural observers argue that the political philosophy of Rawls effectively renders people of faith second-class citizens simply because their own preferred ways of moral reasoning, informed by their love of God, can have no place in the public square. In other words, Democratic liberalism itself, retooled in the works of Rawls in an unacknowledged ideological way and richly informed by pluralism, has become the chief narrative of society such that religion has now become problematic. Such an understanding of democracy, however, clearly departs from the political wisdom of the founding fathers. Cromartie elaborates:

> The claim that the faith of American Christians should always be only an intensely private affair between the individual and God would have been surprising news to such diverse persons as John Winthrop, Jonathan Edwards, Abraham Lincoln, the abolitionist of slavery, fifteen generations of the black church, civil rights leaders, and antiwar activists.[107]

In championing the political conception of the self, Rawls has strengthened the argument for the privatization of religion in a way not dissimilar from the position of the American Civil Liberties Union when its lawyers argued before the Supreme Court that "religion is not a civil function or a public matter."[108] Those who take on the political conception of the self in the public arena are now emboldened to look upon religion as an intrusion and its adherents, if they refuse to drop their moral and religious reasoning, as intolerant. However, in an ironic twist Jean Bethke Elshtain points out that "to tell political and religious believers to shut up for they will interfere with my rights by definition, simply by speaking out, is an intolerant idea."[109] Putting forth a much different perspective than Rawls, Michael Novak maintained that the pluralistic structures of modern capitalist societies

---

[107]Michael Cromartie, "The Evangelical Kaleidoscope: A Survey of Recent Evangelical Political Engagement," in *Christians and Politics Beyond the Culture Wars*, ed. David P. Gushee (Grand Rapids: Baker, 2000), p. 27.

[108]Martin E. Marty, *Modern American Religion: The Noise of Conflict 1919-1941* (Chicago: University of Chicago Press, 1991), 2:211.

[109]Jean Bethke Elshtain, "Religion and American Democracy," in *Christians and Politics Beyond the Culture Wars*, ed. David P. Gushee (Grand Rapids: Baker, 2000), p. 74.

must be "checked by a political and a moral-cultural system."[110]

Since, in the view of Rawls, no comprehensive doctrine is permitted, whether moral or religious, this means that individuals are free to pursue what goods they deem to be worthy of their attention. "It is left to citizens individually as part of their liberty of conscience," Rawls notes, "to settle how they think the great values of the political domain are related to the other values they accept."[111] Or as Ronald Dworkin has put it, "the central doctrine of modern liberalism is the thesis that questions about the *good life* for [humanity] or the ends of human life are to be regarded from the public standpoint as systematically unsettlable."[112] So, then, in the absence of any overarching goal or purpose in democratic, pluralistic societies (the loss of teleology), citizens are free to define the good life as they see fit. What is lost in such an understanding, however, is not simply the recognition of a few, basic common goals that are in accordance with the dignity of human existence but also what virtues would lead to such goals. As such men and women are free to pursue a diversity of lifestyles and to discard them just as quickly, like last year's clothes.

With a political conception of what is appropriate in play and with questions of moral desert, moral worth and even virtue bracketed out in the name of democratic pluralism, no rational moral defense can be offered for the lifestyles that people invariably choose other than the popularity of such, an element that can be translated into raw political power. In other words, to neglect in some sense what traditional societies have considered the normal constraints on personal liberty, such as "religion, morality, law, family, and community,"[113] for the sake of public peace or what some call political expediency may come at a very high price. Neglecting the counsels of prudential reasoning, a democratic society so conceived will no doubt be made up of many people who will pursue what "goods" are championed by the culture (press, media and films) but that in the end, after sorrowful and painful experience, are revealed to be not real goods at all but simply apparent ones. In other words, there are no sound moral

---

[110]Michael Novak, *The Spirit of Democratic Capitalism* (New York: Touchstone, 1982), p. 15.

[111]Rawls, *Justice as Fairness*, p. 190.

[112]Ronald Dworkin, cited in Alasdair MacIntyre, *After Virtue*, 3rd ed. (Notre Dame, Ind.: University of Notre Dame Press, 2007), p. 119.

[113]Bork, *Slouching Towards Gomorrah*, p. 61.

reasons that inform particular lifestyle choices or behaviors at the highest level in democratic societies. All such choices and behaviors are simply the expression of *preferences*—a state of affairs that moral philosophers refer to as "emotivism."[114] Such an approach not only undermines the very basis for genuine community (a point readily conceded by Rawls) but it also results in radical individualism.[115]

WHERE THE EVANGELICAL LEFT FALTERS

When the evangelical left reflects on the two culturally significant issues of abortion and human sexuality, it appears that it draws not simply from the resources of its own comprehensive doctrine of biblical faith but also from a liberal understanding of a modern democracy in which its own comprehensive doctrine is rendered somewhat ineffective in terms of sound, prudential guidance as to what form a human life should take. Put another way, the substance of who Jesus Christ is, as an ever-present Lord and moral guide, is deflected, at least in some sense, by careful attention to the individualistic liberty that is so valued by modern democracies as expressed in the key political value of tolerance, or what some on the evangelical left have called "generosity." Indeed, the mixing of frameworks, the going back and forth between a comprehensive doctrine that celebrates religious faith and a public order that silences its very voice in the name of individualistic liberty, diversity and tolerance is confusing at times. Simply put, you cannot slap the name of Jesus on top of political and social policy that in the end is aiming at little other than the political conception of self, in which teleology and the virtues have been effectively discarded, and then call it Christian.

For one thing, the evangelical left has failed to see just how oppressive liberal democracies as defined by Rawls (and others) can be to people of faith and just what clashes are virtually inevitable. Though Rawls, for example, liked to claim that the political conception of self (in which comprehensive doctrines are repudiated at the national level) would lead to a peaceful and orderly society in the face of rampant diversity, he failed to realize that in the end the touted political value of tolerance may itself

---

[114]MacIntyre, *After Virtue*, p. 12.
[115]Rawls, *Justice as Fairness*, p. 3.

become problematic. In other words, in a move marked by irony and riddled with contradictions, the political conception of self and its associated value of tolerance will in time *become* the overarching narrative of the culture, with oppressive results. Indeed, the consequence of this move, as Rawls himself admitted, was that "political values, that under . . . reasonably favorable conditions . . . make democracy possible, normally outweigh *whatever* values oppose them."[116]

Thus, if a group in a modern liberal society is engaging in a practice or a lifestyle that the Christian community finds deeply offensive, given its own pursuit of the good, then all the coercive power of the state may be employed in the very names of tolerance and diversity to insure acquiescence or even acceptance by the church. In other words, the political conception of the self in the end becomes a comprehensive doctrine. The state, as with nature, abhors a vacuum. To illustrate, in 2006 the state of Massachusetts ordered Catholic Charities (with its long history of charitable work) to place children in the homes of same-sex couples, who claimed that they were entitled to be a family just like heterosexual couples. Catholic Charities refused this request since it violated basic moral principles articulated by its theologians going back millennia. The state of Massachusetts, however, was not impressed with the reply of the Catholic Church and therefore began to issue threats. Caught precisely in the clash of values that Rawls had not properly envisioned in his own theoretical work, Catholic Charities had little choice but to close its doors.[117] So much for the liberal idea that individuals and groups should be free to pursue what goods or values they themselves choose. And the evangelical left was largely silent.

The Manhattan Declaration

But not all evangelicals remained silent. Indeed, several leaders such as Timothy George and J. I. Packer came together with fourteen Roman

---

[116]Ibid., p. 194.

[117]Most recently the Obama administration sought to require church-affiliated institutions to include free birth control in their insurance packages for employees. Several U.S. Catholic bishops decried these bureaucratic procedures as an unnecessary government intrusion into the life of religious institutions. See editor, "Obama Decision on Birth Control Sparks Battle with U.S. Bishops," *Church and State* 65, no. 3 (March 2012): p. 17.

Catholic bishops and a couple of Eastern Orthodox bishops to stand up and be counted against this and other intrusions by a liberal democratic state. They therefore issued the Manhattan Declaration in 2009, a carefully crafted and well-balanced document richly informed by the moral principles of Scripture, human reason and natural law.[118] Ron Sider made it clear during the initial promulgation of the Declaration that it was neither "partisan," nor a "political ploy."[119] Instead, it sought to bring together all people, regardless of political persuasion, in order to protect the intrinsic dignity of a human being and to stand for the common good.[120] Along these lines, the crafters of this document wisely appealed to the work of John Wesley in the eighteenth century, as this noted evangelical employed the normative power of the natural law in his own efforts to abolish the vicious practice of the slave trade and to insure that men and women enjoy those goods, liberty among them, that pertain to all human beings.[121]

The Manhattan Declaration focused on three areas of concern in which the actions of liberal democratic states have proved to be especially troubling of late: abortion, marriage and religious liberty. In terms of the first concern, abortion, the authors of the document explored both the positive and negative aspects of this prominent cultural issue. That is, these leaders underscored on the one hand the value of fostering a culture of life such that the appropriate response to problem pregnancies "is for all of us to love and care for mother and child alike," while on the other hand they revealed their resolve to be "united and untiring in our efforts to roll back the license to kill that began with the abandonment of the unborn to abortion." Rightly noting that many in the Obama administration "want to make abortions legal at any stage of fetal development," the signers of this Declaration continued to seek to put in place appropriate policies that will protect the very least of all.[122]

Marked by openness to correction and deep humility, these same advo-

---

[118]"Manhattan Declaration: A Call of Christian Conscience," Manhattan Declaration.org, October 20, 2009, www.manhattandeclaration.org/home.aspx.

[119]"Catholics Join Evangelicals to Resist Abortion, Gay Marriage," *National Catholic Reporter* 46, no. 4 (2009): 13.

[120]"Manhattan Declaration."

[121]For more on the issue of Wesley's efforts against slavery see Kenneth J. Collins, *John Wesley: A Theological Journey* (Nashville: Abingdon, 2003), pp. 209-10.

[122]"Manhattan Declaration."

cates confessed with respect to the second issue of marriage that Christians as well as their institutions "have too often scandalously failed to uphold the institution of marriage and to model for the world the true meaning of marriage."[123] Evangelical sexual scandals at the national level have been especially troubling: from Jim Bakker to Jimmy Swaggart and on to Ted Haggard. In fact, virtually all of the demographic evidence indicates that the church has been inordinately influenced by the dysfunctional, relationship-destroying attitudes and practices that hail from the sexual revolution of the 1960s. Not surprisingly, the divorce rates among Christians are little different from those of the broader American population. It is therefore difficult in this area to gather up the moral capital necessary to offer a strong prophetic word. Nevertheless, mindful of the personal and social malaise left in the wake of culturally championed aberrant sexual behaviors, promiscuity and infidelity among them, this coalition of concerned religious leaders believed it was necessary to challenge the erosion of the marriage culture with its out-of-wedlock birth rate hovering at around 40 percent.[124] Beyond this, the signers of the Manhattan declaration challenged the popular cultural tendency of modern democracies to revision basic, longstanding institutions—such as marriage—and to reconfigure them abruptly in terms of the likes and dislikes of various populations within the culture whose chief argument for such radical change, by the way, is little more than some form of emotivism or political pressure.

In terms of the third concern of religious liberty there have been a number of distressing cases of late whereby cultural expectations, fostered by a liberal democratic state, are in the end inimical to the religious freedoms of physicians and even clergy. Archbishop Justin Rigali of Philadelphia, for example, has pointed out the overweening expectations and the resultant pressure that doctors often feel to toe the line, so to speak, and to perform abortions despite their own significant moral and religious objections.[125] Moreover, in New Jersey a Methodist institution was stripped of its tax exempt status simply because its minister refused to have the facility

---

[123]Ibid.
[124]Ibid.
[125]"Catholics Join Evangelicals," p. 13.

used for "ceremonies blessing homosexual unions."[126] Elsewhere in Canada and Europe, as indicated in the Manhattan Declaration, Christian clergy have been dragged into court "for preaching biblical norms against the practice of homosexuality."[127] In short, the signers of the declaration perceived an abuse of power by the state, inching toward nothing less than tyranny, as it employed "anti-discrimination statutes to force religious institutions, businesses and service providers of various sorts to comply with activities they judge to be deeply immoral or go out of business."[128]

Precisely because it contains a bold, prophetic word, especially in that it refuses to be swept away by popular, though vice-inducing cultural trends, the Manhattan Declaration has been greeted by both cheers and jeers alike. In terms of the former, in an important article in *Touchstone* James Mark Kushiner lauded the document in its goal of protecting communities, associations and churches, and their right to enjoy religious freedom as well as to maintain "long-held views about . . . marriage," such that they are not "coerced to adopt the new views of the secular state."[129] Others, however, were less impressed. Rob Boston, for example, assistant director of communications for Americans United for Separation of Church and State, and a board member of the American Humanist Association, opined: "Let's face it, we're a far cry from medieval Spain—and that really, really bothers the signers of the Manhattan Declaration." Offering more of an expression of personal dissatisfaction than anything else, Boston caricatured the reflections of the signers of the Declaration in the following way: "We're right about religion, so you have to do what we say. Yawn."[130]

Remarkably enough, key leaders of the evangelical left, such as Wallis, Campolo, McLaren and Carter, have not signed the document to date. In fact, McLaren in a piece in *Sojourners* actually sought to undermine the whole effort in his loose, amorphous and largely idiosyncratic way. With all the moral force he could muster, McLaren repeatedly complained, "Nobody *I've* ever met likes abortion. . . . Nobody *I've* ever wants to

---

[126]"Manhattan Declaration."
[127]Ibid.
[128]Ibid.
[129]James Mark Kushiner, "Where We Stand," *Touchstone* 23, no. 1 (2010): 3.
[130]Rob Boston, "Of Declarations and Tea Parties: A New Birth for the Religious Right," *Church and State* 70, no. 2 (2010): 30.

weaken the institution of marriage. . . . Nobody *I've* ever met wants to deny the basic freedoms of speech, conscience or religious faith."[131] Many others, of course, disagreed. At any rate, without an appeal to sound moral principles either culled from Scripture or derived from moral and natural law (more on this in chapter six) or without even the use of much reasoned argumentation, in the end all that McLaren had to offer his readers was his own deeply held opinion that "extending marriage to gay and lesbian couples would strengthen, not weaken, marriage as a desirable and socially respected way of life."[132] But perhaps, just perhaps, McLaren as with others of the evangelical left have confused the bromides of a liberal democratic state in its supposed lack of a comprehensive doctrine (though the reality is actually quite different) and in its inattentiveness to the requisites of human nature (a consideration of which would lead to genuine flourishing), with the precepts of the gospel itself.

THE EVANGELICAL LEFT AND POLITICAL SOLUTIONS

Beyond the cultural accommodation of the evangelical left, as the narrative of liberal democracies is at times exchanged back and forth with the story of the gospel, a second major problem emerges as this same political and religious community thinks about social justice. Just as in chapter three we explored the weaknesses of the religious right in terms of its own social and political policy by drawing from MacIntyre's description of what we called "persons A," so too must we now consider the shortcomings of the evangelical left by employing MacIntyre's description of "persons B."[133] However, first recall the criticism of the religious right cited earlier:

> [Person] A holds that principles of just acquisition and entitlement set limits to redistributive possibilities. If the outcome of the application of the principles of just acquisition and entitlement is gross inequality, the toleration of such inequality is a price that has to be paid for justice.[134]

---

[131]Brian McLaren, "Can We Talk? The Manhattan Declaration's Harder Challenge," *Sojourners* 39, no. 3 (2010): 13 (emphasis added).

[132]Ibid.

[133]McIntyre actually uses the designation of "A" and "B." I have personalized this typology through the employment of "person A" and "person B." See McIntyre, *After Virtue*, p. 245.

[134]Ibid., p. 245.

The difficulty in this view is that those who hold it are often heedless with respect to the enormous human suffering, at times leading to impoverishment, even death, that is left in the wake of libertarianism or meritocracies played out, for example, in freewheeling capitalism. The right of acquisition, in other words, cannot be an absolute one, nor can it edge out other equally important considerations especially when the wealthy will not freely take on their social responsibilities and duties in terms of the less fortunate. Put another way, it is simply unacceptable for the good and just society to sit back and do little or nothing while the rich contemplate, for example, what trim they will purchase for their yachts while children in America are both malnourished and suffer for lack of decent medical care.

The ongoing problems of the evangelical left with respect to social justice are therefore much different from this preceding description, to be sure, but no less troubling. Such shortcomings, and they are numerous, can be clearly seen in MacIntyre's following portrayal of "persons B":

> [Person] B holds that principles of just distribution set limits to legitimate acquisition and entitlement. If the outcome of the application of the principles of just distribution is interference . . . with what has up till now been regarded in this social order as legitimate acquisition and entitlement, the toleration of such interference is a price that has to be paid for justice.[135]

On one level, social justice as conceived through the eyes of persons B, especially as they take into account the needs of all, especially the poor, is a viable and reasonable way of moral reflection. So construed this perspective takes into account precisely those social and political elements often neglected by persons A. Nevertheless, difficulties remain. One problem, for example, is that equality of results has been so emphasized in this view that other factors, such as moral worth, merit and achievement, have all been minimized if not outright repudiated. In his own economic and political ethic, in particular his labor theory of appropriation, John Locke wrote about the value of mixing labor with a product, an action that in turn led to increasing claims of entitlement whereby common property would soon become private property. From the perspective of persons B, however, whatever rights to private property emerge would have to be im-

---

[135]Ibid.

mediately limited in accordance with one's basic needs, and a little more, so long as inequality in the broader society remained.

Second, social justice as conceived by persons B not only uses entire classes of people as a *means* to politically expedient ends but it also strips these same classes of some of the social goods (such as money, status and promotions) that they have legitimately earned through the exercise of talent and significant effort, giving them instead to others who have not earned them. This practice, though touted by the political left, the evangelical left among them, often leads to mediocrity on the social level, as well as to the wasting of numerous gifts and talents that should be employed for the larger good of society. There is, after all, a sense in which the "best and the brightest" are to be preferred, without of course neglecting the poor, since the genuinely gifted will bless the larger society in so many ways. Simply put, if you suppress the talented few or inhibit them in the name of social justice you will invariably hurt all.

Third, impressed with the "arbitrariness of the inequalities in the distribution of wealth," whether through inheritance, the application of intellectual talent or a character marked by abundant discipline, persons B want to set limits to what inequalities will naturally emerge in society by enhancing the powers of the state.[136] Therefore, persons B favor redistributive taxation (the managing of tax dollars of which Campolo wrote[137]) to "finance welfare and social services" with the goal of bringing about greater equality.[138] However, since in this view the state has been greatly empowered to bring into being a conception of social justice required by a particular political philosophy not shared by all in the society, then the possibility of oppression or outright tyranny is great. As one social commentator put it, an "enormous bureaucratic despotism . . . would be required to enforce that principle" of justice.[139]

In light of the preceding, just as the *right of acquisition* cannot be the nearly exclusive consideration with respect to the perspective of persons A, so too the *right of redistribution* cannot be a nearly absolute one in terms

[136]Ibid.
[137]Tony Campolo, *Red Letter Christians: A Citizen's Guide to Faith and Politics* (Ventura, Calif.: Regal, 2008), pp. 156-7.
[138]MacIntyre, *After Virtue*, p. 245.
[139]Bork, *Slouching Towards Gomorrah*, p. 79.

of persons B, for it violates basic concepts of fairness that render to persons their due in accordance with what they have achieved or earned, precisely what persons A so clearly see. When this move occurs, when evangelicalism is confused with leftist politics, then other evangelicals who hold different, though no less valuable, views on social and economic justice will only feel alienated in such an evangelical church. And so *as I have already indicated in terms of the evangelical right* in chapter three, so too I now point out with respect to the evangelical left: Here a particular political and economic ideology runs the risk of displacing in some important ways the universal nature of the gospel. And though the evangelical left likes to paint its thought and practices as the coming of the kingdom of God, as money and social goods are redistributed, and though it in some sense speaks with the voice of Jesus as a vibrant Christian community, the good news of Jesus Christ is far greater than any political ideology; its vision is far more extensive than the insights of the Democratic Party.

6

Beyond Ideology

The Renewal of Catholicity and the Challenges
of a Modern, Liberal Democratic State

BY 2008 THE EVANGELICAL LEFT ALREADY BEWAILED what political power the Christian right had amassed during the administration of George W. Bush, and the movement continued to define itself in a contrarian way with respect to conservative groups such as the now weakened Christian Coalition. With hope for change in the offing, Jim Wallis employed a strategy that he had tried earlier, and not only announced that the Christian right was dead (was this more the expression of a desire than a reality?) but also that his particular brand of leftist politics was nothing less than the movement of God upon the nation, giving evidence of what he called "a great awakening."[1] Indeed, the title of his recently published book during this election year says it all: *The Great Awakening: Reviving Faith and Politics in a Post-Religious Right America*.

Actually at the beginning of this presidential year the outlook did not look very promising for the evangelical left. Granted it had made some headway with its ongoing criticism of the war in Iraq, especially since most Americans had by now grown weary of the conflict, but it continued to struggle for a greater share of the evangelical audience, only to find that

---

[1]See Jim Wallis, *The Great Awakening: Reviving Faith and Politics in a Post-Religious Right America* (New York: HarperOne, 2008).

many young people, college students in particular, had already learned how to spell the word *Republican*. And when at times the evangelical left broke out of its oppositional rhetoric ("please don't mistake us for the Christian right") to articulate its own positive program, many began to wonder how enhancing the powers of the state would usher in the kingdom as promised. Indeed, the evangelical left chaffed under the on-going reality that when most Americans outside the evangelical community thought about born again Protestants and what they stood for (both politically and religiously) they hardly had the names of Wallis, Campolo, McLaren or even Carter in mind. Back in early 2008 the fortunes of this wing of evangelicalism were never as bright as its own spin doctors had imagined. But all of this was about to change.

THE RISE OF BARACK OBAMA

While still serving the thirteenth district in the Illinois Senate in July 2004, Barack Obama was tapped to be the keynote speaker at the Democratic Convention in Boston. Bright, articulate and poised, Obama thundered from the podium, "We worship an awesome God in the Blue States."[2] Attempting to bring the values of religious faith back into a conversation that had gone flat during John Kerry's primary campaign, Obama reassured the delegates that evening that "Those of us on the political left . . . trust that big government can be a tool of righteousness—we also love God."[3] The crowed roared in approval.

Many evangelicals were surprised, and some were outright stunned, by this engaging speaker from the state senate in Illinois. Growing up in churches that had become overly identified with the Republican Party, they had been schooled on the notion that Democrats simply do not appeal to faith in the national arena. At first glance, when evangelicals looked at Obama back in 2004 they saw much with which they could identify. The Harvard Law School graduate had claimed in an unabashed way, for example, that he had "a personal relationship with Jesus Christ."[4]

[2]Barack Obama, cited in Stephen Mansfield, *The Faith of Barack Obama* (Nashville: Thomas Nelson 2008), p. xiv.
[3]Ibid., p. xv.
[4]Ibid., p. 50.

Chronicling what many evangelicals would likely identify as a conversion narrative, Obama revealed that he needed "a vessel for [his] beliefs,"[5] throwing off his mother's agnostic/atheistic views, and so he knelt beneath a cross on the South Side of Chicago during the mid 1980s and submitted his life to Jesus Christ: "I felt God's spirit beckoning me," he noted, "I submitted myself to His will, and dedicated myself to discovering His truth."[6] Beyond this, the language of Scripture flowed easily from Obama's lips, even when he ran for the U.S. Senate seat in Illinois in 2004, and Cal Thomas, the popular evangelical journalist, opined that "Obama is better at biblical language and imagery than any Democrat in modern times."[7] But then the noted columnist wryly added that perhaps this was not such a significant achievement after all, given that Howard Dean, who eventually became the chairman of the Democratic National Committee, had lowered the bar considerably by identifying Job "as his favorite New Testament book."[8]

A couple of years later, the junior Senator from the state of Illinois (Obama had won his election in 2004) published a popular call to action in his *The Audacity of Hope*. The title of this book was taken from a key sermon preached by the controversial Reverend Jeremiah Wright in Chicago during the 1980s. In this work, Obama—now very much a national figure—gave expression to the hopes and aspirations of so many evangelicals when he declared, "Surely, secularists are wrong when they ask believers to leave their religion at the door before entering the public square."[9] And Obama drove home his point from the pages of American history that included the voices of a former slave, a war-torn president, an evangelical reformer, a Roman Catholic activist, and a civil rights leader straight out of the black church: "Frederick Douglass, Abraham Lincoln, William Jennings Bryan, Dorothy Day, Martin Luther King Jr.," he pointed out"—indeed, the majority of great reformers in American history—not only were motivated by faith but repeatedly used religious

---

[5]Barack Obama, *The Audacity of Hope: Thoughts on Reclaiming the American Dream* (New York: Three Rivers Press, 2006), p. 206.
[6]Ibid., p. 208.
[7]Cal Thomas, "Obama Is No Joshua," *Human Events* 64, no. 21 (2008): 501.
[8]Ibid.
[9]Obama, *Audacity of Hope*, p. 218.

language to argue their causes."[10] Moreover, in this same account Obama stressed the importance of talking to average Americans whereby one would quickly learn that "most evangelicals are more tolerant than the media would have us believe."[11] Indeed, Ron Sider later pointed out that Obama "understands evangelicals better than any Democrat since Carter."[12]

When Barack Obama won the presidency in 2008 not only did he invite the popular evangelical leader the Reverend Rick Warren to deliver the prayer at the inaugural ceremony, but upon taking office he also continued a Bush initiative (though it was somewhat modified) and established the White House Office of Faith-Based and Neighborhood Partnerships, to the chagrin, by the way, of the secular left in his own party. The task of this partnership was to help "religious groups get federal dollars for social service projects for the needy."[13] Undeterred by this opposition, Obama chose Joshua DuBois, a twenty-six-year-old campaign worker and engaging Pentecostal minister, to head up the project.[14] In order to strengthen further his ties to the religious community, Obama also put together a spiritual cabinet, so to speak, a group of religious leaders that would advise him on occasion, including Denis McDonough, Joshua DuBois, Rashad Hussain, Melissa Rogers, Joel Hunter, Sharon Watkins and Lt. Carey Cash.[15] Who was this man who seemed to be so gifted and so religious? Evangelicals, as with most Americans, eagerly wanted to know.

Many cultural observers and political analysts, from essayists to bloggers, from newspaper reporters to authors, did indeed do their homework and took a closer look at this leader from Chicago. Several evangelicals, especially moderates and those from the Christian right, apparently did not like what they soon discovered. Upon closer examination it was revealed that perhaps many had mistaken the nature of Obama's earlier conversion, after all, since he subsequently claimed "that there are

---

[10]Ibid., p. 218.
[11]Ibid., p. 51.
[12]Ron Sider, cited in John Kennedy, "The Faith Factor," *Christianity Today*, October 2008, p. 28.
[13]Dan Gilgoff, "A New Role for Religion," *US News and World Report*, June 2009, pp. 45-46.
[14]Joseph Conn, "Civil Rights and Civil Liberties," *Church and State* 62, no. 3 (2009): 4.
[15]Ibid.

many paths to the same place."[16] And when he was pressed with the specific issue of the exclusivity of the Christian claim in terms of Jesus Christ ("I am the way and the truth and the life. No one comes to the Father except through me" [Jn 14:6 NIV]), Obama glibly retorted, "This is only a particular verse."[17] Indeed, in a telling autobiographical account Obama related that as he was growing up, his household (no doubt reflecting his mother's amorphous and eclectic interests) contained many Scriptures drawn from several different faiths: "The Bible, the Koran, and the Bhagavad Gita sat on the shelf alongside books of Greek and Norse and African mythology."[18] In addition, the way that Obama interpreted the Bible left some in doubt about his basic approach (his hermeneutic) to Scripture: "When I read the Bible, " he observed, "I do so with the belief that it is not a static text but the Living Word and that *I must be continually open to new revelations*—whether they come from a lesbian or a doctor opposed to abortion."[19]

In addition to these difficulties, many Americans, not simply evangelicals, were stunned to learn just how radical Obama's views were on the topic of abortion. Back in 2002 when he was a member of the Illinois senate, Obama had voted against the Induced Infant Liability Act, a piece of legislation that would have required medical care for those babies that *survive* abortion. In other words, these infants would be given the same medical treatment and human concern as those who were born prematurely.[20] Later when he became a U.S. Senator, Obama voted against similar legislation at the federal level (The Born-Alive Infants Protection Act) even though NARAL (National Abortion and Reproductive Rights Action League) established in 1969 in the midst of the sexual revolution had no objection to such bills.[21] Without appropriate legal protections in place these babies that survived abortion would "be exposed and left to die."[22] So then, in his views on this controversial topic Obama had outdone

---

[16]Mansfield, *Faith of Barack Obama*, p. 55.
[17]Ibid., p. 57.
[18]Obama, *Audacity of Hope*, p. 203.
[19]Ibid., p. 224 (emphasis added).
[20]Mansfield, *Faith of Barack Obama*, p. 96.
[21]Ibid., p. 97.
[22]Ibid., p. 98.

even one of the most radical abortion groups in the nation. Not surprisingly, he declared that one of his first acts as president would be to sign the Freedom of Choice Act, which would "again legalize partial-birth abortions and would use tax funds to pay for abortions."[23]

Conservative Roman Catholics were by now deeply offended as well, and so when Obama gave the commencement address at Notre Dame in the spring of 2009, some students protested and seventy bishops spoke out against extending the invitation to one who held such morally troubling views. Beyond this, some moderate and conservative evangelicals began to wonder if Obama's pronouncements on politics and religion were carefully thought out after all, but actually represented at times an unthinking rhetorical flourish in which the values compared were clearly mismatched. In his *Audacity of Hope*, for instance, Obama remarked, "But our democracy might work a bit better . . . if conservatives recognized that most women feel as protective of their right to reproductive freedom as evangelicals do of their right to worship."[24]

The American electorate became more keenly aware of Obama's political and economic views through a gaffe that had occurred while the candidate was campaigning in the swing state of Ohio in 2008. Engaging in small talk with Joe ("the plumber") Wurzelbacher, Obama remarked, "It's not that I want to punish your success. I want to make sure that everybody who is behind you, that they've got a chance for success, too."[25] And then he added, "I think when you spread the wealth around, it's good for everybody."[26] This last comment was immediately picked up by some political commentators around the country, who had a virtual field day criticizing the presidential candidate for his failure to recognize that just acquisition, especially in the form of hard work, sacrifice and significant achievement, should indeed set some limits to any government program of redistribution (though Obama had mentioned none), and that politicians who champion such plans of giving the resources of some to others (who have not worked for them) are often ideologically driven, ever with an eye

---

[23]Kennedy, "Faith Factor," p. 28.
[24]Obama, *Audacity of Hope*, p. 57.
[25]Tommy Newberry, *The War on Success: How the Obama Agenda Is Shattering the American Dream* (Washington, D.C.: Regnery, 2010), p. 60.
[26]Ibid.

on a slice of the electorate that is all too eager to keep them in office.[27] Granted some form of redistribution must occur in any society to help those who fall through the gaps of the particular economic system, and some forms of sharing the wealth can indeed be morally justified. Obama's problem, however, was that this approach seemed to be the only card in his deck. Indeed, on the campaign trail he repeatedly pointed out the causes of poverty (as well as his plans to solve them), but he rarely indicated what are the causes of wealth. In the end both concerns, however, warrant attention in any balanced political posture.

Schooled in the economic theory of John Maynard Keynes, the British economist who argued that government must intervene in the private sector to regulate some of the inefficient outcomes of modern capitalist societies, Obama maintained in his own writings that "an active national government has also been indispensable in dealing with market failures—those recurring snags in any capitalist system that either inhibit the efficient workings of the market or result in harm to the public."[28] Looking to Franklin Delano Roosevelt in some sense as his economic and political mentor, Obama argued that the thirty-second president had actually saved capitalism from itself "through an activist federal government that invests in its people and infrastructure, regulates the marketplace, and protects labor from chronic deprivation."[29] Such views, according to political moderates, conservatives and some independents, turned back the economic and political clock to the days prior to Bill Clinton, who in his State of the Union address back in 1996 had proclaimed "the era of big government is over."[30]

Throughout his first term in office, Obama repeatedly championed the merits of a large, activist government whereby bureaucrats would regulate the marketplace (some of whom, by the way, understood very little about business) rather then let the numerous free choices of Americans in exercising their buying power determine what shape markets would in fact

---

[27]See Alasdair MacIntyre, *After Virtue*, 3rd ed. (Notre Dame, Ind.: University of Notre Dame Press, 2007), p. 245

[28]Obama, *Audacity of Hope*, p. 153.

[29]Ibid., p. 155.

[30]Rick Perlstein, "A New New Deal," *New York Times*, January 25, 2004, www.nytimes.com/2004/01/25/books/a-new-new-deal.html?scp=15&sq=rick+perlstein&st=nyt.

take. Among other things, the president failed to realize that "the state which does not recognize limits to its power in the economic sphere," as Novak pointed out in his classic text *The Spirit of Democratic Capitalism,* "inevitably destroys liberties in the political sphere."[31] Rejecting the principle of *subsidiarity* (that a central authority should only perform those tasks which cannot be done more efficiently at a lower, local level), the Obama administration was almost immediately faced with the annoying problem of not knowing the specific conditions and circumstances of the very markets it sought to regulate. As Friedrich Hayek (1889-1992), Austrian-born economist, put it in his earlier book *The Road to Serfdom,* "The state should confine itself to establishing rules applying to general types of situations . . . because only individuals concerned in each instance can fully know these circumstances and adapt their actions to them."[32] Washington was a long way from the cattle ranchers of Wyoming.

With the passage of health care legislation and with the establishment of guaranteed loans for college education, whereby private banks were stripped of their roles as middlemen to be replaced by the federal government, the Obama administration extended Washington's obligations "on the scale of an LBJ or an FDR."[33] Few Americans realize that by now thousands of new Internal Revenue Service agents have been hired "to crack down on employers and workers alike to collect healthcare taxes and to impose penalties."[34] And though the political pundits have not yet come up with a catchy phrase, such as "the Great Society" or "the New Deal," to describe Obama's economic and social initiatives, the dreaded "S" word has often been bandied about. Stoking the fires of the debate, *Newsweek* editor Jon Meacham mocked the president's detractors "for considering him to be a "crypto-socialist" (no doubt in an attempt to clear the field of all such language),[35] and Alan Wolfe in a article in the *New Republic* offered the shockingly contrary view that if Obama succeeds in implementing his program "There would be no greater blow to socialism—

[31]Michael Novak, *The Spirit of Democratic Capitalism* (New York: Touchstone, 1982), p. 15.

[32]F. A. Hayek, *The Road to Serfdom* (Chicago: University of Chicago Press, 2007), p. 114.

[33]Jacob Weisberg, "The Staying Power of the S Word," *Newsweek*, March 16, 2009, p. 39.

[34]David Lambro, "Obama Plots Assault on Non-Union Business," *Human Events* 66, no. 14 (2010), p. 9. This turn of events has occurred by the time of the publication of this book.

[35]Jonah Goldberg, "What Kind of Socialist," *Commentary* 129, no. 5 (2010): 10.

in America, in Europe, or anywhere else."[36]

Contrary to some of the president's sharpest critics, it must be quickly noted that Obama is no Marxist.[37] As a political liberal going back to the time of his community organizing days in Chicago, Obama upholds the basic institutions that make up a modern, liberal democratic state, but he also believes that such institutions must ever bend "to the needs of the underprivileged and the downtrodden in the name of social justice," in which a premium is placed not only on equality but also on the instruments of the government required to bring about such a vision.[38] Jonah Goldberg, therefore, entertains the language of "socialism," "social democracy" and even "progressive" to describe the current administration.[39] His own preference is for the term "neo-socialism," in order to suggest a difference between his terminology and the all too glib, almost unthinking, designation of socialist.

The reference point then, by which to gauge Obama's neo-socialism (if that's the most helpful and accurate term), would not be the former Soviet Union or modern China, but a contemporary European social democracy such as Sweden, Great Britain or even Germany. Here the comparisons are far more helpful and informative. To illustrate, if the total amount of government spending against the backdrop of the gross domestic product (GDP) of the United States is compared with similar statistics in Europe, it is remarkably clear that America is becoming much more like a European welfare state. According to Michael Freedman, for example, about a decade ago total government spending in the United States constituted "34.3 percent of the GDP, compared with 48.2 percent in the euro zone—roughly a 14 point gap."[40] Today, however, during Obama's tenure in office, that gap has declined considerably, such that in 2010 spending in the United States is expected to be "39.9 percent of [the] GDP, compared with 47.1 percent in the euro-zone—a gap of just 7.2 points."[41] Put another way, the federal government in the United States, with its numerous tax-funded

---

[36]Alan Wolfe, "Obama vs. Marx," *New Republic* 240, no. 5 (2009): 23.

[37]Goldberg, *What Kind of Socialist*, p.14.

[38]Ibid.

[39]Ibid.

[40]Michael Freedman, "Big Government Is Back—Big Time," *Newsweek*, February 16, 2009, p. 26.

[41]Ibid.

programs, is edging out private industry in the makeup of the GDP. Such a move will likely increase the national debt. Some economists argue that the creation of wealth, a weak suite of the federal government, has to be the engine that supplies the power for any redistribution plan.

Moreover, armed with social and economic legislation that was replete with government regulations issuing in a growing paternalism, the Obama administration cut taxes on key populations of its constituency (Republicans, for their part, tended to cut taxes across the board) such that the number of Americans who pay no federal income tax at all is rising from "the current one-third of all households to more than half."[42] Simply put, one half of America is becoming increasingly dependent on the other. This is a prescription not for equality (which is how it is often presented and justified) but for polarization. Indeed, despite the rhetoric of the president, the details of his policies along with the economic data that flows from his office suggest that he has, in the words, of Andrew Potter, "put his ship in a hard left turn."[43] Focusing almost unswervingly on social and political justice understood as setting limits on legitimate acquisition in the name of equality, Obama would no doubt like to see his *particular* political judgments become a part of the national heritage, that is, safely ensconced above any change that could be offered by those who think otherwise. In fact, Obama believes that the Supreme Court itself erred "by refusing to mandate redistribution."[44] The president obviously believes that his particular brand of politics should always be considered the story of the American nation. Some, then, are beginning to think that Obama is not only an able and effective politician (which he clearly is) but also something of an ideologue, although he has been revealing a far more pragmatic side of late. Indeed, when David Alinsky, the son of the leftist Saul Alinsky (who founded the modern community organizing movement), considered the political themes of the 2008 Democratic Convention he observed, "Obama learned his lesson well."[45] Earlier David's father, Saul, had articu-

---

[42]Dick Morris and Eileen McGann, "The Obama Presidency: Here Comes Socialism," *Human Events* 65, no. 4 (2009): 6.

[43]Andrew Potter, "How Did America Become the New Canada," *Maclean's* 122, no. 13 (2009): 14.

[44]Newberry, *War on Success*, p. 60. Newberry also points out that "the top 10 percent of American households now pay approximately 70 percent of the taxes" (ibid., p. 58).

[45]L. David Alinsky, "Son Sees Father's Handiwork in Convention," *Boston Globe*, August 31, 2008,

lated what was to become the emblem of the political left: "*The Prince* was written by Machiavelli for the Haves on how to hold power. *Rules for Radicals* is written for the Have-Nots on how to take it away."[46]

THE PUBLIC VOICE OF THE CHURCH

Many Americans, regardless of their politics, were happy to see an African American, after years of searing discrimination, take the highest office in the land. And not a few were pleased with the personality and demeanor of the new president. He was, after all, a very likeable and affable man. But beyond these considerations, the evangelical left was elated with the election of Barack Obama because its own political thinking, at least in part, now had the possibility of being enacted. Welcomed to the hallways of political power, Jim Wallis soon met with the new president and shared his vision.

Having few reservations about exercising political power in contrast to the historic Anabaptist community (which viewed governing as infected with a sinful struggle of interests that is best left alone), the evangelical left was delighted that its day in the sun had finally come. The rhetoric of renewal, awakening and social justice filled the pages of *Sojourners* with renewed energy. But did the evangelical left actually have something different to offer the country other than what looked to many political observers like just another evangelical spin on leftist politics? James Davison Hunter, for his part, apparently thought not. In his insightful new book *To Change the World*, the distinguished professor from the University of Virginia argued on the one hand that "Wallis and others *do* take issue with the secular left for not taking religion seriously," but on the other hand he concluded that "in substance the perspective they offer is not an alternative to the ideology of the secular left, but a faith-based extension of its discourse."[47]

---

www.boston.com/bostonglobe/editorial_opinion/letters/articles/2008/08/31/son_sees_fathers_handiwork_in_convention.

[46]Saul D. Alinsky, *Rules for Radicals: A Pragmatic Primer for Realistic Radicals* (New York: Vintage Books, 1971), p. 3. Hillary Clinton, for example, wrote, "Many of you are well enough off. . . . We're going to take things away from you on behalf of the common good" (Hillary Clinton, cited in Newberry, *War on Success*, p. 56).

[47]James Davison Hunter, *To Change the World: The Irony, Tragedy, and Possibility of Christianity in the Late Modern World* (Oxford: Oxford University Press, 2010), p. 145.

Indeed, although the evangelical left likes to tout its political prefer-ences as a kingdom ethic or as the politics of the Bible, its relatively facile movement from the first to twenty-first century is fraught with several missteps along the way, errors of judgment that affect the *entire* evangelical community. Beyond the basic historiographical mistake in which all sorts of twenty-first-century constructions are placed on the lips of Jesus and the early church, as noted in chapter five, the evangelical left has become embroiled in an equally problematic mistake in judgment. The basic error here, from which so many others flow, is that this community has reduced the public voice of the church in some important ways largely to a political idiom, thereby becoming complicit in evangelicalism's own subjugation by a modern liberal democratic state.

To illustrate this last claim we must first of all point out that politics in America of late has come to mean two basic things: first, the power to *coerce* by means of the state with respect to such things as taxes (supporting the operations of the state *and* redistributing wealth), a host of laws and regula-tions (many affecting business and industry), the power of imprisonment (for example placing pro-life protestors in jail for waging public demonstra-tions). Second, politics as it seeks to influence if not outright control the legislative arm of the state has in effect become interwoven with the power to grant or restrict access to key (and limited) social goods that are desired by all citizens, such things as housing, educational benefits, grants, job op-portunities and promotions, to name a few. Who gets what today is rarely a matter of a judicious assessment of worth or simple achievement. The logic and fruit of this political reasoning is then *enforced* by the state to the pros-pering of some groups and to the diminishment of others. Antagonized by the Christian right in general, and frustrated in particular by the Christian Coalition, the evangelical left has become all the more eager to embrace this political world. *Its influence* on the levers of power will make a dif-ference for the kingdom—or so it is claimed.

Entering the public arena with the name of Jesus on their lips and with public policies that enhance the power of the federal government (moving in a statist direction), the evangelical left may not get a hearing from those outside the church simply because many nonbelievers, independents among them, don't like Campolo's and McLaren's politics. Developing new plans for the redistribution of social goods (which in many instances will violate the legitimate acquisition and entitlement of some), and undermining key values that would actually lead to the liberation of the poor (instead of making them increasingly dependent on the public dole), the evangelical left may portray the public face of Jesus in a way that the non-churched may feel compelled to reject. That is, in this branch of evangelicalism Christ has become so identified with a particular conception of social justice and with the public policies that support it (*God's Politics* as Wallis puts it in the title of a recent book) that some beyond the walls of the church may now want little to do with the Christian faith.[48] Such a stumbling block, however, should not be placed in the path of those for whom Christ has died. The church is much larger, and its story is far greater, than the deflecting, oppositional and polarizing narrative of the evangelical left. The public voice of the church must not be reduced to politics.

In a similar way, the Christian right, some of whom are politically conservative evangelicals, has reduced the public voice of the church largely to a political idiom. In this the evangelical right and left are on the same page. The politics and the players are different, to be sure, but the larger script remains the same. Like the evangelical left, the evangelical right has confused its own particular political judgments with the coming of the kingdom. These conservatives, for example, have stressed the freedom of acquisition, often celebrating American free enterprise, but they have not underscored the *duties* and *obligations* entailed in the acquisition of wealth with equal force. Moreover, its association with fiscal conservatives of the Republican Party, some of whom are libertarians, has distorted its moral vision. The right to earn and save as much as one can must be matched by the social, moral and religious obligations to give as much as one can, as the eighteenth-century evangelical John Wesley understood so well in his own day.[49] In fact, Wesley cautioned his hearers against the danger of increasing riches since wealth could so easily work its way into the human heart in an idolatrous fashion and thereby undermine both the love of God

---

[48]See Jim Wallis, *God's Politics: Why the Right Gets It Wrong and the Left Doesn't Get It* (San Francisco: HarperSanFrancisco, 2005).

[49]John Wesley, "The Use of Money," *Sermons*, vol. 4 of *The Works of John Wesley*, ed. Albert C. Outler (Nashville: Abingdon, 1984), p. 277.

and neighbor.[50] Just how many sermons on the dangers of wealth have been proclaimed from the pulpits of the evangelical right of late?

Clearly, evangelical political conservatives have at times failed to appreciate that modern capitalist societies often function in a way that is grossly unfair to whole segments of society who, through no fault of their own ("the slings and arrows of outrageous fortune"), cannot compete. As Reinhold Niebuhr pointed out years ago, "A conservative class which makes 'free enterprise' the final good of the community . . . [is] perilous to the peace of the community."[51] The good community that goes beyond the individualism of a consumerist culture cares for the impoverished widow, the orphan and the homeless. Moreover, it reaches out in mercy and genuine human concern toward those who in their current condition are slaves of forces (grinding poverty, drugs, alcohol and mental disturbance) beyond their control. The government can and should play a role that no private charity, however well-motivated, can match. Indeed, some of the goods of society *must* be redistributed by the state to lend a helping hand simply because, on the one hand, the rich so often neglect their rightful duties to the broader community and, on the other hand, the downtrodden evidence such great and dire need. A more just and equitable distribution should, at times, set limits to legitimate acquisition and entitlement. To fail in this is simply to stoke the fires of an irresponsible selfishness that will undermine most any community.

Here, however, is where the evangelical right and left part company, for the former encounters a problem hardly faced by the later, namely, an unbalanced and uncritical embrace of the American way of life that can so easily result in some disturbing forms of nationalism. To illustrate, the evangelical right's embrace of the recent war in Iraq (even dashing off letters of support to the president!) in which so many innocent Iraqis lost their lives in what can be described as a cruel (and ultimately ill-informed and misguided) display of American military power was at the very least morally troubling. Who will tell the Iraqi mother who has lost her children

---

[50]"The Danger of Riches" *Sermons*, vol. 3 of *The Works of John Wesley*, ed. Albert C. Outler (Nashville: Abingdon, 1984), pp. 227ff.

[51]Reinhold Niebuhr, *The Children of Light and the Children of Darkness* (New York: Charles Scribner's, 1944), p. 149.

that this war has been enthusiastically supported by American evangelical Christians, those who having been born again of the Spirit of the living Christ and for that reason are supposed to be known for how they love their neighbor as themselves? The public face of Jesus in this setting, caught up in the politics of the day, likewise looks greatly marred.

About a decade ago Cal Thomas and Ed Dobson, both of whom had been very active in the earlier and now defunct Moral Majority, warned the evangelical community that when you start to mix religion and politics in very partisan ways, you end up with some strange concoctions. "When the church engages in the political system, using the weapons of that system," they wrote, "then it becomes just another lobbying group and ceases to be the church."[52] Even more forcefully these two former political activists pointed out that in their opinion the Christian Coalition and other Christian political groups "are selling their religious priorities for a mess of political pottage. In the process, they are harming the gospel."[53] Neither the Christian right nor the evangelical left has a corner on the kingdom of God. The grace of Christ is greater.

YODER TO THE RESCUE?

Although John Howard Yoder's writings call into question the church and state configurations expressed in both the evangelical right and left, and are in some respects similar to Thomas and Dobson, this body of work nevertheless does not depart from a political idiom as one of the chief expressions of the faith. That is, although Yoder very perceptively observed that "What in the Middle Ages was done by Roman Christianity or Islam is now being attempted . . . by democratic nationalism," he nevertheless maintained that the public expression of Christianity is best understood as politics, though of a different order to be sure, one that challenges the Constantinian state.[54] This neo-Anabaptist vision, then, opposes all forms of Constantinianism (where the church is "responsible" for the state) "while being dependent on it for its self-understanding."[55]

---

[52]Cal Thomas and Ed Dobson, *Blinded by Might* (Grand Rapids: Zondervan, 1999), p. 180.
[53]Ibid., p. 80.
[54]John Howard Yoder, *The Politics of Jesus* (Grand Rapids: Eerdmans, 1972), p. 238.
[55]Hunter, *To Change the World*, p. 280.

In his *Politics of Jesus* Yoder reached out to the long-haired youth of the early 1970s and claimed that "Jesus was, like themselves, a social critic and an agitator, a drop-out from the social climb, and the spokesman of a counterculture."[56] Indeed, the politicization of the New Testament is everywhere apparent in this celebrated book. In reworking the Gospel of Luke for a better fit to his own social location and its problems, Yoder argued, for instance, that "the cross of Jesus was a political punishment"; he then quoted the speculation of Oscar Cullmann that "perhaps as many as half of the twelve [disciples] were recruited from among the ranks of the Zealots," a radical and often violent political group; and to top off his political reading he declared that "Both Jewish and Roman authorities were defending themselves against a real threat [in Jesus]."[57] In making this last claim, however, one can only wonder if Yoder had properly considered the awesome military presence of the Romans in the Middle East in the first century, with its vaunted ability to crush and kill *any* opposition. They hardly feared the humble, donkey-riding Jesus of Nazareth. At any rate, in this vision as well, and in a way *similar* to the evangelical left and right, the public voice of the Christian faith has by and large been rendered political. Indeed, Yoder even went so far, as Hunter points out, to argue that "the only suffering that has spiritual meaning is political suffering."[58] This is not a "third way," an option that resolves the dilemma faced by contemporary evangelicals and others, especially in terms of polarization, but is very much a part of the problem. Like so many modern people, "Christians . . . have politicized every aspect of public life and private life as well."[59] They are adept, even artful, in taking the penultimate and making it ultimate. They have learned to speak the language of Babylon.

COME TO CHURCH AND GET ALIENATED

The unenviable predicament that American evangelicalism finds itself in today has been a long train coming. When liberals of the early twentieth century such as Harry Emerson Fosdick were faced with the intellectual

---

[56]Yoder, *Politics of Jesus*, p. 1.
[57]Ibid., pp. 125, 39, 49.
[58]Hunter, *To Change the World*, p. 163.
[59]Ibid., p. 275.

challenges of both higher criticism of the Bible and Darwinism, they basically folded up their intellectual tents, so to speak, and moved to different quarters. In other words, the presentation and justification of the Christian faith would henceforth, for the most part, not be intellectual but *moral*. With the success of the Social Gospel as championed by Walter Rauschenbusch, Washington Gladden and others, not only did the modern liberal democratic state itself become something of a focus but also the moral, public voice of the church became increasingly identified with politics and economics of a particular sort. Evangelicals, for their part, were also influenced by these broad cultural trends (perhaps more than they were willing to admit), although not to the extent that their liberal, mainline cousins had desired.

Then something strange happened on the way to the kingdom in the midst of these cultural shifts. The public, diminished voice of the church that had become increasingly political and partisan was then brought into the church itself, in the pulpit as well as in the classroom, such that this highly touted political narrative had now become an ecclesiastical one. This move was clearly evident in mainline denominations, although it found expression, to a lesser extent, in evangelical churches as well. To illustrate, a Sunday bulletin insert sponsored by the United Methodist church during the late 1980s celebrated the wonders of the Sandinista revolution in Nicaragua, and it wistfully opined that the careful observer will see within it the coming kingdom of God.[60] And Stephen Carter recounts the story when he and his wife attended a church in New Haven, Connecticut, shortly after moving there. The preacher that Sunday morning, a divinity student, was going to set the congregation straight because she believed than many "were misunderstanding God's plan and therefore falling into sin."[61] Animated and determined, she was "a sort of left-wing Oliver North," as Carter points out, "whose evident view was that it was our Christian duty to support the good (left-wing) terrorists in their holy struggle to massacre the bad (right-wing) terrorists." In this pulpit-

---

[60]I recall sitting in a pew in a United Methodist Church in Fayetteville, North Carolina, and reading this insert that had been passed out to the entire congregation. I immediately crumpled it up. See also Mark D. Tooley, "Missions and Marxism," *FrontPageMag.com*, July 22, 2009, http://archive .frontpagemag.com/readArticle.aspx?ARTID=35659.

[61]Stephen L. Carter, *The Culture of Disbelief* (New York: Basic Books, 1993), p. 69.

delivered spanking the young woman apparently had no conception of "the possibility of a faith not guided by her prior political commitments."[62]

Not to be outdone, the Christian right, with its wedding of "the political and religious world"[63] (and in a context where "more than 75 percent of professing 'evangelical Christians' now classify themselves as Republicans")[64] ascended the pulpit on Sunday mornings and proclaimed a message that at times confused American consumerism with the fruits of the kingdom, and free enterprise with the freedom of the gospel.[65] Pulpit fare around the Fourth of July tended to be particularly offensive with nationalism approaching idolatrous heights and with its ethnocentric themes actually interlaced in the hymns. And wars, if they were supported by a popular Republican president, took on a glow of righteousness that was unwarranted not only in the judgment of the international community but also through a consideration of the ugly realities on the ground.

The pulpit mishmash in such culturally accommodated churches, whether from the left or the right, is at times a thing to behold. Neglecting the sacred traditions of the church, such politicized preachers employ all the language of historic Christianity such as *Christ, gospel* and *salvation*, but then they redefine every one of these terms in light of their preferred political narrative, which actually constitutes the heart of their message. As Ballor notes, "It is indeed a sorry statement on the present state of the Christian church that economic opinions or political allegiances become more definitive of unity than the spiritual bond shared as followers of Jesus Christ."[66] Here the very catholicity of the church is at stake. Put another way, that which is penultimate (politics and economics, which constitute areas in which rational people will no doubt disagree) has become ultimate, and the fleeting configurations of the day have been declared eternal with the result that the church has lost its gospel voice that should have consisted in a bold declaration of the *universal* love of God manifested in Jesus Christ. Through no stretch of the imagination can the

---

[62]Ibid.

[63]Jimmy Carter, *Living Faith* (New York: Three Rivers Press, 2001), p. 186.

[64]George G. Hunter, *Christian, Evangelical and Democrat?* (Nashville: Abingdon, 2006), p. 2.

[65]See the argument in Lisa R Withrow, "Success and the Prosperity Gospel: From Commodification to Transformation," *Journal of Religious Leadership* 6, no. 2 (2007): 15-41.

[66]Jordan J. Ballor, *Ecumenical Babel* (Grand Rapids: Christian's Library Press, 2010), pp. xvi-xvii.

gospel be ably expressed in political speech that is tribal, limited and in the end divisive. Again, partisan politics, whether from the left or the right, must not become "much more determinative of fellowship than ecclesiastical unity,"[67] for the narrative that the church holds dear is broader, more inclusive and, in contrast to its nagging substitutes, leads to genuine human flourishing. In his own day H. Richard Niebuhr pointed out how the gospel proclamation of the church, its catholicity and generous outreach, can be readily deflected by lesser concerns (petty idolatries) such as ethnicity, race, social class and economics.[68] To that mix we must now add particular political judgments as well, which, when elevated to the level of the basic story of the church, *ever* become divisive. Simply put, partisan politics invariably forgets how to spell the word *catholic*.

Though evangelicals have kept the gospel story alive in pulpit and classroom, they have not been beyond intermixing it with very partisan views with respect to social justice. I recall the time when one of the leading pundits of the evangelical left spoke at Asbury Theological Seminary. After criticizing our pietist heritage, with a little humor thrown in, the speaker then moved on to "more important matters," as he put it, namely, the maintenance needs of the poor. A couple of the faculty at the time reckoned that if the American government actually put in place the statist solutions being offered that morning, then the number of poor in the country would likely *increase*. The rule here as elsewhere is that you invariably get more of what you subsidize, thereby creating unintended dependency. Indeed, billions of dollars have been spent since the anti-poverty programs of the Great Society of the Johnson era, and yet the number of poor people in America remains virtually the same: 39 million in 1959, 37 million in 2004.[69] What was equally disturbing, however, was the preacher's intimation that if we as a community did not embrace his well-worked belief of the superiority of a government-administered economy, then somehow or other we were less than adequate Christians, nothing but ersatz evangelicals.

---

[67]Ibid., p. 16.

[68]See H. Richard Niebuhr, *The Social Sources of Denominationalism* (New York: New American Library, 1957).

[69]Jerome R. Corsi and Kenneth Blackwell, "Democrats' War on Poverty Has Failed," *Human Events*, September 6, 2006, www.humanevents.com/article.php?id=16860.

This same basic error, however, is likewise committed by the evangelical right that easily confuses the freedom of the gospel with the wonders of free markets, not taking into account, of course, the multitude of people who will be left behind in such a system. This approach mistakes American free enterprise with all its supposed advantages and enticements for the Christian way. In this setting, private property has virtually become a right-wing shibboleth. Though the historic church has informally entered into some very troubling arrangements with states in the past, especially in Europe, it has never declared as dogma for all the faithful to believe any particular conception of social justice that devolves on partisan politics, whether it be the celebration of a government-led economy *or* free markets. Political and economic *preferences* must not be mistaken for the "normative claims of Christian ethics."[70] Believers will demonstrate all sorts of political philosophies as they minister to the poor. These matters are best left open.

Good and reasonable arguments can be made for social justice conceived in either of the following forms, which would then be implemented, at least in part, by the state: (1) just acquisition and entitlement should set limits to redistribution, and (2) just distribution should set limits to legitimate acquisition.[71] The church, however, should not throw its entire weight behind one side of the argument, for to do so would invariably transform the body of Christ in two key ways: First, the sacred community would become increasingly ideological (shunting aside the wisdom of the other approach). Second, in becoming ideological the church would necessarily raise penultimate judgments to an ultimate level (where they simply do not belong) and thereby commit idolatry (speaking the language of Babylon) and alienate real Christians sitting in its pews on Sunday mornings. The church then must learn to live in the midst of two worlds, so to speak, with tensions ever present.

One of the good things about the American evangelical community is that there are significant numbers on both sides of this issue such that there is dialogue, even if it is often heated or at times descends into name calling. However, on the boards of many mainline denominations today

[70]Ballor, *Ecumenical Babel*, p. 18.
[71]MacIntyre, *After Virtue*, p. 253.

or on the even higher level of the World Council of Churches, there remains a stultifying monologue on these very issues. As Ballor observes, "the leaders of the World Council of Churches have addressed selective aspects of the economic question almost exclusively from an ideological perspective that asserts the superiority of a government-administered economy over the market."[72] The message at this level is remarkably clear: get on board or get out. But while the evangelical right and left were throwing rhetorical brickbats at each other, they failed to realize that the ground under their feet was slowly shifting—and in a way that, in the end, could easily topple them both.

THE CHALLENGES OF THE MODERN LIBERAL DEMOCRATIC STATE

The transition in political philosophy that began with Thomas Hobbes (1588-1679)—who was clearly *not* a classical liberal—resulted in the increasing separation between "the political order and the divine nexus," with an inordinate emphasis on all-too-human power.[73] In contrast, traditional societies, medieval Christendom in Europe for example, were held together by the common ties of a carefully articulated political theology, with its robust belief in God, as well as by a philosophy of history that went back at least to the time of Augustine in his *City of God.* Though the harshness of Hobbes in terms of his call for an awesome human power, a leviathan, to govern society was put aside by the Enlightenment, its champions nevertheless "stayed well within the philosophical orbit that Hobbes had circumscribed," in that Locke and others realized what dangers religious passions could pose to the public order.[74]

The critique and eventual elimination of political theology as a viable discipline (in which national life had been understood in terms of a larger, transcendent purpose) was a gradual process, especially in America. Much more influenced by the moderate Enlightenment of Locke than the skeptical (and anticlerical) Enlightenment of Voltaire (1694-1778) and David Hume (1711-

---

[72]Ballor, *Ecumenical Babel*, p. 17.
[73]Mark Lilla, *The Stillborn God: Religion, Politics and the Modern West* (New York: Alfred A. Knopf, 2007), p. 219.
[74]Ibid., pp. 218-19.

1776), the founders of the nation continued to appeal to God to explain in part what form the American experiment (with its disestablishment of religion) would take.[75] The Declaration of Independence, for example, contains four specific references to the Almighty as a Lawmaker, Creator, Supreme Judge and Protector.[76] Especially telling is the language with respect to the divine role in creation, since it affirms that citizens are "endowed by their Creator with certain unalienable rights," indicating not only that the state itself is not the origin of such rights but also that it does not, and should not, have the power to take them away.[77] A year earlier Charles Carroll (1737-1832), a wealthy planter and early advocate of liberation from England, had observed that the sacred rights of humanity are written, "as with a sun beam, in the whole volume of human nature, by the hand of divinity itself; and can never be erased or obscured by mortal power."[78]

During his inauguration as the nation's first president, George Washington (1732-1799) placed his right hand on the Bible and concluded the oath of office with his own addition: "So help me God," at which point he bent forward and "kissed the Bible before him."[79] Later, during a Thanksgiving Proclamation of October 3, 1789, the new president affirmed before the American people that "It is the duty of all Nations to acknowledge the Providence of Almighty God, to obey His will, to be grateful for His benefits, and humbly to implore His protection and favor."[80] Expressing the limited powers of government, John Adams (1735-1826), the second president, declared that "We have no government armed with power capable of contending with human passions unbridled by morality and religion."[81] And in the following century, Abraham Lincoln (1809-1865) remarked in his Gettysburg Address that "this nation, *under God*, shall have a new birth of freedom."[82]

As the preceding examples demonstrate, political theology in America

---

[75]Henry F. May, *The Enlightenment in America* (Oxford: Oxford University Press, 1976), pp. 359-60.

[76]Newt Gingrich, *Rediscovering God in America: Reflections on the Role of Faith in Our Nation's History* (Nashville: Thomas Nelson, 2006), p. 30.

[77]Ibid., p. 29.

[78]Charles Carroll, cited in ibid., pp. 19-20.

[79]Gingrich, *Rediscovering God in America*, p. 15.

[80]George Washington, cited in ibid., p. 16.

[81]John Adams, cited in Gingrich, *Rediscovering God in America*, p. 19.

[82]Abraham Lincoln, cited in Gingrich, *Rediscovering God in America*, p. 22 (emphasis added).

was not yet dead, and the transcendent dimension, greater than the nation itself, was by no means empty. Indeed, the appeal to God by the founding fathers and presidents was the preferred means by which they comprehended the life of the nation at its highest reaches, a practice that lent greater meaning to the national enterprise as it basked in the light of the transcendent. Beyond this, these earlier leaders understood that religion itself would, after all, provide the lion's share of the moral capital through which the nation would prosper. Indeed a well-functioning democracy that emphasized freedom was ever dependent on such capital. "The Founders saw religion as vital to the survival of republican government," as Gingrich, a former assistant professor of history at West Georgia College (now the University of West Georgia), observes, "because they believed the maintenance of liberty requires virtue."[83] All that was excluded by the First Amendment before the legal revisionism of the twentieth century was the sectarian option that a particular group's faith (whether Protestant, Catholic or Jew) would become the established religion for all.

A NEW KIND OF SECULARISM

Philip Roth, the novelist of *Portnoy's Complaint* fame, referred to the period between 1960 and 1970 as the "demythologizing decade."[84] The countercultural movement at the time, both in terms of its pop and elite forms, not only undermined traditional notions of authority (family, church and educational standards) but it also looked askance at the wealth of human wisdom from the past, especially in terms of early American history. Celebrating the present possibilities for cultural revolution and repeatedly deprecating tradition, radical groups like the SDS (Students for a Democratic Society, established in Chicago in 1962); the Youth International Party (the Yippies), the brain child of Abbie Hoffman and Jerry Rubin; along with the Black Panther Party, headed up by Bobby Seale and Huey Newton, all gave a sharp edge to the ongoing cultural conflict. And though most Americans would reject the basic teachings of these radicals, they nevertheless were affected by the ongoing cultural viability of these

---

[83]Newt Gingrich, *To Save America: Stopping Obama's Secular-Socialist Machine* (Washington, D.C.: Regnery, 2010), p. 38.

[84]Susan Jacoby, *Freethinkers: A History of American Secularism* (New York: Henry Holt, 2004), p. 319.

groups, who throughout much of the decade repeatedly contended through their ideology and actions that there was nothing higher than raw political and cultural power. Jerry Rubin, for example, was better known and more celebrated than many key evangelical leaders. And when religion did become the topic of discussion during this turbulent decade in a university setting or on the streets it was often viewed from the distortions of a Marxist (religion is the opium of the people) or a Freudian (religion is a childish illusion) lens, with all of its borrowed misunderstandings of faith going back to the time of Ludwig Feuerbach.[85] Indeed, at the beginning of the decade only "2 percent of the population claimed not to believe in God."[86] Today around 12 to 14 percent of Americans would call themselves "secularists."[87] The transitional decade of the 1960s goes a long way in explaining much of that increase.

Earlier, in 1947, a crucial turn in the understanding of religion and its relation to the state was made by the Supreme Court in its decision of *Everson v. Board of Education*. In this ruling religious freedom was "radically recast between religion and irreligion, much to the benefit of irreligion."[88] Moreover, when the Warren court outlawed school prayer in *Engel v. Vitale* in 1962, as noted in chapter three, it continued this trend and demonstrated a different understanding of the relation between religion and national life than did earlier leaders, presidents among them. This variance is evident in the court's conception of the term *secular*, as expressed, for example, in the lengthy opinion of Judge Hugo Black, revealing once again that it is the cultural winners who get to define the terms of the debate.[89] In a way that would have likely received the rebuke of the founding fathers and mothers of the nation, the federal government encroached upon "the public space" of childhood education, seeing it not so much as the cultural phenomenon that it was but as a matter of the state

---

[85]See Ludwig Feuerbach, *The Essence of Christianity*, trans. George Eliot (New York: Harper Torchbooks, 1957). Neither Marx nor Freud is original in his critique of religion. Both writings are clearly dependent of the writings of Feuerbach, who maintained that theology equals anthropology.

[86]Hunter, *To Change the World*, p. 19.

[87]Ibid.

[88]Richard John Neuhaus, *American Babylon: Notes of a Christian Exile* (New York: Basic Books, 2009), p. 39.

[89]"Engel v. Vitale - 370 U.S. 421 (1962)," Justia.com, http://supreme.justia.com/us/370/421/case .html.

(where all sorts of political narratives would come into play). Indeed, the Supreme Court had been goaded along these lines (it is a myth to think that the court is above such influences) by an activist American Civil Liberties Union whose lawyers repeatedly insisted that "religion is not a civil function or a public matter."[90]

Accordingly, when Justice Black, in his judicial ruling, operated from an understanding of the term *secular* that was set in sharp contrast to *any* sort of religious influences, he in effect mandated that henceforth the public, cultural space of American education must not only be dominated by the state (as a cultural gatekeeper) but it must also be devoid of religion. In his dissent from this opinion Justice Potter Stewart, underscoring the importance of freedom of speech observed, "I think the Court has misapplied a great constitutional principle. I cannot see how an 'official religion' is established by letting those who want to say a prayer say it."[91] A generation later the Supreme Court overturned an Alabama law that simply set aside one minute for "meditation or voluntary prayer."[92] The pretense of neutrality was by now long gone, for this judgment put the court in the very odd position of eliminating the *voluntary* prayers of Americans who were slowly, so it seemed, being stripped of their unalienable rights.

The term *secular*, of course, can be defined much differently than Hugo Black had done, and in a way that does not set it in sharp contrast to religion. This comes as a surprise to many people who have grown used to the well-worn definition. Early medieval definitions of *secularis*, for example, upon which our contemporary term is based, suggest that the contrast is not *between* a "naked public square," to borrow a phrase from Richard John Neuhaus, *and* religion, but *between* the temporal *and* the eternal.[93] This is the so-called eschatological use of the term.[94] Indeed, clergy were and are still often called secular, not because they are devoid of

---

[90]Martin E. Marty, *Modern American Religion: The Noise of Conflict 1919-1941* (Chicago: University of Chicago Press, 1991), 2:211.

[91]"Engel v. Vitale: The Issue: Prayer in Public Schools," PBS.org, www.pbs.org/jefferson/enlight/prayer.htm.

[92]Carter, *Culture of Disbelief*, p. 191.

[93]See Richard John Neuhaus, *The Naked Public Square* (Grand Rapids: Eerdmans, 1984), pp. 1ff. See the eighth definition of *secular* in *The Random House Dictionary of the English Language Unabridged*, ed. Stuart Berg Flexner (New York: Random House 1987), p. 1731.

[94]Douglas Farrow, "Three Meanings of Secular," *First Things* (2003): 22.

religion, to be sure, but because they minister in the midst of the mundane, fleeting affairs of life where religion is present as well. Properly understood, religion has both a temporal and an eternal dimension, and it can gather up various cultural forms and expressions that will not bear the test of time. Thus, the term *secular*, understood in this second way, highlights what is fleeting, what will not endure (in contrast to the eternal), and it can *include* religious expression. Such an understanding does not target religion in a discriminatory or prejudicial way but sees a contrast between the present, transitory nature of life, the provisional character of existence, and "that which is to come."[95] As Stephen Carter notes, "a secular public space," the kind that discriminates against religion, "is a late-twentieth-century invention."[96]

Though many of the recent secular trends in America are ideologically driven, not all are so motivated. The work of George Marsden, especially his *Secularization of the Academy*, has been very helpful in comprehending the variegated and systemic challenges that modern liberal democracies pose to religious faith. Drawing upon a distinction between ideological and methodological secularism, this Notre Dame professor ably demonstrated that the cultural power of secularism also grows out of the very nature and structure of modern universities and other cultural entities due to constantly shifting frameworks, a phenomenon otherwise known as pluralism.[97] That is, with the loss of any overarching value or center (whether God or moral philosophy), universities have spun out discipline after discipline with the result that a plural, decentralized curriculum structure does not even have the wherewithal, the common vocabulary, necessary to discourse on the transcendent. Here, structure—in other words, universities going about their various particular interests—has philosophical and cultural consequence. Granted, some professors would indeed take the ideological turn, as both Francis Schaeffer (1912-1984) and Harold Lindsell had warned, and interlace their disciplines with their own metaphysical views.[98] Nevertheless, Marsden's basic point remains: secu-

---

[95]Ibid.

[96]Carter, *God's Name in Vain*, p. 72.

[97]George M. Marsden and Bradley J. Longfield, *The Secularization of the Academy* (New York: Oxford University Press, 1992), pp. 21-37.

[98]Francis A. Schaeffer, *A Christian Manifesto* (Westchester, Ill.: Crossway, 1981), pp. 53ff; and Harold

larism is far more complicated and culturally rooted than mere ideological (or philosophical) analyses can allow.

REVISIONING SEPARATION OF CHURCH AND STATE

In order to appreciate the precise challenge of secularism in its various forms, especially as it has been reflected in Supreme Court decisions, it will be helpful to consider just what the much-disputed phrase *separation of church and state* might have meant in the eighteenth century, during the founding of the nation, and what it has come to mean today. At the outset, it must be noted that the first ten amendments of the Constitution, known as the Bill of Rights, were introduced by James Madison (1751-1836) at the first Congress in 1789, in order to *limit the power of the federal government* with respect to the states and its citizens. In fact, the Bill of Rights was composed, in part, in order to garner support for the Constitution itself, since some critics had charged that it failed to protect, in some instances, the fundamental principles of human liberty. The First Amendment, which not only *restrains* the federal government from establishing a state religion (a rejection of the Old World European model) but also insures that American citizens will have full religious liberty (as well as freedom of speech), reads as follows: "Congress shall make no law respecting an establishment of religion, or prohibiting the free exercise thereof."[99]

When the historical context of this amendment is taken into account it becomes abundantly clear that it was drafted "in an effort to protect religion from the state, not the state from religion."[100] This noble intent, however, was turned on its head by the early 1970s such that the First Amendment was now frequently cited not in order to protect religion from an intrusive federal government but in order to safeguard an increasing number of secularists (who held significant cultural power) from coming into any sort of contact with religion publicly. "The wall of separation is no longer for the protection of the people of the garden," as Carter cautions,

---

Lindsell, *The New Paganism: Understanding American Culture and the Role of the Church* (San Francisco: Harper & Row, 1987), p. xi.

[99]*The Constitution of the United States*, ed. Floyd G. Cullop (New York: New American Library, 1984), p. 113.

[100]Carter, *Culture of Disbelief*, p. 105.

"it is for the protection of the people of the wilderness."[101] Operating once again with a definition of *secular* that stacked the deck, so to speak, many on the political left argued for a clean sweep of religion in the public square in the name of pluralism. Giving a new twist to an old argument, the left's appeal to pluralism here was not with the intent to be inclusive (for then religious voices would have to be a part of the discussion) but to be *exclusive*. That is, if anyone in a diverse American society was offended by *any* public expressions of faith (as not representing the beliefs or reasoning of their own community, for instance) then that language had to be shut down or censored.

One way of grappling with the full-throttled reworking of the First Amendment that took place in the late twentieth century in both the courts and in the broader culture is to consider the nation as a two-story house in which the bottom floor represents the life of the nation in its on-going temporal existence and the top floor corresponds to a transcendent, eternal dimension occupied by God, through whom the bottom floor in some sense is understood. Such a description mirrors to a certain extent the earlier understanding of secularism already detailed. Accordingly, the early American history just chronicled reveals that leaders such as Washington, Adams, Carroll and Lincoln clearly affirmed that the top floor was not and should not be empty. They all acknowledged the reality of something higher than the state. Indeed, the good of the nation in terms of its moral integrity and its larger, more enduring purposes required an occupied second floor. The chief concern of these early leaders, then, was that no *particular* or partisan conception of God (whether Roman Catholic, Protestant, Jewish or Muslim) should be declared the nation's faith. In other words, they wanted to avoid the oppression of an established religion. Simply put, the top floor was occupied but not specified.

In contrast to this understanding, radical secularists such as Sam Harris maintain that the top floor has always been empty in the nation's history (or at the very least that it was a matter of broad indifference) by trading on a distinction that subtly redefined the whole debate on terms much more to an agnostic's or atheist's liking. Citing the late historian

---

[101]Carter, *In God's Name*, p. 80.

Stephen Henry Roberts (1901-1971), Harris declared, "I contend that we are both atheists. I just believe in one fewer god than you do. When you understand why you dismiss all the other possible gods, you will understand why I dismiss yours."[102] In other words, Harris, in this pointed observation, like so many in the secular left, effectively rendered the following contrasts equivalent: (1) Christian-Muslim, and (2) theist-atheist. However, the choice between options *within* theism is not, after all, equal to the choice in which *theism itself is held in the balance.* This latter contrast represents nothing less than a *categorical* difference slipped in by Harris and Roberts to foster their atheist views. Again, if these contrasts are accepted as the same thing, in an unthinking way, then atheism (or radical secularism) will be placed on a footing never imagined in either the Declaration of Independence or by early American presidents, and belief in God will thereby be rendered just another option, one among many in a whirligig pluralism that in the end is aiming at nothing (the "no comprehensive" doctrine of John Rawls)—or as little as what modern liberal democracies have become. Put another way, the top floor of the house has become empty. Nothing higher than the liberal democratic project exists, and it has now become godlike it its pretentions. This is exactly the kind of error that the Supreme Court made in 1947 and during the 1960s when it interpreted the First Amendment in a manner that enhanced the power of the federal government and restricted the scope of religious expression.

Work the contrast theist-atheist in the right way, throw in an emphasis on pluralism and not offending culturally powerful groups, trade on the considerable authority of some scientists who intermix their professional work with their own atheism, place judges on the federal bench who have never taken a course on religion, and a climate in which the state will forcefully discriminate against religious expression in the name of being impartial will inevitably emerge. The old judgment that the state cannot establish any *particular* religion has now become the state must be indifferent to *all* religion, an indifference that never just sits on the fence, so to

---

[102] See Sam Harris's blog, "Edge: The Third Culture," www.edge.org/3rd_culture/harris06/harris06_index.html. Also see Sam Harris, *Letter to a Christian Nation* (New York: Alfred Knopf, 2006), p. 7.

speak, but as recent court cases clearly attest, actively inhibits, frustrates and at times eliminates the voice of religion in public life.

PEOPLE OF FAITH AS SECOND-CLASS CITIZENS

Law professors at some of the best schools in the country (e.g., Yale University) are beginning to warn that "Many people of deep religious commitment, especially but not exclusively evangelical Christians [will find it] . . . harder . . . to practice their religion, and harder for them to pass it on to their children."[103] With a script that was drafted by the political left and that masquerades as the nation's own constitutional heritage, people of faith are being repeatedly discriminated against in public life. Due to the reworking of the nation's heritage during the last quarter of the twentieth century, it has by now become standard practice in public discourse to consider religious voices "as though they were a threat to democracy."[104] In fact, in the midst of some of these tectonic cultural shifts, the Williamsburg Charter Survey of Religion and Public Life revealed back in 1988 that "nearly one out of three academics said that Evangelicals are a 'threat to democracy.'"[105] Not surprisingly, government bureaucrats who apply the codes that ban political involvement by 501(c)(3) organizations often end up expressing their own partisan political preferences by targeting the religious right while "the left is all but immune."[106] Moreover, a few years later, in 1993, the Internal Revenue Service eliminated the tax exemption of Jerry Falwell's *Old-Time Gospel Hour* and fined it $50,000 for failing "to devote themselves to spiritual causes alone," as if federal government workers were the best judges to determine just what the nature and extent of spiritual causes actually were.

The antireligious attitudes that affect the judiciary as well as government agencies (and that seek to privatize all religious speech as not suitable for public consumption) are being disseminated throughout the culture, trickling down, if you will, especially in the media and academia. With funding from the federal government, National Public Radio's re-

---

[103]Carter, *God's Name in Vain*, p. 2.

[104]Ibid., p. 31.

[105]David Limbaugh, *Persecution: How Liberals Are Waging War Against Christianity* (Washington, D.C.: Regnery, 2003), p. 111.

[106]Carter, *God's Name in Vain*, p. 70.

porters, for example, have become known not only for their political bias but also for their animus toward religion. To illustrate, on December 19, 1995, shortly before Christmas, an *All Things Considered* commentator made the following remark with respect to the evangelical belief in the rapture of the church: "The evaporation of four million [people] who believe in this [Christian] crap would leave this world a better place."[107] However, if the word *Jewish* had been substituted for Christian in this observation, then the listener perhaps would have been able to get a better sense of just where this kind of thinking leads. Protestations of being open and tolerant take such strange forms today when the topic is Christianity in general or evangelicalism in particular.

As bad as things are in the media, they are even worse in the public school system due to its strong ties to the government. Here the recently revised narrative of the separation of church and state is being applied to school children with a vengeance. Pitting religious faith *against* democracy and in a way the founders of the nation would never have done, Amy Gutmann, in her book *Democratic Education*, has urged that the American school system be used by administrators and teachers as an effective instrument "to limit the ability of parents to raise their children in intolerant religious beliefs."[108] And Suzanna Sherry has cautioned that educational policy henceforth must be drafted so as to "limit the effect of the bad choices that religious parents will *inevitably* make for their children."[109]

What is especially troubling about the *cultural environment* in public education is that the children from diverse backgrounds and values are being subjected to the on-the-spot, ad hoc and confused reflections of teachers and administrators as to how the understanding of "separation of church and state" should be applied in the classroom. To illustrate, the New Jersey Department of Education felt compelled to rewrite American history (perhaps out of fear of an ACLU lawsuit) and so it removed references "to the Pilgrims and the *Mayflower* from its history standards for school

---

[107]Limbaugh, *Persecution*, p. 200. The commentator was specifically referring to Christians who read the Left Behind series.

[108]Carter, *God's Name in Vain*, p. 181.

[109]Ibid. (emphasis added).

textbooks."[110] What was the reason offered for this bold move? Assessing the situation, Brian Jones replied, "The problem is that 'Pilgrim' suggests religion."[111] Simply put, the mere mention of the "R" word is justification enough. Educators can then fill in the blanks as they see fit.

School officials in the same state also prevented a student from reading his favorite story (the assignment given to the whole class) because "it came from the Bible."[112] This action targets both Christians and Jews. Students were free to read from novels whose story lines were critical of or even mocked religion (no doubt any excerpt from the historical hodgepodge *Inherit the Wind* would have been most welcomed), and students could, of course, even read from plays that touted the intellectual superiority of atheism (Sartre's *No Exit*, for example), but not from the Bible. Since when, however, has the public school system in the United States been granted the authority to throw its weight behind one side of an argument that in the end is largely philosophical? Such is the inanity that emerges when separation of church and state is not understood in terms of the federal establishment of a *particular* religion over all others, but when religion itself is in the docket, so to speak, by being contrasted with atheism or with the kind of clean-sweep secularism that the political left prefers. Indeed, "A Colorado high school valedictorian," as one cultural observer points out, "was refused a diploma unless she apologized for mentioning Jesus in her commencement speech."[113] However, hell should freeze over before any American should have to apologize for or publicly hide who she is as a religious person, whether she is a Christian, Jew, Muslim, Hindu or Buddhist. This high school girl is a religious person twenty-four hours a day, seven days a week. If she is like many evangelicals, her faith is more important to her than her race, gender, economic status, ethnicity or social location. As a child of God she has certain unalienable rights that the state, any state, must recognize. This young girl does not have to get the permission of the state or a school board to express who she is in terms of her deepest loyalties and

[110]Limbaugh, *Persecution*, p. 68.
[111]Ibid., p. 68.
[112]Gingrich, *To Save America*, p. 40.
[113]Ibid., p. 40.

affections. The unreasonable demand for the utter privatization of religion by *one segment* of American society upon another surely violates the free exercise clause of the First Amendment. Where is the Supreme Court when you actually need it?

SEPARATION OF CHURCH AND STATE HAS BECOME
SEPARATION OF CHURCH AND CULTURE

Culture is one of the means by which we order our experience on a number of levels. It embraces knowledge, ideas, customs, traditions, folkways, mores, language, notions of right and wrong, beliefs, skills, artifacts, social and political values, institutions, and organizations.[114] In a real sense, culture takes into account the full, rich and variegated life of a given society. It gives expression to the aspirations and goals of its members in terms of what they "cherish, honor and worship."[115] At its heart culture is a yearning for goodness and truth, however misdirected at times such desire may be. Again, culture is a "normative order by which we comprehend others, the larger world and ourselves," and it therefore holds the power "to define what is real."[116] Thus culture, as we are defining the term, in a modern liberal democratic state, though it includes polities, is much larger, more encompassing, than politics, as noted in chapter five. For one thing, politics entails making an appeal to authority, to the commanding and coercive power of the state, an appeal that would be seen as nothing less than intrusive in whole swaths of culture. Such areas of society are therefore best left with a minimum of political involvement in the celebration of human freedom, diversity and creativity.

Precisely because the narrative of American society has in effect been reworked to embrace the "no comprehensive" doctrine of Rawls (such that no transcendent dimension above the state is postulated and *individuals* are therefore free to pursue what goals or lifestyles they desire), the loss of a common culture is in the offing. But since culture abhors a vacuum, especially in terms of cult, that is, with respect to what people actually

---

[114]Samuel P. Huntington, *Who Are We? The Challenges to America's National Identity* (New York: Simon & Schuster, 2004), p. 30. I have expanded his definition.

[115]George Weigel, *The Cube and the Cathedral: Europe, America, and Politics Without God* (New York: Basic Books, 2005), pp. 41-42.

[116]Hunter, *To Change the World*, pp. 32, 178.

cherish, politics almost immediately fills in the gaps as it politicizes larger areas of cultural life. Throughout much of the twentieth century and on into the twenty-first, the federal government has taken over broad segments of culture especially in the areas of charity, education, and human sexuality, even attempting to redefine marriage in terms of the fleeting, political pressures of the day. In this setting, politicization means the "predisposition to interpret all of public life through the filter of partisan beliefs, values, ideals and attachments."[117] As the late Roman Catholic political philosopher John Courtney Murray (1904-1967) pointed out in his own day, "the state is distinct from society and limited in its office toward society." However, this principle, he cautioned "was cancelled out by the rise of the modern omni-competent society-state."[118] Indeed, when the American state politicizes a cultural area, such as charity, for example (an area, by the way, in which the church used to play a much larger role), it immediately brings its reworked narrative of separation of church and state to displace the heretofore cultural power of religion. Tax dollars that are collected from *all* Americans now have to be distributed to the needy (community rehab programs, for example) in accordance with a viewpoint that seeks to wipe clean any vestige of religious motivation and understanding. To his credit Barack Obama has backed away from the conclusions of this logic (as did George W. Bush), but this is a narrative that will undoubtedly surface again.

Evangelicals, of course, have been painfully aware of these cultural missteps by an overweening state, especially when the muscle of the Internal Revenue Service is applied, but they have been for the most part ineffective in stemming the tide. One of the paradoxes of American evangelicalism (and there are several!) is that as a movement it has exercised considerable political clout, especially during the last quarter of the twentieth century; nevertheless it has remained culturally weak, and not simply because of the federal government's grasping, encroaching ways. Oddly enough, evangelicals (and conservative Roman Catholics, for that matter) have been largely excluded from the structures of cultural power, espe-

---

[117]Ibid., p. 102.
[118]John Courtney Murray, *We Hold These Truths: Catholic Reflections on the American Proposition* (New York: Sheed & Ward, 1960), p. 35.

cially at its highest levels, because the prejudicial attitudes toward religion, which are inculcated day in and day out in public (government dominated) education, are touted as an appropriate way of proceeding *culturally* in a liberal and diverse democracy. Such attitudes, in which religion is considered a plutonium-like subject not to be handled beyond the walls of churches, synagogues or mosques, have influenced academia, the media, the courts and, of course, arts and entertainment. Though more than 80 percent of Americans would identify themselves as Christian, that large voice is rarely depicted culturally in its full weight. Here is a wall of separation as prodigious as any. In fact, if the offerings on American television of late are any guide, then an alien from outer space who visited this country and simply watched TV all day would have to conclude that Christians, indeed religious folk in general, were an obscure minority. So then, if culture is in some sense a window on truth and reality, on what is actually happening in the country, especially on Sunday mornings, then what is offered to Americans in several cultural venues is nothing short of a matrix. That is, it's an artful and sophisticated way of lying. The mistake of evangelicals, especially from the Christian right, is to think that political power easily translates into broader cultural power. It does not.

American cultural institutions, and the elites who lead them, have considerable power in that they have a corner on the market in the production of the symbols and paradigms that hold sway in society. In other words, "culture is embedded in structures of power," whose chief currency is expressed in the form of symbolic capital, the ability to draft a vision of reality whose only metaphysical support may be that it is repeated often enough.[119] Operating out of a "dynamics of exclusion," high status and privileged groups will restrict access into "*their* circle and their benefits."[120] The result of all this gate keeping according to Hunter is that "The culture-producing institutions of historic Christianity are largely marginalized in the economy of culture formation in North America."[121] How many books written about evangelicals and published by evangelical presses, for example, will be reviewed in the *New York Times Book Review* this year? You

---

[119]Hunter, *To Change the World*, p. 27.
[120]Ibid., p. 258 (emphasis added).
[121]Ibid., p. 89.

probably don't even need one hand to do the counting. Again, how many times will the Bible appear on the best-seller list in this leading newspaper, though this book continues to outsell all others? Answers to these and similar questions reveal something of the cultural ghetto where elites believe Christians in general, and evangelicals in particular, belong.

Exclusion by cultural elites, however, is only one part of the story. Evangelicals have actually barred themselves from high culture due to the attitudes, beliefs and practices they hold dear. In other words, evangelicals are not participating in the high arts of dance and theater in great numbers, for example, because they quite literally have not shown up. Held back by self-defeating attitudes that suggest these endeavors are too polluted, too sin-laden, to allow for their participation, evangelicals have helped to build the walls of their own cultural ghettos brick by brick.

In terms of academic life, the acids of anti-intellectualism continue to eat away at evangelical participation at the very highest levels of achievement. Would evangelicals, for example, like to change the figure cited in chapter four that only 7 percent of the members of the prestigious and exclusive cultural institution of the National Academy of Sciences believe in God? This can, after all, be done; it is not out of the realm of possibility. Part of the problem, however, is that the evangelical community has apparently not been willing to pay the price. What would the cost be? Send your evangelical sons and daughters off to prestigious universities to acquire doctorates in science, urge them to participate at the highest levels of their disciplines (where all sorts of socializing forces come into play) and several of these same evangelicals will likely join the ranks of the 93 percent instead of the 7. That is, they will have been socialized out of the faith. Granted evangelical entrance to this exclusive society would likely make a difference (if there was a concerted effort) and the number of members of the NAS who believe in God would perhaps change to 9 or even to 12 percent—but at what cost?

It's this sort of reckoning in which the *preeminent value* of faith is repeatedly set in contrast to academic excellence, in the form of elite privilege and status, that has kept the forces of anti-intellectualism very much in place in the evangelical community. From our perspective, however, when all is said and done, the life of the mind is not in conflict with that of the soul, and evangelicals should indeed pursue academic degrees at the highest levels. But they should do so supported and sustained by a believing community at least some of whose members are intellectually deep, even prodigious.

THE PRIORITY OF THE CHURCH OR DEMOCRACY?

Cultural elites on the judicial bench, in university classrooms, and in newspaper offices have sought to co-opt religion by making it merely instrumental to the alleged larger narrative of a liberal democracy. As Richard Rorty has remarked, not only is the conversation in American society about democracy as the highest goal, but religion, itself, must now be seen as an intrusion, as a genuine "conversation stopper."[122] Such an approach, once again, renders the second floor of the house empty. It therefore privileges radical secular and atheistic approaches by essentially defining religion out of existence such that it has no voice in the larger conversation in society about the good, the true and the beautiful. And so while the evangelical right and left were arguing about appropriate conceptions of social justice, and what forms their public voices would take, the broader cultural institutions and the elites who manage them were determined not to hear their voices at all. Speak the language of democracy (as *we* have defined it) or speak not at all.

Richard John Neuhaus clearly recognized the particular nature and threat of these ascendant views in American society, which is one of the reasons why he titled his journal *First Things*. In other words, to put first things first must surely mean understanding liberal democracies as pointing beyond themselves to a transcendent God; though God, of course, should not be defined in the form of any particular group's sectarian preference. That is, democracy should be instrumental to higher values, even God; and not the other way around. As such, democracy in the view of Neuhaus needs the voice of religion precisely to come to terms with its own penultimate status. It's the second thing, not the first. It keeps democracies from becoming a veritable Babylon heedless of anything higher and more worthy.

---

[122]See Richard Rorty, "Religion as Conversation-Stopper," *Common Knowledge* 3 (1994).

What is the consequence of holding views that in effect deny anything higher than the state, and contend that religion, if it is accorded any role in a modern liberal democracy, must find its way as just another instrument in the celebration of a democracy reconceived in an ever-accompanying narrative of secularism? The fruit of such culturally championed views can be illustrated, once again, in the political philosophy of Rawls, which has significant implications with respect to understanding what a human being is (anthropology). Severing the link between God and humanity both philosophically and procedurally, Rawls ends up with a greatly diminished view of a human being, one that can only be expressed (due to the loss of transcendence) in a rigid determinism. For example, denying a meritocratic system of justice (in which distribution of income would be in accordance with natural assets), Rawls went so far as to contend that even such elements as personal discipline and effort were morally arbitrary (equivalent to being born into a wealthy family) and did *not* strengthen the claim to acquisition and entitlement.[123] The state is therefore free to step in and redistribute the fruits of this labor. Put another way, men and women can be stripped of what goods they acquire simply because there is no longer any basis (moral worth has been excluded) that can possibly trump the egalitarian operations of Rawls's difference principle (inequalities to the benefit of the marginalized with significant redistribution). Describing the position of Rawls, Michael Sandel observes, "Encourage the gifted to develop and exercise their talents, but with the understanding that the rewards these talents reap in the market *belong* to the community as a whole."[124]

If nothing belongs to persons, if even their own talent and effort is viewed in a way that strips it of moral worth, then their pockets, so to speak, are able to be picked clean by an overly empowered state far better than any thief could have ever done. It is so much easier to begin with a deterministic philosophy, with a diminished view of a human being (that denies a transcendent self), and declare as a basic presupposition that persons really don't own anything at all. With nothing higher than the

---

[123]Michael J. Sandel, *Justice: What's the Right Thing to Do?* (New York: Farrar, Straus & Giroux, 2009), p. 155.

[124]Ibid., p. 156 (emphasis added).

modern democratic state that can be appealed to, all citizens have been rendered ripe for fleecing. Such is the logic of an empty second floor.

WHAT'S AN EVANGELICAL TO DO?

Evangelicals as well as conservative Roman Catholics are like the proverbial canary in the coal mine because both groups contain some of the first people to have experienced what the modern, liberal American democratic state has become, especially in its discriminating, prejudicial and coercive possibilities. In grappling with this predicament both communions of faith have taken a serious look at the theology of Stanley Hauerwas: evangelicals, likely because many of their number have been influenced by Anabaptist views, especially on issues of war and peace; Roman Catholics, in part, because Hauerwas was a professor at Notre Dame from 1970 to 1983, at which point he moved to Duke Divinity School. Such attention is clearly warranted; there is indeed much to appreciate in the reflections of this gifted scholar.

Critical of the liberal project of Rawls, Hauerwas observes that this modern approach, embracing some of the mistakes that go back to the time of the Enlightenment, has failed to offer a *narrative* and a *vision* that are commonly held to be true.[125] When principles are purported to be both abstract and universal, and are viewed *apart from stories*, then they are subject to "perverse interpretation," since they can then be gathered up into immoral stories.[126] Beyond this, Hauerwas calls into question the role that the state has played of late in taking over "the functions of the family." In particular, "few developments have been more deleterious for the family," he cautions, "than what we now call 'public education.'"[127] In light of these and other mistakes, the church must refuse "to continue the illusion that the larger social order knows what it is talking about when it calls for justice."[128]

An equal opportunity critic, Hauerwas offers numerous objections

---

[125]John Berkman and Michael Cartwright, eds., *The Hauerwas Reader* (Durham, N.C.: Duke University Press, 2001), p. 288 (emphasis added).

[126]Ibid., p. 170.

[127]Ibid., p. 509.

[128]Stanley Hauerwas, *After Christendom: How the Church Is to Behave If Freedom, Justice and a Christian Nation Are Bad Ideas* (Nashville: Abingdon, 1991), p. 68.

when he faces the church. Calling into question some of the teachings of the Social Gospel in its attempt to strengthen Christianity by supporting democracy, Hauerwas holds up the work of Rauschenbusch for special censure. What is the difference between a redeemed and an unredeemed society? "From Rauschenbusch's perspective," Hauerwas notes, "it is quite simple: saved social orders and institutions are democratic"; unsaved ones are not.[129] So understood, the mission of the church, at least in part, is to save the world and bring in social justice, not only by supporting liberal democracy but also by providing an ethos for its outworking. As a consequence of these and other trends, the seminaries of the modern liberal church ended up producing clergy who became "agents of modernity."[130] That is, they had learned how "to detach themselves from the insights, habits, stories, and structures that make the church the church."[131] Moreover, in his book *Resident Aliens*, coauthored with Will Willimon, Hauerwas contends that both the conservative and liberal church, "the so-called private and public church, are basically accommodationist (that is, Constantinian) in their social ethic." In other words, *both* wrongly assume that "the American church's primary social task is to underwrite American democracy."[132]

THE BEGINNINGS OF A POLITICAL PHILOSOPHY

If evangelicals want to shape the future of American politics by serving their neighbors (love your neighbor as yourself) then according to Stephen Lazarus they need to develop "not only a Christian mind, but also a Christian political mind."[133] Having a normative framework as found in Scripture and moral and natural law, in other words, is simply not enough, for it must be guided, at least to some extent, by a political philosophy that accurately reflects the cultural values cherished by the church. Ron Sider has articulated four key elements that constitute just such a philosophy:

---

[129]Berkman and Cartwright, *Hauerwas Reader,* p. 465.
[130]Ibid., pp. 114-15.
[131]Ibid., p. 116.
[132]Stanley Hauerwas and Will Willimon, *Resident Aliens: A Provocative Christian Assessment of Culture and Ministry for People Who Know That Something Is Wrong* (Nashville: Abingdon, 1989), p. 32.
[133]Stephen Lazarus, "Evangelicalism and Politics," in *The Futures of Evangelicalism,* ed. Craig Bartholomew, Robin Parry and Andrew West (Grand Rapids: Kregel, 2003), p. 286.

(1) a normative framework, (2) a broad study of society and the world, (3) a political philosophy, and (4) a detailed social analysis.[134] The third element needs special care, especially in the Christian community, so that the political philosophy that is chosen does not function in an ideological, partisan, nearly idolatrous, way. In other words, key insights from those political philosophies not chosen (whether they emphasize freedom or equality) must somehow be factored in since these insights correspond to the rights and needs of real people, those for whom Christ died. And in terms of the evangelical community in particular, the polarization of the left and right must be transcended. Consequently, if liberal or conservative political philosophies rule the day, it may be best for the church to become bilingual, so to speak, and avoid the considerable injustice that emerges when one of these philosophies is chosen in a flat-footed and nearly exclusive way. A Christian political philosophy, then, in contrast to others, will undoubtedly be motivated by the universal love of God that embraces *all* people, and it will therefore break out of the tribal mentality of the ideologues. On the political level in which so many elements come into play, and as Reinhold Niebuhr pointed out in his own generation, it will continually seek justice as the best expression of that love.[135]

Evangelicals (right, left and moderate) have important contributions to make at the political level, since their faith offers them a vantage point through which they can challenge the power of the state in terms of a "higher authority." As Stephen Carter observes, "At its best, religion in its subversive mode provides the believer with a transcendent reason to question the power of the state and the messages of the culture."[136] If, however, the state were viewed as the highest authority, the final court of appeal, then this would be nothing less than a prescription for oppression in various forms and, in the worst cases, outright tyranny. This was the kind of state (in Alabama, for instance) that Martin Luther King Jr. challenged on the basis of natural law when it had failed to accord to blacks those things that should pertain to *all* human beings. Lose that universal

---

[134]Ronald J. Sider, "Toward an Evangelical Political Philosophy," *Evangelical Review of Theology* 28, no. 2 (2004): 143-44.

[135]See Reinhold Niebuhr, *Moral Man and Immoral Society* (New York: Charles Scribner's, 1932).

[136]Carter, *God's Name in Vain*, p. 30.

dimension and the arguments tied to it, and there is hardly anything that the state cannot take away. Raw political and cultural power can always find a way (and a justification to go along with it) to exclude and deny. And so whereas Hauerwas has argued that when principles are viewed as abstract and universal apart from stories, "they can be subject to perverse interpretation," as noted earlier,[137] we must now add to this basic truth that stories understood apart from universal principles (expressive of human nature and moral and natural law) are likewise subject to perverse interpretation. The church then *must* become involved in the political life of the nation precisely in order to protect those who, in the days ahead, will likely be shorn of so much, due to the outworking of what modern, liberal democratic states have become. Not to become involved, to desire clean hands above all else, would simply be irresponsible. But when the church does speak publicly it can never be simply with a stripped down political voice, for the body of Christ has far more to say, even beyond its walls, than can be contained in such an idiom.

---

[137]Berkman and Cartwright, *Hauerwas Reader*, p. 170.

Conclusion

What Kind of Power?

THE STUDY OF AMERICAN EVANGELICALISM IS SO ENGAGING precisely because it is an important window on the shifting tides of cultural power. This complex movement went from significant cultural strength during the nineteenth century, prior to the Civil War (as the ongoing effects of the Second Great Awakening made their presence felt throughout American life), to considerable weakness in the twentieth century, when the once unified movement not only broke up but also was in cultural decline. Many evangelical Protestants, for example, took part in the heady progressive movement from the 1890s to 1920s only to find that their cultural overreach and subsequent rejection had became abundantly evident with the repeal of the Eighteenth Amendment, putting an end to the "holy" experiment of Prohibition. Immigration, of course, played its role in weakening Protestant power, and the Great Depression of 1929 and thereafter hurt all forms of religion. But none of these factors (as significant as they are) is sufficient to explain the extensive and lasting fall from cultural grace sustained by the broad Protestant evangelical consensus of the nineteenth century, informed as it was by a rich heritage of revivalism. For that story we must look elsewhere.

The cultural currents that led to the displacement of evangelical Protestantism were actually centuries old and were deeply rooted in the European culture that was passed along to Americans. Generally speaking, that inheritance entailed the *loss of teleology* (goals, purposes and ends) as one area of human endeavor after another was subsumed under a scientific, empirical method: from astronomy to physics to chemistry to sociology (the positivism of Auguste Comte) and on to psychology (Freud). Methodologically speaking, a diminished teleology had been there all along, in Europe at least from the sixteen hundreds, but it would take centuries both in Europe and later in the United States for that worldview to find *significant and powerful cultural expression.* That's precisely where Darwinism came in and why, at least in America, it resulted in nothing less than a cultural crisis. In offering an explanation of human life itself that rooted out any appeal to God at the outset, Darwinism and later neo-Darwinism created the intellectual capital by means of which the loss of teleology (already present in the other sciences) would at last find its powerful cultural and intellectual voice. The church could by no means confront Darwin in the same way it had (mistakenly!) challenged Galileo. The cultural tide had by now greatly shifted. Indeed, Darwin's ongoing voice can be readily heard in the numerous attempts to apply evolutionary thought, often in a reductionist way, to almost every form of human inquiry (evolutionary psychology, for example), and why Richard Dawkins has boasted of late, "Darwin made it possible to be an intellectually fulfilled atheist."[1]

The challenge of Darwinism as well as higher criticism (which in a certain sense is the application of a scientific methodology to the Bible) resulted in theological modernists giving up the intellectual ghost, so to speak, and with it much cultural power. Henceforth their defense of the Christian faith would devolve upon political ethics, often expressed in the form of social justice. The problem, of course, was that hardly anyone beyond the church was listening any longer. That is, the mainline denominations, as with fundamentalists (and later the neo-evangelicals), *all* lost a national cultural voice by the mid 1930s, when the quest for a Christian (read Protestant) America was clearly over.[2] Hereafter, all forms of Protestantism, from liberal to fundamentalist, would increasingly be reduced to subcultures in American life.

---

[1]Richard Dawkins, *The Blind Watchmaker: Why the Evidence of Evolution Reveals a Universe Without Design* (New York: W. W. Norton, 1996), p. 6.
[2]See Robert T. Handy, *A Christian America, Protestant Hopes and Historical Realities* (New York: Oxford University Press, 1971), p. 214.

Culturally weak in some important ways, both Protestant theological liberals and later neo-evangelicals (to a much lesser extent) developed a political idiom to address some of the salient issues at the national level in order to achieve, among other things, a larger hearing. This political idiom was employed so often by the church that it was eventually interlaced with the gospel itself in novel twentieth-century configurations (that would not bear the test of time), and this idiom oddly enough was then brought back into the church. Among theological liberals throughout most of the twentieth century, Marxism supplied much of the substance as well as the reasoning for the church's political ethic as expressed in numerous liberation theologies that operated with the divisive polar tensions developed by Marx of oppressor-oppressed. As this tribal script of bad-good (fill in the blanks with the preferred groups of your choice) increasingly replaced the church's larger, more gracious and inclusive narrative, some actually began to wonder why the church itself was becoming so divided and alienated. Moreover, the judgment of these liberal theologians was in many instances skewed by the philosophical materialism of Marx, once again with its loss of *teleology*. One of the more troubling results of this shift was that the maintenance needs of the poor were given an ultimacy that they simply could not bear. The church's concern for the downtrodden was therefore delimited—in a fashion that undermined the good news of the gospel that addresses human beings on so *many* levels.

In addition, while the cultural power of Protestants (and later on of all theists) was being displaced, the institutional power of the federal government was growing by leaps and bounds: from the New Deal of Franklin Delano Roosevelt to the Great Society of Lyndon Baines Johnson and on to the health care system of Barack Obama. This growth was unprecedented in the relatively brief history of the United States, and it changed the relation between the government and its citizens in ways that the founders would likely have opposed. The growth of federal power weakened the church by displacing its role in key areas, charity among them. What complicated matters even further was that by the 1960s the knowledge class, aware of the cultural weakness of religion since the 1930s, set about to revise the nation's history in light of the preferences of their own by a now well-ensconced social location. The earlier revisioning of the

First Amendment (which now *increased* the intrusive power of the federal government) whereby religion was contrasted with agnosticism and atheism helped government bureaucrats to spawn the myth of neutrality, all of which had the consequence of emptying out the second story of the American house. Put another way, this retooling, along with a distinct understanding of secularism, insured that theists would never break out of their subculture status, that the public dimension of American life (with all its cultural implications) would henceforth be swept clean of nearly every vestige of religion (even down to textbooks), to mirror the preferences not of the majority of Americans but of a culturally powerful minority, the knowledge class. Religion would still have some forms of public expression, but they would be far more limited. That all of this was accomplished in a relatively brief period of time, and with little significant opposition, is one of the wonders of recent American history.

The displacement of the heretofore cultural power of religion by enlarging the area of the political, increasing the reach of the state and then applying reworked scripts (many of which hailed from the 1960s), represented nothing less than the death of political theology, and with it, once again, the loss of teleology, this time in terms of how the nation itself was understood. In other words, unlike the vision of the founders, the modern, liberal American democratic state now acknowledges little of anything higher than itself. American democracy as refashioned by cultural elites has become the grand narrative beyond which no other lofty story exists. Religion, if it has any voice at all, is simply *instrumental* to something greater. In the nineteenth century, religion roared like a lion; it was a cultural power to be reckoned with, and it created nothing less than a benevolent empire. Today's religion, for the most part, chirps like a bird. And that chirping is viewed as an annoyance by secularists who want to, as they put it, focus on "the real issues" of life or who refer to religion as a "conversation stopper." Though such judgments are often hailed as profound by a secular knowledge class that has grown to be increasingly insular, viewed from another perspective, they are remarkably flat-footed, tedious and in the end boring.

The loss of teleology, then, is one of the common threads in this complicated history that helps to tie together the aftermath of the Scopes Trial, in which intellectual and cultural life were increasingly secularized—the loss of political theology by 1947 in the Supreme Court decision (*Everson v. Board of Education*) and on through the 1960s as the American state itself was no longer understood against the backdrop of anything greater. These two movements of the loss of teleology—one that has by and large played out in the academy, and the other in the courts—have resulted in an American cultural experience that in a real sense renders American theists second-class citizens, whether Christian, Jew or Muslim. Real Americans, according to this new way of thinking, view either the democratic way of life itself or its procedural expressions in the form of tolerance as their highest allegiance. And many religionists have jumped on board, especially in the mainline denominations. The modern liberal democratic state that considers nothing higher than itself constitutes a veritable Babylon. Those faiths that by and large accommodate their own stories to the feigned ultimacy of liberal democracies, developing a nearly exclusive political idiom, whether from the left or the right, make up Babylonian religion. Of course, communions of faith can participate in the political life of modern democracies without taking up Babylonian religion, but only if they remain insistent on keeping "first things first."

Given these shifts, conservative evangelicals, some of whom looked to the Christian right for leadership, took up the only real power left to them at the national level (or so it was claimed), that is, *political power*. They mistakenly thought, however, that this would be the avenue to significant cultural change whereby they would inevitably play a greater role. The Nazarene conservative icon James Dobson, for example, boasted that "in one generation, you [can] change the whole culture," not realizing, of course, that political and cultural power are very different animals.[3] Underscoring the complexity of cultural transformation, James Davison Hunter maintains that cultures are resistant to intentional change by "ordinary individuals or by a well-organized movement of individuals." He therefore viewed Dobson's boast as "nothing short of ludicrous."[4]

---

[3]James Dobson, cited in James Davison Hunter, *To Change the World: The Irony, Tragedy, and Possibility of Christianity in the Late Modern World* (Oxford: Oxford University Press, 2010), p. 45.
[4]Hunter, *To Change the World*, p. 45.

At any rate, conservative evangelicals pursued political power with an intensity that caused alarm among several cultural elites. From the rise of the Moral Majority and on to the Christian Coalition, key leaders sitting on judicial benches, in university classrooms and in the media were determined that these religious activists would remain well within their subcultures and therefore not develop a national voice that would make any difference—or be respected. Actually the fears of such left-leaning groups as People for the American Way proved to be for the most part unfounded, for even the political power of conservative evangelicals, though often celebrated, was remarkably thin. Republican candidates needed evangelicals to win, to be sure, but once elected they rarely sought to implement anything from a conservative or even a moderate evangelical social agenda. And the election of the Democrat Jimmy Carter as a born again president may have in the end done the overall movement more harm than good, especially since he favored the revisionism going back to 1947, which resulted in the further privatization of religion. The election of Carter, then, was like winning the beauty pageant without getting the scholarship.

When the evangelical left resurged later on, they often liked to paint themselves, especially to the younger generation, as being avant garde, cutting edge and groovy. Working the contrast, for example, between themselves and the administration of George W. Bush to the hilt, the evangelical left maintained that it was a viable, countercultural option for committed evangelicals and in a way, we must add, not very different in some important respects from the radicals of the 1960s.[5] However, when the evangelical left was not immediately compared to the Bush administration (in an attempt to hype the contrast as much as possible) and a much larger swath of American history was entertained (running from FDR to LBJ to Obama), it then emerged as very much a part of establishment trends in the sense that it participated in and even championed the ongoing growth of the federal government with hardly a peep of opposition and with little awareness of any danger, especially to religion. This was hardly countercultural. One only has to change the lens to discover this truth rather quickly.

---

[5]See Jim Wallis, *The Great Awakening: Reviving Faith and Politics in a Post-Religious Right America* (New York: HarperOne, 2008).

The grasping after political power on the part of the evangelical left and right for the sake, among other things, of a greater public voice has unfortunately hurt both movements. For one thing, both wings of the evangelical household are far greater than their public political expressions could ever suggest. Each is composed of people, for instance, who are more kind, gracious, caring and more respectful of human dignity and freedom than what could be assumed from their political posture. In other words, the politics of the evangelical left and right is like a mask that is offered those beyond the church; it is a public expression that invariably distorts not only their own image but that of Jesus Christ as well. How many Americans, for example, who lack a knowledge of the beauty of the church, are attracted to the Christian faith precisely due to the political agendas of the evangelical left and right? That both movements, each in its own way, have been complicit in the reduction of their public voice to a largely political one, even if a vaunted appeal is made to Scripture, is very much a part of the problem. And that this reduced political voice was ever brought back into the church to function at times as a major narrative and in a partisan way was mischievous beyond expression. Evangelical moderates had always been aware of these ideological dangers and with them the specter of idolatry and painful alienation.

Beyond this, the evangelical community unfortunately followed some of the practices of mainline denominations by privileging particular conceptions of social justice and politics, whether from the left or the right, and then it placed such judgments in the highest rank where they simply did not belong. The universality and catholicity of the gospel, in contrast, transcend such second rank, less-than-ultimate judgments. In other words, social and political justice can be variously conceived in viable and legitimate ways, and one is no less Christian or evangelical for differing in this area so long as the basic precepts of the moral law and orthodoxy are affirmed. In light of this, it is important not only to overcome some of the earlier nagging divisions of Reformed and Wesleyan evangelicalism in a generous way (there is so much that unites these two movements) but also to go beyond the fragmentation of the evangelical household that is currently taking place *across the theological traditions* because a particular brand of politics is, in effect, being made decisive.

How then shall evangelicals, with their various political judgments, minister in a twenty-first-century context? The evangelical right, left and middle can richly affirm their own particular conceptions of politics and social justice realizing, of course, that others who are no less Christian or evangelical will think remarkably otherwise.[6] What's more, an awareness of the strengths (not simply the weaknesses) of the views of the evangelical right, left and middle should be readily acknowledged by those who in the end hold much different views. Indeed, it is in living with this "disturbing knowledge" and embracing an at-times "annoying tension" that will keep each group of American evangelicals from taking the flat-footed, neighbor-denying ideological turn.

With political judgments in their proper place, with social visions not immediately equated with the kingdom of God in crude, idolatrous ways, evangelicals of all persuasions can be free to acknowledge their brothers and sisters of differing views around the Lord's Table, celebrating a God of holy love who transcends them all. Clearly, far more unites American evangelicals than what divides them. Such a gracious truth, however, can only be obscured when disparate political judgments or social visions displace the richness of the gospel, that is, the universal love of God manifested in Jesus Christ. Indeed, secularists and atheists often attached ultimate importance to their own partisan, fleeting political and social views, thinking that they have reached the heights of transcendence and meaning. They then expected the church to play this same game, so to speak. The body of Christ, however, in its rich ecumenical posture knows far better than this. The church therefore should live according to the wisdom that it has been granted by a gracious, ever-loving Lord, especially in its evangelical communions: not ideology but theology; not partisan separation but universal embrace.

Finding themselves culturally alienated, many evangelicals championed the work of Phillip Johnson, William Dembski and Michael Behe, with the hope that it too might somehow be a pathway to their

---

[6]I am assuming that all corners of evangelicalism acknowledge the guiding and illuminative power of the moral law as revealed in the Ten Commandments and in the Sermon on the Mount and that finds particular expression in natural law, the same law that Dr. Martin Luther King Jr. appealed to in order to turn back racism, and that right-to-life committees, in their own way, have cited to defend the unborn.

own cultural power through greater intellectual respectability. In this, however, they were grossly mistaken. In studying this complex movement very carefully, we observe that many of the champions of intelligent design, like their evangelical supporters, underestimated all that is required for even a modicum of cultural change. They too committed the error of James Dobson.

The advocates of intelligent design, as we have argued, wanted a clean intellectual battle; they ended up with a messy cultural war and traipsed into a wasp's nest of trouble ranging from the board of the Smithsonian Institution to the editors of leading scientific journals to opinionated and ill-informed judges and on to the morass of political, social and cultural confusion that constitutes what the American public school system has become. In all of this the intelligent design movement, in our judgment, has been naive, not realizing that cultural change is so very resistant to frontal assaults. Indeed, a case can be made that the intelligent design movement actually has *less* cultural power today than when it first began simply because it has raised the hackles of those who do indeed hold significant power, and they are now steeled in their opposition to the ID movement.

Though the pursuit of intellectual, cultural and political power is marked by struggle, opposition, setbacks and at times even counterproductive results, we by no means argue for a theology of retreat in which the church would, in effect, settle into an enclave under the banner of purity or under the guise of maintaining its distinct narrative. While such considerations are vital and necessary, they must, in our judgment, be held in tension with others as well. That is, the church as the body of Christ is not only a community *called out* of the world, but it is also called *back into* that same world, in all its messiness, for the sake of witness and, at its highest level, for communion. In other words, the church holds together (and in tension!) strong themes of separation (for the sake of purity and beauty) and engagement (for the sake of love and communion) as expressed in holy love, a love that is distinct, transformative and ennobling. To focus on purity and retreat to the exclusion of all else would result in new forms of separation; to focus on engagement as the only viable end in a modern, liberal democratic state would result in a very accommodated religion.[7] The church has its life, then, in tension, ever avoiding one-sided responses. The church lives in the midst of not only numerous fleeting cultural expressions but also what endures, what will last millennia and beyond. The way forward, then, is in terms of *both* engaging resistance (holiness) *and* resisting engagement (love).

Given this understanding, how can the church in general and evangelicals in particular be heard in a cultural and national climate that has become teleologically challenged, focused on *individualistic* freedom (the backside of pluralism) that defines the good in nearly any way, some of which actually undermine relationships and community in the long run (emotivism), and riven with scripts that in their outworking are prejudiced against virtually any public religious expression that is not immediately reduced to political considerations? A twofold approach is warranted.

First, evangelicals, along with Roman Catholics, must lead the way and demonstrate convincingly that the vision of a human being touted in elite American culture, informed by many sources, is in reality inadequate. Reigning cultural expressions of the nature of a human being, in other words the anthropological question, ranging from the denial of a human essence to the many diminishments offered by scientific empiricism (a human being is nothing but . . .) falter when compared to the rich wisdom that has been in the church for millennia: a human being is created in *nothing less* than the image and likeness of God. To consider human beings forthrightly, then, in all the dimensions in which they live is *in some sense* to discern the handiwork of God. That is, the anthropological and the theological, the human and the divine, are not utterly discontinuous, for both immanence and transcendence mark this vital relationship as Emil Brunner, the gifted Swiss theologian, knew all along. This connection between God and humanity, however, must ever be understood within the context of grace.

Moreover, this dignity of a human being, which is not something conferred by the state but reflects the ultimate source of human life, was celebrated by Martin Luther King Jr. as he challenged the vicious and de-

---

[7]See Charles Yrigoyen, John G. McEllhenney and Kenneth A. Rowe, *United Methodism at Forty: Looking Back Looking Forward* (Nashville: Abingdon, 2008) for a fine example of what an acculturated church looks like.

grading statutes of Southern states that failed to acknowledge that dignity, specifically in terms of African Americans. In employing a natural law argument, King's approach was both Thomistic and teleological. He understood that given human origins, properly understood, something higher than the state (or science, for that matter) must be recognized especially when that very same state fails to acknowledge, given the politics and cultural powers of the day, *all* that pertains to the dignity of a human being. Our current predicament, however, is that the very ingredients necessary to make this kind of moral and natural law argument (reflective of the moral law) are hardly in place. The acids of modernity, for example, have eaten away so much that moral justification today is seen as little more than an expression of the *preferences* of individuals or the pulls and tugs of political pressures. Beyond this, that which is common among human beings (in terms of a distinct essence, a humanness if you will) is likewise hardly recognized. Not surprisingly King's appeal to transcendence (going beyond the state to something higher) would be seen today by cultural shakers and movers as quaint at best and unnecessary at worst. The procedures and reasoning of democratic societies are, of course, sound and sufficient—or so it is claimed. In light of such views, we suffer few illusions about the considerable difficulty of making natural law arguments today. So many prerequisites must be put in place before this approach can even be understood. Yet without such arguments in play little remains to check the state in the future from becoming oppressive in ways not yet even imagined. Seeing itself as corresponding to the highest allegiance, the state and its narrative, in turn would become god-like, adjudicating all, a virtual Babylon.

Second, while many Christians have focused on the importance of political (*coercing*) and intellectual (*convincing*) power of late, the church once again in its wisdom has ever been aware of a far greater power, that is, the power of the Spirit. Showing up as a blank on both an empiricist and a secular lens, considered as nothing by unswerving materialists, the Spirit is yet that awe-evoking reality through which so many Americans comprehend the outworking of their own lives. And here, interestingly enough, we encounter the modern paradox in terms of meaning and proof: That which is insignificant is readily capable of empirical proof (the weight of a pencil for example), and that which is enormously significant (such as the Spirit expressed in the form of evoking love) is not capable of such proof at all. Therefore, to limit the expanse of human vision and interest simply to what can be empirically proved is to take up a reductionism that in the end will be oppressive to the human spirit itself, created as it is in nothing less than the *imago Dei*. Put another way, human beings are far greater and have more dimensions to their being than what some cultural leaders have ever acknowledged. Such insights, then, must not be lost. It is high time to employ the terminology of *homo spiritualis* as one of the best descriptions of what it means to be a human being.

Inviting all people to genuine transcendence in order to get out of themselves, so to speak, and to live *into* something more, the Holy Spirit, who ever bears witness to Jesus Christ, invites, entices and transforms men and women making them both remarkably beautiful and holy. Contrary to some popular misconceptions in American culture, to be transformed by the Holy Spirit is not the taking on of a crutch but issues in genuine and broad freedom. Where earlier a divided will was in place, often resulting in abject forms of bondage, now freedom, the liberty of the Spirit, reigns. Evangelicals and Pentecostals have celebrated this participatory knowledge in their joint focus on the importance of conversion, or to use the language of Jesus, on the necessity of being born again or born from above.

To be born again of the Holy Spirit, to be called to transcendence and freedom, to love not only God as the highest end of our being but also our neighbors as ourselves is not an invitation to the individualism so rampant in modern cultures. On the contrary, such transformation is best understood as taking place in the communal life of the church in general and in the setting of both Word and sacrament in particular. In knowing oneself in this transforming way as part of a vital community, one realizes that such knowledge is meant for all people, all those who in some sense bear the face of God. As the community is transformed and liberated by the Spirit, free to love the neighbor and even the enemy, the hard, divisive walls of groups, and the vulgar ethnocentrism that goes along with it, begin to melt away in the vision of something far greater. That is, when the miracle of this transforming power of the Spirit takes place, the elements of race, ethnicity, gender, social class, economic status and political persuasion that earlier boasted of being of ultimate importance in the skewed philosophies and theologies of our time begin to slip away and find their proper penultimate place in the glorification of a God of holy love who transcends us all. The walls of Babylon are beginning to crumble. There is, after all, no greater power than holy love, a holiness that speaks of the enchanting beauty of the Most High, and a love that is emblematic of communities drawn together and marked by this numinous, radiating divine presence. This was the same power and presence that toppled the walls of race at Azusa Street in the early twentieth century, when one filled with the Spirit proclaimed, "The color line was washed away in the blood."[8] And this was the same power that graciously marked Billy Graham, who humbly acknowledged in his own evangelistic ministry: "at the foot of the Cross, there are no racial barriers."[9] Yes, indeed, at the foot of the cross there are no racial barriers. Here then is wisdom and power in abundance.

[8]Vinson Synan, *The Holiness-Pentecostal Movement in the United States* (Grand Rapids: Eerdmans, 1987), p. 109.

[9]Billy Graham, cited in Michael D. Hammond, "Conscience in Conflict: Neo-Evangelicals and Race in the 1950s" (Ph.D. diss., Wheaton College Graduate School, 2002), p. 29.

Select Bibliography

BOOKS

Adams, Fred. *Our Living Multiverse.* New York: Pi Press, 2004.

Ahlstrom, Sydney E. *A Religious History of the American People.* 2 vols. Garden City, N.Y.: Image Books, 1975.

Alinsky, Saul D. *Rules for Radicals: A Pragmatic Primer for Realistic Radicals.* New York: Vintage Books, 1971.

Allen, Frederick Lewis. *Only Yesterday: An Informal History of the Nineteen-Twenties.* New York: Harper, 1931.

Askew, Thomas A., and Richard V. Pierard. *The American Church Experience: A Concise History.* Grand Rapids: Baker, 2004.

Ballor, Jordan J. *Ecumenical Babel.* Grand Rapids: Christian's Library Press, 2010.

Balmer, Randall. *Encyclopedia of Evangelicalism.* Waco, Tex.: Baylor University Press, 2004.

———. *The Making of Evangelicalism: From Revivalism to Politics and Beyond.* Waco, Tex.: Baylor University Press, 2010.

Behe, Michael J. *Darwin's Black Box: The Biochemical Challenge to Evolution.* New York: Simon & Schuster, 1996.

Bennett, William J. *America the Last Best Hope: Volume II: From a World at War to the Triumph of Freedom.* Nashville: Thomas Nelson, 2007.

Berger, Peter L. *The Sacred Canopy: Elements of a Sociological Theory of Religion.* New York: Anchor Books, 1990.

Berlinski, David. *The Deniable Darwin.* Edited by David Klinghoffer. Seattle: Discovery Institute Press, 2009.

———. *The Devil's Delusion: Atheism and Its Scientific Pretensions.* New York: Basic Books, 2009.

Bloesch, Donald G. *The Future of Evangelical Christianity: A Call for Unity Amidst Diversity.* Colorado Springs: Helmers & Howard, 1988.

Bork, Robert H. *Slouching Towards Gomorrah: Modern Liberalism and American Decline.* New York: Regan Books, 1996.

Brunner, Emil. *The Divine-Human Encounter.* Westport, Conn.: Greenwood, 1943.

Butterfield, Herbert. *The Origins of Modern Science.* New York: Free Press, 1957.

Campolo, Tony. *Letters to a Young Evangelical.* New York: Basic Books, 2006.

———. *Red Letter Christians: A Citizen's Guide to Faith and Politics.* Ventura, Calif.: Regal, 2008.

———. *Speaking My Mind: The Radical Evangelical Prophet Tackles the Tough Issues Christians Are Afraid to Face.* Nashville: W Publishing, 2004.

Carpenter, Joel A. *Revive Us Again: The Reawakening of American Fundamentalism.* New York: Oxford University Press, 1997.

Carter, Jimmy. *Living Faith.* New York: Three Rivers Press, 2001.

———. *Our Endangered Values: America's Moral Crisis.* New York: Simon & Schuster, 2005.

———. *Palestine: Peace Not Apartheid.* New York: Simon & Schuster, 2006.

Carter, Stephen L. *The Culture of Disbelief.* New York: Basic Books, 1993.

———. *God's Name in Vain: The Wrongs and Rights of Religion in Politics.* New York: Basic Books, 2000.

Case, Riley B. *Evangelical and Methodist: A Popular History.* Nashville: Abingdon, 2004.

Colling, Richard G. *Random Designer: Created from Chaos to Connect with the Creator.* Bourbonnais, Ill.: Browning Press, 2004.

Collins, Francis S. *The Language of God.* New York: Free Press, 2006.

Collins, Kenneth J. *John Wesley: A Theological Journey.* Nashville: Abingdon, 2003.

———. *The Evangelical Moment: The Promise of an American Religion.* Grand Rapids: Baker Academic, 2005.

Conser, Walter H., Jr. *God and the Natural World.* Columbia: University of South Carolina Press, 1993.

Coyne, Jerry A. *Why Evolution Is True.* New York: Penguin, 2009.

Cuneo, Terence, and Rene Van Woundenberg, eds. *The Cambridge Companion to Thomas Reid.* Cambridge: Cambridge University Press, 2004.

Darwin, Charles. *The Descent of Man.* New York: A. L. Fowle, 1874.

———. *The Origin of Species.* New York: Penguin, 1958.

Dawkins, Richard. *The Blind Watchmaker: Why the Evidence of Evolution Reveals a Universe without Design.* New York: W. W. Norton, 1996.

———. *The God Delusion.* London: Black Swan, 2006.

———. *The Greatest Show on Earth: The Evidence for Evolution.* New York: Free Press, 2009.

Dayton, Donald W. *The Theological Roots of Pentecostalism.* Grand Rapids: Francis Asbury Press, 1987.

Dembski, William. *The Design Revolution: Answering the Toughest Questions About Intelligent Design.* Downers Grover, Ill.: InterVarsity Press, 2004.

———. *Intelligent Design: The Bridge Between Science and Theology.* Downers Grove, Ill.: InterVarsity Press, 1999.

———. *Intelligent Design Uncensored: An Easy-to-Understand Guide to the Controversy.* Downers Grove, Ill.: IVP Books, 2010.

Dembski, William A., and Sean McDowell. *Understanding Intelligent Design: Everything You Need to Know in Plain Language.* Eugene, Ore.: Harvest House, 2008.

Denton, Michael. *Evolution: A Theory in Crisis: New Developments in Science Are Challenging Orthodox Darwinism.* Bethesda, Md.: Adler & Adler, 1986.

DeWolf, David, et al. *Traipsing into Evolution: Intelligent Design and the Kitzmiller vs. Dover Decision.* Seattle: Discovery Institute Press, 2006.

D'Souza, Dinesh. *Ronald Reagan: How an Ordinary Man Became an Extraordinary Leader.* New York: Touchstone 1997.

El-Faizy, Monique. *God and Country: How Evangelicals Have Become America's New Mainstream.* New York: Bloomsbury, 2006.

Ellingsen, Mark. *The Evangelical Movement: Growth, Impact, Controversy, Dialog.* Minneapolis: Augsburg, 1988.

Emerson, Michael O., and Christian Smith. *Divided by Faith: Evangelical Religion and the Problem of Race in America.* New York: Oxford University Press, 2000.

Feuerbach, Ludwig. *The Essence of Christianity.* Translated by George Eliot. New York: Harper Torchbooks, 1957.

Flew, Antony. *There Is a God: How the World's Most Notorious Atheist Changed His Mind.* New York HarperOne, 2007.

Gaustad, Edwin Scott. *A Religious History of America.* Rev. ed. New York: Harper & Row, 1990.

Giberson, Karl W. *Saving Darwin: How to Be a Christian and Believe in Evolution.* New York: HarperOne, 2008.

Giberson, Karl W., and Francis S. Collins. *The Language of Science and Faith.* Downers Grove, Ill.: InterVarsity Press, 2011.

Gingrich, Newt. *Rediscovering God in America: Reflections on the Role of Faith in*

Our Nation's History. Grand Rapids: Thomas Nelson, 2006.

Gonzalez, Guillermo, and Jay W Richards. *The Privileged Planet: How Our Place in the Cosmos Is Designed for Discovery*. Washington, D.C.: Regnery, 2004.

Gushee, David P. *Christians and Politics Beyond the Culture Wars: An Agenda for Engagement*. Grand Rapids: Baker, 2000.

———. *The Future of Faith in American Politics: The Public Witness of the Evangelical Center*. Waco, Tex.: Baylor University Press, 2008.

Handy, Robert T. *A Christian America, Protestant Hopes and Historical Realities*. New York: Oxford University Press, 1971.

Hankins, Barry N. *American Evangelicals: A Contemporary History of a Mainstream Religious Movement*. Lanham, Md.: Rowman & Littlefield, 2008.

Harris, Sam. *Letter to a Christian Nation*. New York: Alfred A. Knopf, 2006.

Hart, D. G. *That Old Time Religion in Modern America: Evangelical Protestantism in the Twentieth Century*. Chicago: I. R. Dee, 2002.

Hatch, Nathan O. *The Democratization of American Christianity*. New Haven, Conn.: Yale University Press, 1989.

Hauerwas, Stanley. *After Christendom: How the Church Is to Behave If Freedom, Justice and a Christian Nation Are Bad Ideas*. Nashville: Abingdon, 1991.

Hauerwas, Stanley, and Will Willimon. *Resident Aliens: A Provocative Christian Assessment of Culture and Ministry for People Who Know That Something Is Wrong*. Nashville: Abingdon, 1989.

Hawking, Stephen, and Stephen Mlodinow. *The Grand Design*. New York: Bantam Books, 2010.

Hayek, F. A. *The Road to Serfdom*. Chicago: University of Chicago Press, 2007.

Henry, Carl F. H. *The Uneasy Conscience of Fundamentalism*. Grand Rapids: Eerdmans, 1947.

Himmelfarb, Gertrude. *Darwin and the Darwinian Revolution*. Chicago: Elephant Paperbacks, 1959.

———. *One Nation, Two Cultures*. New York: Alfred A. Knopf, 1999.

Hodge, Charles. *Systematic Theology*. Vol. 2. Peabody, Mass.: Hendrickson, 1999.

Hofstadter, Richard. *Anti-Intellectualism in American Life*. New York: Vintage Books, 1962.

Hudson, Winthrop S. *Religion in America: An Historical Account of the Development of American Religious Life*. New York: Charles Scribner's, 1973.

Hunter, George G. *Christian, Evangelical and Democrat?* Nashville: Abingdon, 2006.

Hunter, James Davison. *Culture Wars: The Struggle to Define America*. New York: Basic Books, 1991.

———. *To Change the World: The Irony, Tragedy, and Possibility of Christianity in the Late Modern World.* Oxford: Oxford University Press, 2010.

———. *Evangelicalism: The Coming Generation.* Chicago: University of Chicago Press, 1987.

Huntington, Samuel P. *Who Are We? The Challenges to America's National Identity.* New York: Simon & Schuster, 2004.

Jacoby, Susan. *Freethinkers: A History of American Secularism.* New York: Henry Holt, 2004.

Johnson, Phillip E. *Darwin on Trial.* Downers Grove, Ill.: InterVarsity Press, 1991.

———. *Reason in the Balance: The Case Against Naturalism in Science, Law and Education.* Downers Grove, Ill.: InterVarsity Press, 1995.

———. *The Wedge of Truth: Splitting the Foundations of Naturalism.* Downers Grove, Ill.: InterVarsity Press, 2000.

Kenyon, Dean H., and Charles B. Thaxton. *Of Pandas and People.* Dallas: Houghton, 1989.

Kimball, Roger. *The Long March: How the Cultural Revolution of the 1960s Changed America.* San Francisco: Encounter Books, 2000.

Koester, Nancy. *The History of Christianity in the United States.* Minneapolis: Fortress Press, 2007.

Kostlevy, William. *Holiness Manuscripts: A Guide to Sources Documenting the Wesleyan Holiness Movement in the United States and Canada.* Metuchen, N.J.: Scarecrow Press, 1994.

Kyle, Richard. *Evangelicalism: An Americanized Christianity.* New Brunswick, N.J.: Transaction, 2006.

Land, Steven J. *Pentecostal Spirituality: A Passion for the Kingdom.* Sheffield, U.K.: Sheffield Academic Press, 2001.

Larson, Edward J. *Summer for the Gods: The Scopes Trial and America's Continuing Debate over Science and Religion.* New York: Basic Books, 1997.

Laughlin, Robert B. *A Different Universe: Reinventing Physics from the Bottom Down.* New York: Basic Books, 2005.

Lewis, C. S. *The Problem of Pain.* New York: Macmillan, 1962.

Lewis, Sinclair. *Elmer Gantry.* New York: Harcourt, Brace, 1927.

Lichtman, Allan J. *White Protestant Nation: The Rise of the American Conservative Movement.* New York: Grove, 2008.

Lilla, Mark. *The Stillborn God: Religion, Politics and the Modern West.* New York: Alfred A. Knopf, 2007.

Limbaugh, David. *Persecution: How Liberals Are Waging War Against Christianity.* Washington, D.C.: Regnery, 2003.

Lindsay, D. Michael. *Faith in the Halls of Power: How Evangelicals Joined the American Elite.* New York: Oxford University Press, 2007.

Lindsell, Harold. *The New Paganism: Understanding American Culture and the Role of the Church.* San Francisco: Harper & Row, 1987.

Linker, Damon. *The Theocons: Secular America under Siege.* New York: Anchor Books, 2006.

Lippmann, Walter. *The Public Philosophy.* New Brunswick, N.J.: Transaction, 1989.

Machen, J. Gresham. *Christianity & Liberalism.* Grand Rapids: Eerdmans, 1990.

MacIntyre, Alasdair. *After Virtue.* 3rd ed. Notre Dame, Ind.: University of Notre Dame Press, 2007.

Mansfield, Stephen. *The Faith of Barack Obama.* Nashville: Thomas Nelson, 2008.

Marsden, George. *Fundamentalism and American Culture.* New York: Oxford University Press, 1980.

———. *Reforming Fundamentalism: Fuller Seminary and the New Evangelicalism.* Grand Rapids: Eerdmans, 1987.

———. *Religion and American Culture.* New York: Harcourt, Brace & World, 1990.

———. *Understanding Fundamentalism and Evangelicalism.* Grand Rapids: Eerdmans, 1991.

Marsden, George M., and Bradley J. Longfield. *The Secularization of the Academy.* New York: Oxford University Press, 1992.

Marsh, Charles. *Wayward Christian Soldiers: Freeing the Gospel from Political Captivity.* Oxford: Oxford University Press, 2007.

Marty, Martin E. *Modern American Religion: The Irony of It All 1893-1919.* Vol. 1. Chicago: University of Chicago Press, 1986.

———. *Modern American Religion: The Noise of Conflict 1919-1941.* Vol. 2. Chicago: University of Chicago Press, 1991.

———. *Modern American Religion: Under God Indivisible 1941-1960.* Vol. 3. Chicago: University of Chicago Press, 1996.

———. *Pilgrims in Their Own Land.* Harrisonburg, Va.: Penguin, 1984.

Mathews, Shailer. *The Faith of Modernism.* New York: Macmillan, 1925.

May, Henry F. *The Enlightenment in America.* Oxford: Oxford University Press, 1976.

McCune, Rolland D. *Promise Unfulfilled: The Failed Strategy of Modern Evangelicalism.* Greenville, S.C.: Ambassador International, 2004.

McGrath, Alister E. *Science and Religion: An Introduction.* Malden, Mass.: Blackwell, 1999.

———. *The Twilight of Atheism.* New York: Doubleday, 2006.

McLaren, Brian. *A Generous Orthodoxy.* Grand Rapids: Zondervan, 2004.

———. *The Secret Message of Jesus: Uncovering the Truth That Could Change Everything.* Nashville: Thomas Nelson, 2006.

Medawar, Peter. *The Limits of Science.* Oxford: Oxford University Press, 1984.

Moberg, David. *The Great Reversal.* Philadelphia: Holman, 1972.

Moore, Scott H. *The Limits of Liberal Democracy.* Downers Grove, Ill.: IVP Academic, 2009.

Murray, Iain H. *Evangelicalism Divided: A Record of Crucial Change in the Years 1950-2000.* Edinburgh: Banner of Truth, 2000.

Murray, John Courtney. *We Hold These Truths: Catholic Reflections on the American Proposition.* New York: Sheed & Ward, 1960.

Neuhaus, Richard John. *American Babylon: Notes of a Christian Exile.* New York: Basic Books, 2009.

———. *The Naked Public Square.* Grand Rapids: Eerdmans, 1984.

Newberry, Tommy. *The War on Success: How the Obama Agenda Is Shattering the American Dream.* Washington, D.C.: Regnery, 2010.

Niebuhr, H. Richard. *The Social Sources of Denominationalism.* New York: New American Library, 1957.

Niebuhr, Reinhold. *The Children of Light and the Children of Darkness.* New York: Charles Scribner's, 1944.

———. *Moral Man and Immoral Society.* New York: Charles Scribner's, 1932.

Noll, Mark. *A History of Christianity in the United States and Canada.* Grand Rapids: Eerdmans, 1992.

———. *The Old Religion in the New World: The History of North American Christianity.* Grand Rapids: Eerdmans, 2002.

———. *American Evangelical Christianity.* Malden, Mass.: Blackwell, 2001.

Noll, Mark, and Carolyn Nystrom. *Is the Reformation Over? An Evangelical Assessment of Contemporary Roman Catholicism.* Grand Rapids: Baker Academic, 2005.

Novak, Michael. *The Spirit of Democratic Capitalism.* New York: Touchstone, 1982.

Nugent, Walter. *Crossings: The Great Transatlantic Migrations, 1870-1914.* Indianapolis: Indiana University Press, 1992.

Obama, Barack. *The Audacity of Hope: Thoughts on Reclaiming the American Dream.* New York: Three Rivers Press, 2006.

————. *Dreams from My Father*. New York: Crown Publishers, 1995.

Olasky, Marvin. *Compassionate Conservatism: What It Is, What It Does, and How It Can Transform America*. New York: Free Press, 2000.

Olasky, Marvin, et al. *Freedom, Justice, and Hope: Toward a Strategy for the Poor and the Oppressed*. Westchester, Ill.: Crossway, 1988.

Olson, Roger E. *Reformed and Always Reforming*. Grand Rapids: Baker Academic, 2007.

Outler, Albert C. *The Works of John Wesley*. Vols. 1-4: *Sermons*. Bicentennial ed. Nashville: Abingdon, 1984-1987.

Penning, James M., and Corwin E. Smidt. *Evangelicalism: The Next Generation*. Grand Rapids: Baker Academic, 2002.

Pickering, Ernest D. *The Tragedy of Compromise: The Origin and Impact of the New Evangelicalism*. Greenville, S.C.: Bob Jones University Press, 1994.

Quebedeaux, Richard. *The Worldly Evangelicals*. San Francisco: Harper & Row, 1978.

————. *The Young Evangelicals*. New York: Harper & Row, 1974.

Rausch, Thomas P. *Catholics and Evangelicals: Do They Share a Common Future?* Downers Grove, Ill.: InterVarsity Press, 2000.

Rauschenbusch, Walter. *Christianity and the Social Crisis*. New York: Macmillan, 1907.

————. *A Theology for the Social Gospel*. Nashville: Abingdon, 1981.

Rawls, John *Justice as Fairness: A Restatement*. Cambridge, Mass.: Belknap Press, 2001.

Reed, Ralph. *Active Faith: How Christians Are Changing the Soul of American Politics*. New York: Free Press, 1996.

Robertson, Pat, and Bob Slosser. *The Secret Kingdom: Your Path to Peace, Love and Financial Security*. Nashville: W Publishing, 1992.

Sagan, Carl. *Cosmos*. New York: Random House, 1980.

Sandeen, Ernest R. *The Roots of Fundamentalism: British and American Millenarianism, 1800-1930*. Grand Rapids: Baker, 1978.

Sandel, Michael J. *Justice: What's the Right Thing to Do?* New York: Farrar, Straus & Giroux, 2009.

Schaeffer, Francis A. *A Christian Manifesto*. Westchester, Ill.: Crossway, 1981.

Sider, Ronald J. *Fixing the Moral Deficit: A Balanced Way to Balance the Budget*. Downers Grove, Ill.: InterVarsity Press, 2012.

————. *Just Generosity: A New Vision for Overcoming Poverty in America*. Grand Rapids: Baker, 1999.

Singham, Mano. *God vs. Darwin: The War Between Evolution and Creationism in the Classroom*. New York: Rowman & Littlefield Education, 2009.

Smidt, Corwin E. *Contemporary Evangelical Political Involvement*. Lanham, Md.: University Press of America, 1989.

———. *Pulpit and Politics: Clergy in American Politics at the Advent of the Millennium*. Waco, Tex.: Baylor University Press, 2004.

Smith, Christian. *American Evangelicalism: Embattled and Thriving*. Chicago: University of Chicago Press, 1998.

———. *Christian America? What Evangelicals Really Want*. Berkley: University of California Press, 2000.

Sowell, Thomas. *The Housing Boom and Bust*. New York: Basic Books, 2009.

Stein, Harry. *How I Accidently Joined the Vast Right Wing Conspiracy (and Found Inner Peace)*. New York: Harper Paperbacks, 2001.

Stenger, Victor J. *God: The Failed Hypothesis: How Science Shows That God Does Not Exist*. Amherst, N.Y.: Prometheus, 2008.

Stone, Jon R. *On the Boundaries of American Evangelicalism: The Postwar Evangelical Coalition*. New York: St. Martin's Press, 1997.

Sweeney, Douglas A. *The American Evangelical Story: A History of the Movement*. Grand Rapids: Baker Academic, 2005.

Sykes, Charles J. *A Nation of Victims: The Decay of the American Character*. New York: St. Martin's Press, 1992.

Synan, Vinson. *The Holiness-Pentecostal Movement in the United States*. Grand Rapids: Eerdmans, 1987.

Thaxton, Charles B. *The Mystery of Life's Origin: Reassessing Current Theories*. New York: Lewis & Stanley, 1992.

Thomas, Cal, and Ed Dobson. *Blinded by Might*. Grand Rapids: Zondervan, 1999.

Tillich, Paul. *The Courage to Be*. New Haven, Conn.: Yale University Press, 1952.

Tipton, Steven M. *Public Pulpits: Methodists and Mainline Churches in the Moral Argument of Public Life*. Chicago University of Chicago Press, 2007.

Wallis, Jim. *The Call to Conversion: Why Faith Is Always Personal but Never Private*. San Francisco: HarperSanFrancisco, 2005.

———. *God's Politics: Why the Right Gets It Wrong and the Left Doesn't Get It*. San Francisco: HarperSanFrancisco, 2005.

———. *The Great Awakening: Reviving Faith and Politics in a Post-Religious Right America*. New York: HarperOne, 2008.

Ward, Peter D, and Donald Brownlee. *Rare Earth: Why Complex Life Is Uncommon in the Universe*. New York: Copernicus Books, 2000.

Weigel, George. *The Cube and the Cathedral: Europe, America, and Politics Without God*. New York: Basic Books, 2005.

Wilson, A. N. *God's Funeral*. New York: W. W. Norton, 1999.

Woodward, Thomas. *Darwin Strikes Back: Defending the Science of Intelligent Design*. Grand Rapids: Baker, 2006.

Wuthnow, Robert. *The Struggle for America's Soul: Evangelicals, Liberals and Secularism*. Grand Rapids: Eerdmans, 1989.

Yoder, John Howard. *The Politics of Jesus*. Grand Rapids: Eerdmans, 1972.

Yrigoyen, Charles, John G. McEllhenney, and Kenneth A. Rowe. *United Methodism at Forty: Looking Back Looking Forward*. Nashville: Abingdon, 2008.

CHAPTERS IN BOOKS

Bebbington, David W. "Evangelicalism in Its Settings: The British and American Movements since 1940." In *Evangelicalism*, edited by Mark Noll, David W. Bebbington and George A. Rawlyk, 365-88. New York: Oxford University Press, 1994.

Campbell, Dennis M. "Does Methodism Have a Future in American Culture." In *United Methodism and American Culture: Questions for the Twenty-First Century Church*, edited by Russell E Richey, William B. Lawrence and Dennis M. Campbell, 9-23. Nashville: Abingdon, 1999.

Cromartie, Michael. "The Evangelical Kaleidoscope: A Survey of Recent Evangelical Political Engagement." In *Christians and Politics Beyond the Culture Wars*, edited by David P. Gushee, 15-28. Grand Rapids: Baker, 2000.

Dayton, Donald W. "James Dean, Popular Culture and Popular Religion: With Implications for the Study of Evangelicalism." In *From the Margins: A Celebration of the Theological Work of Donald W. Dayton*, edited by Christian T. Collins Winn. Eugene, Ore.: Pickwick, 2007.

Elshtain, Jean Bethke. "Religion and American Democracy." In *Christians and Politics Beyond the Culture Wars*, edited by David P. Gushee, 69-78. Grand Rapids: Baker, 2000.

Miller, Kenneth R. "The Flagellum Unspun: The Collapse of 'Irreducible Complexity.'" In *Debating Design: From Darwin to DNA*, edited by William Dembski and Michael Ruse, 81-97. New York: Cambridge University Press, 2004.

Plantinga, Alvin. "Evolution and Design." In *For Faith and Clarity: Philosophical Contributions to Christian Theology*, edited by James Beilby, 201-17. Grand Rapids: Baker Academic, 2006.

Warfield, Benjamin B. "Evolution or Development." In *Evolution, Science, and*

Scripture: Selected Writings, edited by Mark Noll and David Livingstone, 114-31. Grand Rapids: Baker, 2000.

Edited Books

Abraham, William J., Jason E. Vicker and Natalie B. Van Kirk, eds. *Canonical Theism: A Proposal for Theology and the Church.* Grand Rapids: Eerdmans, 2008.

Ahlstrom, Sydney E., ed. *Theology in America: The Major Protestant Voices from Puritanism to Neo-Orthodoxy.* Indianapolis: Bobbs-Merrill Educational, 1967.

Berkman, John, and Michael Cartwright, eds. *The Hauerwas Reader.* Durham, N.C.: Duke University Press, 2001.

Brockman, John, ed. *Intelligent Thought: Science Versus the Intelligent Design Movement.* New York: Vintage Books, 2006.

————, ed. *What We Believe but Cannot Prove: Today's Leading Thinkers on Science in Age of Certainty.* New York: Harper Perennial, 2006.

Colson, Charles, and Richard John Neuhaus, eds. *Evangelicals and Catholics: Toward a Common Mission.* Dallas, Tex.: Word, 1995.

————, eds. *Your Word Is Truth: A Project of Evangelicals and Catholics Together.* Grand Rapids: Eerdmans, 2002.

Cullop, Floyd G., ed. *The Constitution of the United States.* New York: New American Library, 1984.

Dembski, William, and James M. Kushiner, eds. *Signs of Intelligence: Understanding Intelligent Design.* Grand Rapids: Brazos Press, 2004.

Dembski, William, and Michael Ruse, eds. *Debating Design: From Darwin to DNA.* New York: Cambridge University Press, 2004.

Flexner, Stuart Berg, ed. *The Random House Dictionary of the English Language Unabridged.* New York: Random House 1987.

Pelikan, Jaroslav, ed. *Lectures on Galatians,* Luther's Works 26. Saint Louis: Concordia Publishing, 1963.

Scott, Jack, ed. *An Annotated Edition of Lectures on Moral Philosophy by John Witherspoon.* Newark: University of Delaware Press, 1982.

Torrey, R. A., and A. C. Dixon, eds. *The Fundamentals: A Testimony to the Truth.* Grand Rapids: Baker, 1980.

Washington, James M., ed. *The Essential Writings and Speeches of Martin Luther King, Jr.* New York: HarperCollins, 1991.

Wells, David F., and John D. Woodbridge, eds. *The Evangelicals: What They Believe, Who They Are, Where They Are Changing.* Nashville: Abingdon, 1975.

Wiener, Philip P., ed. *Dictionary of the History of Ideas: Studies of Selected Pivotal Ideas*. New York: Charles Scribner's, 1973.

ARTICLES

Abraham, William J. "The End of Wesleyan Theology." *Wesleyan Theological Journal* 40, no. 1 (2005): 7-25.

"American Theocracy." *Economist* 379, no. 8479 (2006): 32.

Bendyna, Mary E. "Uneasy Alliance." *Sociology of Religion* 62, no. 1 (2001): 52-64.

Berggren, D. Jason. "I Had a Different Way of Governing: The Living Faith of President Carter." *Journal of Church and State* 47, no. 1 (2005): 43-61.

Boston, Rob. "Of Declarations and Tea Parties: A New Birth for the Religious Right." *Church and State* 70, no. 2 (2010): 30-31.

———. "The Religious Right after Falwell." *Church and State* 60, no. 7 (2007): 4-6.

Canipe, Lee. "Under God and Anti-Communist: How the Pledge of Allegiance Got Religion in Cold War America." *Journal of Church and State* 45, no. 2 (2003): 305-23.

"Catholics Join Evangelicals to Resist Abortion, Gay Marriage." *National Catholic Reporter* 46, no. 4 (2009): 13.

Clapp, Rodney. "Bad News Evangelicals." *Christian Century* 126, no. 5 (2009): 53.

Coleman, John. "Left Behind: Who and Where Is the Religious Left in the United States." *America* 194, no. 15 (2006): 11-14.

Collins, Francis S. "Can an Evangelical Believe in Evolution?" *International Journal of Frontier Missions* 20, no. 4 (2003): 109-12.

Collins, Kenneth J. "Is 'Canonical Theism' a Viable Option for Wesleyans?" *Wesleyan Theological Journal* 45, no. 2 (2010): 82-107.

Conn, Joseph. "Civil Rights and Civil Liberties." *Church and State* 62, no. 3 (2009): 52-54.

———. "God, Guns and the GOP." *Church and State* 51, no. 10 (1998): 4-8.

Cottle, Michelle. "Prayer Center: Let's Not Talk About Sex." *New Republic* 232, no. 9 (2005): 21-25.

Cromartie, Michael. "Fixing the World: From Nonplayers to Radicals to New Right Conservatives: The Saga of Evangelical Social Actions." *Christianity Today* 36, no. 5 (1992): 23-25.

Crouse, Eric R. "Popular Cold Warriors: Conservative Protestants, Communism, and Culture in Early Cold War America." *Journal of Religion and Popular Culture* 2, no. 2002 (2002): 1-17.

Curry, Dean C. "Evangelical Amnesia." *First Things* 176 (2007): 15-17.

Davis, Sue. "President Carter's Selection Reforms and Judicial Policymaking." *American Politics Quarterly* 14, no. 4 (1986): 328.

Dayton, Donald. "The Embourgeoisement of a Vision: Lament of a Radical Evangelical." *The Other Side* 23 (1987): 19.

Editor. "Obama Decision on Birth Control Sparks Battle with U.S. Bishops." *Church and State* 65, no. 3 (2012): 17.

Ellingsen, Mark. "Common Sense Realism: The Cutting Edge of Evangelical Identity." *Dialog* 24, no. 3 (1985): 197-205.

Evans, Curtis J. "White Evangelical Protestant Responses to the Civil Rights Movement." *Harvard Theological Review* 102, no. 2 (2009): 245-73.

Farrow, Douglas. "Three Meanings of Secular." *First Things* (2003): 20-23.

Flowers, Ronald B. "President Jimmy Carter, Evangelicalism, Church-State Relations, and Civil Religion." *Journal of Church and State* 25, no. 1 (1983): 113-32.

Freedman, Robert. "The Religious Right and the Carter Administration." *Historical Journal* 48, no. 1 (2005): 231-60.

Goldberg, Jonah. "What Kind of Socialist." *Commentary* 129, no. 5 (2010): 9-15.

Gould, Stephen Jay. "Impeaching a Self-Appointed Judge." Review of Phillip Johnson's *Darwin on Trial*. Scientific American 267 (1992): 118-21.

Green, John. "Evangelical Realignment." *Christian Century* 112, no. 2 (1995): 676-79.

———. "The Undetected Tide." *Religion in the News* 6, no. 1 (2003): 4-6.

Guthrie, Stan. "When Red Is Blue." *Christianity Today* 51, no. 10 (2007): 100.

Harding, Susan. "American Protestant Moralism and the Secular Imagination." *Social Research* 76, no. 4 (2009): 1277-1306.

Harper, Brad. "The Scopes Trial, Fundamentalism, and the Creation of an Anti-Culture Culture: Can Evangelical Christians Transcend Their History in the Culture Wars." *Cultural Encounters* 3, no. 1 (2006): 7-16.

Honey, Charles. "Adamant on Adam." *Christianity Today* 54, no. 6 (2010): 14.

Hoover, Dennis. "Ecumenism of the Trenches." *Journal of Ecumenical Studies* 41, no. 2 (2004): 247-71.

Howell, Leon. "Ups and Downs of the Religious Right." *Christian Century* 117, no. 13 (2000): 462-66.

Hynson, Leon. "The Church and Social Transformation." *Wesleyan Theological Journal* 11 (1976): 49-61.

———. "Religion and Politics, Truth and Toleration: Toward a Wesleyan Political Philosophy" *Evangelical Journal* 15 (1997): 18-32.

Jaschik, Scott. "Academic Freedom and Evolution." *Inside Higher Ed* (2007): 1-3.

————. "Believing in God and Evolution." *Inside Higher Ed* (2009).

Jelen, Ted. "American Clergy on Evolution and Creationism." *Review of Religious Research* 51, no. 3 (2010): 277-87.

Johnson, Phillip E. "Should a Darwinist Bother to Be a Christian?" *Philosophia Christi* 4, no. 1 (2002): 185-88.

Karmarkovic, Alex. "American Evangelical Responses to the Russian Revolution and the Rise of Communism in the Twentieth Century." *Fides et Historia* 4, no. 2 (1972): 11-27.

Kushiner, James Mark. "Where We Stand." *Touchstone* 23, no. 1 (2010): 3-4.

Lambro, David. "Obama Plots Assault on Non-Union Business." *Human Events* 66, no. 14 (2010).

Love, D'Esta. "An Interview with Edward J. Larson, Pulitzer Prize Winning Author of *Summer for the Gods: The Scopes Trial and America's Continuing Debate over Science and Religion*." *Leaven* 17, no. 2 (2009): 67-72.

Marsden, George. "Divine Politics." *Wilson Quarterly* 30, no. 3 (2006): 82.

————. "Fundamentalism as an American Phenomenon." *Church History* 46, no. 2 (1977): 215-32.

McLaren, Brian. "Can We Talk? The Manhattan Declaration's Harder Challenge." *Sojourners* 39, no. 3 (2010): 13.

Miller, Mike. "Community Organizing: Lost among Christians?" *Social Policy* 31, no. 1 (2000): 33-41.

Moran, Jeffrey P. "The Scopes Trial and Southern Fundamentalism in Black and White: Race, Region, and Religion." *Journal of Southern History* 70, no. 1 (2004): 95-120.

Morris, Dick, and Eileen McGann. "The Obama Presidency: Here Comes Socialism." *Human Events* 65, no. 4 (2009): 1-8.

Myra, Harold, and Marshall Shelley. "Jesus and Justice: How Billy Graham Tactfully Led Evangelicals on Race at His First New York City Crusade." *Christianity Today* 49 (2005): 58-59.

Neff, David, ed. "Why Is Latin America Turning Protestant?" *Christianity Today* 36 (1992): 28-39.

Newman, Simon P. "One Nation under God; Making Historical Sense of Evangelical Protestantism in Contemporary American Politics." *Journal of American Studies* 41, no. 3 (2007): 581-97.

Olson, Roger E. "The World Its Parish: Wesleyan Theology in the Postmodern Global Village." *The Asbury Theological Journal* 59, no. 1 (2004): 17-26.

Pierard, Richard. "From Evangelical Exclusivism to Ecumenical Openness: Billy Graham and Sociopolitical Issues." *Journal of Ecumenical Studies* 20, no. 3 (1983): 425-46.

Potter, Andrew. "How Did America Become the New Canada." *Maclean's* 122, no. 13 (2009): 14.

Rabey, Steve. "Conversation or Competition? Pentecostals, Roman Catholics in Long-Standing Talks to Resolve Conflicts, Discover Some Commonalities." *Christianity Today* 42, no. 10 (1998): 22-23.

Ramet, Sabrina. "'Fighting for the Christian Nation': The Christian Right and American Politics." *Journal of Human Rights* 4, no. 3 (2005): 431-42.

Regnerus, Mark D. "Selective Deprivatization among American Religious Traditions: The Reversal of the Great Reversal." *Social Forces* 76, no. 4 (1998): 1347-72.

"Religious Right Holds Too Much Power in the GOP." *Church and State* 58, no. 5 (2005): 16.

Ruse, Michael. "What Darwin's Doubters Get Wrong." *Chronicle of Higher Education* 56, no. 26 (2010): 6-9.

Saberi, Erin. "From Moral Majority to Organized Minority." *Christian Century* 110, no. 23 (1993): 781-84.

Scholtz, Gregory, and Ruth Caldwell. "Academic Freedom and Tenure: Olivet Nazarene University." *Academe: Bulletin of the AAUP* 95, no. 1 (2009): 41-57.

Scott, Julie A. "More Than Just Monkey Business." *Kansas History* 30, no. 2 (2007): 74-91.

Segady, Thomas W. "Traditional Religion, Fundamentalism, and Institutional Transition in the 20th Century." *Social Science Journal* 43, no. 2 (2006): 197-209.

Shermer, Michael. "Darwin on the Right." *Scientific American* 295, no. 4 (2006): 38.

Sider, Ronald J. "Toward an Evangelical Political Philosophy." *Evangelical Review of Theology* 28, no. 2 (2004): 140-55.

Smith, Timothy. "The Evangelical Kaleidoscope and the Call to Christian Unity." *Christian Scholars Review* 15 (1986).

Stassen, Glen. "The New Evangelicals." *Tikkun* 21, no. 5 (2006): 35-37.

Stiver, Dan R. "A Word About . . . Evangelicals on the Left." *Review and Expositor* 104, no. 4 (2007): 715-17.

Tapia, Andres. "Why Is Latin America Turning Protestant?" *Christianity Today* 36, nos. 28-29 (1992): 28-29.

Thomas, Cal. "Obama Is No Joshua." *Human Events* 64, no. 21 (2008): 13.

Tontonoz, Matthew J. "The Scopes Trial Revisited: Social Darwinism Versus Social Gospel." *Science as Culture* 17, no. 2 (2008): 121-43.

Van Frassen, Bas C. "On McMullin's Appreciation of Realism Concerning the Sciences." *Philosophy of Science* 70, no. 3 (2003): 479-94.

Wald, Kenneth D. "The Religious Dimension of American Anti-Communism." *Journal of Church and State* 36, no. 3 (1994).

Wall, James M. "Jimmy Carter, Religion and Public Service." *Christian Century* 102, no. 16 (1985): 459-60.

Wilcox, Clyde. "America's Radical Right." *Sociological Analysis* 48, no. 1 (1987): 46-57.

———. "Rethinking the Reasonableness of the Right." *Review of Religious Research* 36, no. 3 (1995): 263-76.

Withrow, Lisa R. "Success and the Prosperity Gospel: From Commodification to Transformation." *Journal of Religious Leadership* 6, no. 2 (2007): 15-41.

Wolfe, Alan. "Obama Vs. Marx." *New Republic* 240, no. 5 (2009): 21-23.

Yong, Amos. "God and the Evangelical Laboratory: Recent Conservative Protestant Thinking About Theology and Science." *Theology and Science* 5, no. 2 (2007): 203-21.

MAGAZINES AND NEWSPAPERS

Alinsky, L. David. "Son Sees Father's Handiwork in Convention." *Boston Globe,* August 31, 2008.

Begley, Sharon. "Tough Assignment: Teaching Evolution to Fundamentalists." *Wall Street Journal,* December 3, 2004, p. A15.

———. "Despite Appearance, Science Doesn't Deny the Existence of God." *Wall Street Journal,* January 27, 2006.

———. "Can God Love Darwin, Too?" *Newsweek,* September 17, 2007.

Freedman, Michael. "Big Government Is Back—Big Time." *Newsweek,* February 16, 2009, pp. 24-27.

Gilgoff, Dan. "A New Role for Religion." *US News and World Report,* June 2009, pp. 45-46.

Hart, Gary. "When the Personal Shouldn't Be Political." *New York Times,* November 8, 2004, p. 23.

Hout, Michael, and Andrew M. Greeley. "A Hidden Swing Vote: Evangelicals." *New York Times,* September 4, 2004, p. 17.

Kennedy, John. "The Faith Factor." *Christianity Today,* October 2008, pp. 25-30.

Novak, Michael. "The Snoop Report." *National Review,* December 11, 1981, p. 1488.

Weisberg, Jacob. "The Staying Power of the S Word." *Newsweek,* March 16, 2009, p. 39.

DISSERTATIONS

Hammond, Michael D. "Conscience in Conflict: Neo-Evangelicals and Race in the 1950s." Ph.D. dissertation. Wheaton College Graduate School, 2002.

Subject Index